Wittgenstein and Artificial Intelligence, Volume II: Values and Governance

ANTHEM STUDIES IN WITTGENSTEIN

Anthem Studies in Wittgenstein publishes new and classic works on Wittgenstein and Wittgensteinian philosophy. This book series aims to bring Wittgenstein's thought into the mainstream by highlighting its relevance to 21st century concerns. Titles include original monographs, themed edited volumes, forgotten classics, biographical works and books intended to introduce Wittgenstein to the general public. The series is published in association with the British Wittgenstein Society.

Anthem Studies in Wittgenstein sets out to put in place whatever measures may emerge as necessary in order to carry out the editorial selection process purely on merit and to counter bias on the basis of gender, race, ethnicity, religion, sexual orientation and other characteristics protected by law. These measures include subscribing to the British Philosophical Association/ Society for Women in Philosophy (UK) Good Practice Scheme.

Series Editor

Constantine Sandis – University of Hertfordshire, UK

Forthcoming Titles in the Series

Extending Hinge Epistemology

Normativity, Meaning and Philosophy: Essays on Wittgenstein

Practical Rationality, Learning and Convention: Essays in the Philosophy of Education

Wittgenstein and Modernist Fiction: The Language of Acknowledgment

Wittgenstein and the Life We Live with Language

Wittgenstein, Human Beings and Conversation

Wittgenstein on Other Minds

Wittgenstein Rehinged

Wittgenstein, Scepticism and Naturalism: Essays on the Later Philosophy

Wittgenstein and Artificial Intelligence, Volume II: Values and Governance

Brian Ball, Alice C. Helliwell and Alessandro Rossi

ANTHEM PRESS

Anthem Press
An imprint of Wimbledon Publishing Company
www.anthempress.com

This edition first published in UK and USA 2024
by ANTHEM PRESS
75–76 Blackfriars Road, London SE1 8HA, UK
or PO Box 9779, London SW19 7ZG, UK
and
244 Madison Ave #116, New York, NY 10016, USA

British Library Cataloguing-in-Publication Data
A catalogue record for this book is available from the British Library.

Library of Congress Cataloging-in-Publication Data: 2024933809
A catalog record for this book has been requested.

ISBN-13: 978-1-83999-139-4 (Hbk)
ISBN-10: 1-83999-139-9 (Hbk)

Cover Credit: DreamStudio

This title is also available as an e-book.

CONTENTS

INTRODUCTION

Brian Ball, Alice C. Helliwell and Alessandro Rossi

Opening: Crises of Values and Governance in Artificial Intelligence

The twenty-first century has witnessed the rise of 'big data',[1] and the widespread deployment of Artificial intelligence (AI). At the turn of the century, according to Wooldridge, 'AI was a rather niche area with a somewhat questionable academic reputation' (2020: 5). But in 2014, Google bought a 'tiny AI company [DeepMind] for a huge sum […] Artificial intelligence was suddenly big news – and big business' (2020: 167). What happened?

Contemporary AI uses large data sets – which may or may not be representative of the contexts in which the AI trained will be deployed (see below) – to train models using machine learning (ML) techniques,[2] and specifically, 'deep learning' (LeCun et al. 2015). The information processing that results is often opaque: precisely what mapping from inputs to outputs the model supports is unclear, even to the engineers who develop the systems. The AI systems that result are often 'narrow', dedicated to solving a relatively small set of problems.[3] As a result, some might not be inclined to call this true AI – much of it certainly doesn't meet the requirements of Searle's (1980)

1 Within the first 10 years of the century, Twitter (2006) and a number of other companies and products launched: 'Google (2002); YouTube (2006); Wikipedia (2001); the BBC iPlayer (2007); the iPhone (2007); Facebook (2006); Spotify (2009) and […] more' (Rusbridger, 2018: 142). These technologies enabled 'Web 2.0 […] [t]he social web' (Rusbridger 2018, 138), with user participation generating content – and data.

2 'The sudden sea change in attitudes to AI was driven by rapid progress in one core AI technology: machine learning' (Wooldridge 2020, 168).

3 'The mainstream of AI research today,' says Wooldridge, 'is focused around getting machines to do specific tasks which currently require human brains' (2020, 3) even if 'the long-term dream of AI is to build machines that have the full range of capabilities for intelligent action that people have' (2020, 2).

'strong AI', actually possessing the various mental states involved in sapience. But it is also insufficiently general to even simulate much of the variety of human intelligence, and so it fails the requirements for his 'weak' AI too. Nevertheless, for better or worse, the term 'AI' is used in connection with these information processing systems.

Recently, we have seen the emergence of what is known as 'generative' AI[4] – AI that produces outputs of the same kind as its training data. For example, whereas image classifiers take visual images as inputs and produce labels (i.e. words) as outputs (see e.g. Krizhevsky et al. 2012), certain generative systems (such as generative adversarial networks (GANs) and text-to-image models) are able to generate (often novel) images as outputs. Similarly, large language models (LLMs) are trained on vast corpuses of textual data, and are able to generate grammatical, and even meaningful, text (e.g. semantically appropriate answers to questions). Some have suggested that LLMs may be generally intelligent,[5] that is, are not narrow AI; and Chalmers (2023) makes the case that such systems might in principle be conscious, with genuine thoughts, even if they have no sensors and so are not phenomenally conscious. Regardless of how plausible this might be, these generative systems are impressive in what they can do – including with audio-visual data. Cüyaz's chapter in this volume discusses issues arising from the deepfake videos they enable – through the Wittgensteinian lenses of language games and grammar.

As a result of these technical advances and their rapid commercialization, there have been a number of values-based crises. AI systems are being implemented in the world with increasing frequency, and with this we are forced to consider how the race for commercial success conflicts with the need for safe, transparent and trustworthy systems. Take self-driving cars for instance. Many of the world's biggest technology companies are now developing autonomous vehicles, whether for the public market or to use as taxis.[6] Absent within this volume is any discussion of trolley problems, a well-worn feature in debates about the ethics of autonomous vehicles. The very concept of autonomy, however, can be scrutinized through a Wittgensteinian lens (e.g.

4 See e.g. McKinsey's report *The state of AI in 2023: Generative AI's breakout year* (QuantumBlack AI by McKinsey, 2023)

5 See Adam and Carter https://cetas.turing.ac.uk/publications/large-language-models-and-intelligence-analysis

6 Alphabet, Microsoft and Amazon (Gray 2022) are developing self-driving cars.

Collins et al. 2024), and is discussed in the first volume of this collection by Boisseau.

This volume does discuss examples of robots. Like autonomous vehicles, robotics offers another way for AI to venture into the physical world, instead of just the virtual one. This leads to the question of how to consider AI morally (if at all), as moral agents or moral patients. Much effort in the field of AI has been dedicated to the development of artificial moral agents, with the aim to develop virtual or robotic systems that are capable of making and acting upon moral decisions (Misselhorn 2022). However, it is not clear that AI will ever be able to be a moral agent (see Allen and Wallach 2012 for an overview of objections). Rappuoli discusses the moral agency of AI in his chapter in this volume. Similarly, there remains debate about the status of machines as moral patients, particularly in the case of social robots. Sweeney utilizes Wittgensteinian philosophy[7] in her consideration of the status of social robots and any resultant rights in her chapter.

Whilst harms from AI embodied in society might seem obvious (crashing autonomous cars are a glaring example) some harms from AI are more insidious. Many AI systems, upon implementation, reveal troubling biases. Sometimes, this is quickly recognized. Take the example of *Tay,* a bot unleashed by Microsoft onto Twitter in 2016. Tay rapidly acquired a penchant for virulent racism, anti-semitism and misogyny, learnt from interactions with other Twitter users. Tay was quickly taken down, and later replaced with Zo, a bot which would shut down controversial conversation (Schwartz 2019). In reflecting the online behaviour of interacting Twitter users, Tay failed to reflect values we would want to see in AI systems.

Whilst the short-lived rogue Twitter bot was certainly offensive, in some areas of implementation of AI the cost to individuals is far greater, and can take longer to recognize. Algorithmic decision-making is already being implemented in various industries, which, if biased, can exacerbate inequalities in society, particularly in the context of medical and legal decision-making. For example, in the United States, algorithms implemented in the medical and legal sphere have been shown to result in unequal treatment of minority groups. Obermeyer et al. (2019) demonstrated that an algorithm used in the US health system was racially biased: worryingly and inappropriately,

7 Specifically, Sweeney draws on Wittgenstein's remarks on the concepts of *evidence, doing the same as* and *form of life* contained in *Philosophical Investigations*, Zettel and Brown and Blue Books. Further discussions on Wittgenstein's epistemology can be found in his *On Certainty* (Wittgenstein 1972: OC), as well as Moyal-Sharrock (2004, 2021), Pritchard (2012) and Sandis and Moyal-Sharrock (2022).

amongst patients with the same algorithmically determined risk score, black patients were in fact considerably sicker than their white counterparts. The blame, it seems, lay in the choice to use healthcare spending as a proxy for need. Racial bias in AI extends to LLMs, which have been shown to produce biased and nonsensical answers to race-based medical questions, risking the perpetuation of incorrect beliefs in medical professionals (Omiye et al. 2023). Bias can be a particular risk in cases of black-box algorithms, where we are unable to find out what drives each decision. Black-box algorithms and transparency are discussed in this volume by Pelland, Trächtler and Love, particularly in relation to high-stakes fields such as law, and the need for explainable AI (XAI, as it is often abbreviated) is discussed by Schafer.[8] These are areas in which we have embedded value systems. We value safety on our roads, equal access to healthcare and fairness in our courts. The implementation of AI presents areas of potential conflict with the values that we deem central to our society.

Perhaps with fewer obvious harms, we are also witnessing a clash of values in creative fields. For example, the desire to protect the intellectual property of artists and writers is in conflict with developing and training AI systems which can generate impressive outputs (Milmo 2024). Indeed, this conflict is causing issues for attempts to guide AI practice in the creative fields, with the UK government recently shelving its attempt to codify rules for training AI on copyrighted material after a failure of artists and AI companies to agree (Thomas and Criddle 2024).

The potential risks of advancing AI technology turn our focus to the prospect that appropriate governance measures can help protect us. The EU's proposed AI Act, purportedly the first law regulating AI, will attempt to carefully control the use of AI in high-risk areas such as medicine and law enforcement. It also seeks to implement transparency requirements for generative AI (European Parliament 2023). Unfortunately, regulation continues to play catch-up with technology. While the law is at least one instrument for socio-political governance, policies and practice may also be vehicles of governance, albeit on a more localized scale. Ethical principles are used as a tool for governance in specific fields, such as medicine (see the World Health Organization's 'Ethics and governance of AI for health' (2021) and new guidance on LLMs (2024)). Such principles aim to bring our values to the production and implementation of AI.

8 Further discussion of the black-box problem can be found in the chapters by Ground and Galli in volume 1.

These are pressing issues, demonstrating conflict between our values and the values exemplified by the implementation of algorithms in society, and there is much that Wittgenstein's philosophy can contribute to here. Despite having written relatively little on these matters directly, Wittgenstein's ideas have nevertheless been influential in these areas of human concern and the academic disciplines associated with them. A brief sketch of the ways in which they have been so will, we hope, facilitate engagement with their application to the domain of AI.

Ethics

Wittgenstein mentions ethics explicitly in the *Tractatus* (Wittgenstein 1922, 1961, 2021, 2023), and even gave a 'Lecture on Ethics' (Wittgenstein 1965: LE). Yet what is perhaps most notable is that he appears to embrace a kind of quietism in ethics, spawned by transcendentalism concerning its subject matter. Indeed, about the *Tractatus*, Wittgenstein even went so far as to write, 'my work consists of two parts: the one which is here, and of everything which I have not written. And precisely this second part is the important one. For the Ethical is delimited from within, as it were, by my book; and I'm convinced that, strictly speaking, it can ONLY be delimited this way' (Quoted in Fairhurst 2021, 152 – which quotes Monk 1990, 178).

Intriguingly, Wittgenstein's few remarks on aesthetics in the *Tractatus* suggest a similar transcendentalist quietism regarding that domain. We will discuss the influence of his later philosophy on aesthetics presently; but in his earliest published work he says, 'It is clear that ethics cannot be put into words. Ethics is transcendental. (Ethics and aesthetics are one and the same.)' (Wittgenstein 1961: TLP 6.421). Schafer's chapter in this volume discusses 'the ethics and aesthetics of apologising' against this backdrop – but also taking into account Wittgenstein's later views on language games[9] and their potential legal implications in a world comprising AI-powered robots.

In any event, Arrington (2016) nicely lays out the various ways in which Wittgenstein's ideas about ethics have been received, from Ayer's (1936) *Language, Truth, and Logic* treating the claims of ethics as nonsense, through later non-cognitivist, as well as cognitivist, developments and iterations. Rossi's chapter engages with the task of interpreting the view taken by Wittgenstein in the Lecture on Ethics, relating it to worries surrounding the existential risk some find to be associated with AI.

9 In *Philosophical Investigations* (1953) and the *Blue and Brown Books* (1958)

Aesthetics

One way in which Wittgenstein's (later) views have been influential within aesthetics surrounds the discussion in (Part 2 of the Anscombe edition of) the *Philosophical Investigations* of (what has come to be known as) *seeing as.* Wittgenstein there notes, in effect, that it is possible to undergo a *Gestalt* switch when looking at certain figures, such as the Necker cube or the duck-rabbit (see below for more discussion). In the former case, for instance, one brings first one face of the cube, then another, into the perceived foreground, switching which of them one sees as nearer to oneself. Yet there is also a sense in which what one sees remains exactly the same throughout this experience.

This idea of 'seeing as' became influential in aesthetics largely through its use in Wolheim's (1968) book, *Art and its Objects,* to illuminate the notion of pictorial representation.[10] None of the chapters of the present work discuss it, however, and it is perhaps surprising that there has, to the best of our knowledge, been little research on this in relation to computer vision.[11] Nonetheless, it does figure – in a perhaps amusing manner – in an account of the provenance of the cover art for the present collection.

We used stable diffusion to generate the image on the covers of the two volumes of this collection. One idea we had was to generate duck-rabbit images of the kind given in the *Philosophical Investigations* (Wittgenstein 1953: PI II, §xI). What we got was not illustrative of seeing as (or 'aspectual seeing', as it is also sometimes known) at all. Despite the proliferation of the duck-rabbit image online (from which AI training sets are typically drawn), the images generated by Stable Diffusion are not duck-rabbits in the Wittgensteinian sense. Instead, they seem to blend elements of a rabbit and a duck – frequently taking the distorted body of one and adding features of the other (such as the duck with an extra leg and two misplaced rabbit ears, see image 3 below). Interestingly, when we consider AI 'viewing' the illusion, it seems that it does not see a duck-rabbit at all; instead, it simply sees a duck (or, as some have shown, a rabbit when the image is rotated).[12] This may suggest a weakness in

10 Wollheim (1968) also claimed that '[a]rt is, in Wittgenstein's sense, a form of life' (Section 45). Unfortunately, space precludes discussion of this idea here.

11 One exception appears to be Gangopadhyay's talk 'The Duck, the Rabbit, the Robot and the Philosopher', delivered at the conference organized in 2022 in Skjolden (Norway) by Pichler (a participant in the Wittgenstein and AI Conference) and Säätelä entitled 'Wittgenstein and Artificial Intelligence: Towards an Update'. The abstract of Gangopadhyay's talk can be accessed at: https://www.uib.no/en/rg/philtext/154466/wittgenstein-and-artificial-intelligence-towards-update#june-2

12 See the result of one such investigation here: https://improbable.com/2021/02/01/ai-and-the-duck-rabbit-illusion-improbable-experiment/

current AI on two fronts: in generation, and in recognition, these AI systems seem not to be able to reckon with an image where classification depends on our perspective. We cannot pursue this issue further here; but needless to say, we went back to the AI for our cover, and have instead used an image generated with the prompt 'Wittgenstein building a robot print'.

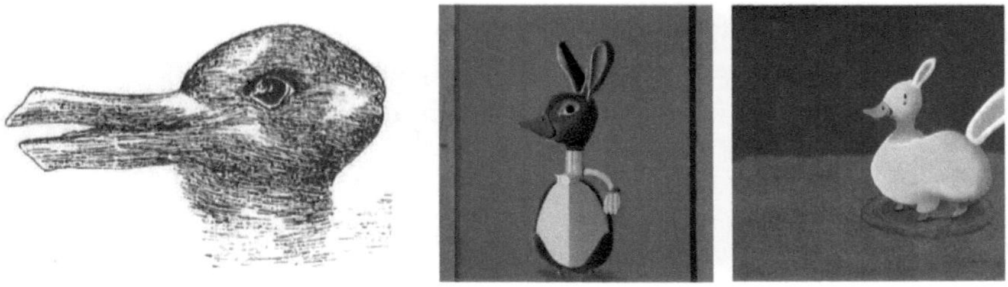

Another area where Wittgenstein's views have been influential is through his discussion of language games in *Philosophical Investigations* (discussed in this volume by Harper, in relation to the changing concept of the user in human–computer interaction (HCI), as well as by Sweeney, Cüyaz and Schafer). Of particular relevance in the present context, where aesthetics is under discussion, is Wittgenstein's notion of 'family resemblance' (in Section 67), and the associated anti-essentialism, according to which no explicit definition of a concept can be given in terms of individually necessary and jointly sufficient conditions characterizing all of its instances. These ideas influenced Waismann's (1945) view that our empirical concepts have a certain characteristic 'open texture'[13] – understood as the *possibility* of vagueness (itself an indeterminacy that can be settled, when necessary, through precisification). In other words, the open texture of a concept is, for Waismann, a certain kind of uncertainty about its application to cases that (only) *might conceivably*

See also the experiments separately conducted in 2019 using Google Cloud Vision by Shane and Woolf, which show that the AI may be sensitive to image orientation – detecting a duck or a rabbit variably as the image is rotated. Shane's report can be accessed here: https://twitter.com/JanelleCShane/status/1103420287519866880

Woolf's report is available here: https://twitter.com/minimaxir/status/1103676561809539072?ref_src=twsrc%5Etfw%7Ctwcamp%5Etweetembed%7Ctwterm%5E1103676561809539072%7Ctwgr%5E9a39b58ccf0269e02a712fe7bae20759121e2976%7Ctwcon%5Es1_&ref_url=https%3A%2F%2Fhub.packtpub.com%2Fresearchers-input-rabbit-duck-illusion-to-google-cloud-vision-api-and-conclude-it-shows-orientation-bias%2F

13 Waismann apparently 'played a key role in the mediation, both personal and intellectual, between Wittgenstein and the other members of the Vienna Circle in the decade from 1927 to 1937' (Makovec & Shapiro 2019, vi). For more on Waismann's philosophy, see the various papers in Makovec and Shapiro (2019).

arise (such as that of something otherwise like a man, but only a 'span' tall, or a cat with the power to come back from the dead), and which therefore cannot be resolved in advance. Weitz then applied this collection of (broadly Wittgensteinian) ideas to the case of the definition of art, which he regarded as an 'open' concept in the sense that 'a situation or case can be imagined or secured which would call for some sort of *decision* on our part to extend the use of the concept or to close the concept and invent a new one to deal with the new case and its new property' (1956, 31, emphasis original).[14] Helliwell's chapter engages with what a so-called cluster account in this tradition might mean in the context of AI-generated art.

Law

Wittgensteinian anti-essentialism (i.e. opposition to explicit definition) has arguably been even more influential in the philosophy of law, thanks to the work of H. L. A. Hart (1907–1992), whose (1961) book, *The Concept of Law*, is widely regarded as the most important work of the twentieth century in this field. According to Schlesinger (1997), Hart tried to find a middle way between the extreme poles of each of two pairs of oppositions. The first opposed those older legal positivists who held that 'law is essentially institutionalized coercion' (1997, 104) with the natural law theorists, who maintained that 'the law is essentially moral' (1997, 104). The second was between the legal formalists, according to whom 'the law will "mechanically" produce just solutions to social problems' (1997, 104), and the legal realists, for whom 'the law is what judges say it is' (1997, 104).[15]

Hart was a legal positivist who insisted on 'the distinction between what is and what ought to be' (Hart 1958, 612) law – a claim sometimes known as the 'separability thesis'.[16] But, unlike earlier positivists, he also distinguished primary from secondary legal rules: whereas the first paradigmatically impose

14 Interestingly, Weitz references Wittgenstein, though his talk of openness is perhaps even more evocative of Waismann, whom he does not cite. Indeed, the Wittgensteinian nature of Weitz's account of art as an open concept might be contested on the grounds that it delivers a theoretical sense of 'family resemblance' (i.e. as pertaining to our decisions on how to use a concept) which was not intended by Wittgenstein. For a line of argument along these lines see McFee (2019).

15 Similarly, according to Bix, Hart aimed 'to defend a middle view on legal interpretation, one that conceded [contra the legal formalists] that the application of legal norms was *sometimes* indeterminate, without accepting the view associated with some American legal realists that legal reasoning was *always* or *generally* indeterminate' (2019, 256, emphasis original), so that – as Schlesinger puts it – 'law is politics' (1997, 103).

16 See Section 2 of Himma's (n.d.) *Internet Encyclopedia of Philosophy* entry on *Legal Positivism*.

'restrictions on freedom backed by the threat of a sanction' (Himma n.d., *Section 1*), the second are meta-rules that are concerned with the primary rules themselves, detailing how they can be recognized, changed or adjudicated. In societies with sophisticated legal systems having both primary and secondary rules, people treat legal rules as in some (non-moral) sense justifying, and not merely forcing, compliance.

Since the law comprises rules (of both of these kinds), it is not simply whatever judges say it is – so the legal realist position is ultimately mistaken. And yet the formalist position on the opposite extreme is also wrong. Moreover, according to Schlesinger, 'Hart uses Wittgenstein as his main ally in the refutation of legal formalists' (1997, 104) – and specifically, the idea that, in Waismann's terms, the 'open texture' of the language in which the rules are articulated requires judgement in its application.[17] For Hart, as Bix explains, '[t]he decision whether a rule applies to a particular situation often turns on delimiting the range of meaning of a general term. For example, the application of the rule, "No vehicles in the park", will usually turn on whether a particular object [e.g. a bicycle] is a "vehicle" for the purpose of the rule' (1991, 52). Of course, much of this has been contested – whether as a matter of legal philosophy,[18] or even of Hart interpretation[19] – and yet it has clearly permeated much contemporary jurisprudential thought.

Indeed, Gori's chapter in the present volume can be viewed in this light: it discusses how AI systems cannot ultimately accommodate the nature of legal rules, whether they belong to the (mnemonically named) 'Good Old Fashioned AI and Law' (GOFAIL) tradition of symbolic AI, or adopt the newer, subsymbolic approach that employs ML and excels in pattern recognition. Obviously, though, the nature of rule-following is already a topic in Wittgenstein's own later work (see e.g. §§ 135–243 of *Philosophical Investigations*): a discussion that figures centrally in Pelland,Trächtler and

17 'Hart argues that the legal formalists were right insofar as they argued that the law is a set of rules, but wrong to argue that these rules provide determinate answers to every case that comes before the bar. Because language is "open-textured", there will be particular cases in the penumbra where judges – not logic – will have to decide how to apply the general rules' (Schlesinger 1997, 104).

18 Schauer (2011), for instance, argues that Hart is mistaken about the defeasibility of the law that purportedly follows from its open texture.

19 Lefebvre (2011), for example, argues that Hart is far more deeply influenced by Wittgenstein's philosophy than the above sketch suggests.

Love's chapter, which raises concerns about the opacity of the rules followed by 'black-box' AI in legal contexts.[20]

Having contextualized the chapters in this volume, it is time to detail the contents of each contribution.

Alessandro Rossi, *Is, Ought and Wittgenstein*

Rossi's chapter offers an interpretation of Wittgenstein's 1929 'Lecture on Ethics' (Wittgenstein 1965: LE), and indicates its relevance to the question of whether AI poses an existential risk to humanity. It begins by noting that the Lecture is the only place where Wittgenstein elaborated at any length on the distinction between normative and descriptive uses of language, and in particular on what von Wright (1951) called the 'deontic' notions, including that of what *ought* to be done. The centrepiece of Rossi's interpretation is the claim that Wittgenstein defended a version of Hume's Thesis, according to which an 'ought' can never be derived from an 'is'.

Consider the argument that the AI singularity – the point at which AI exceeds human intelligence, and is thereby able to create ever more powerful AI – poses an existential risk to humanity. Rossi follows Müller and Cannon (2021) in suggesting that this line of thought draws on two premises, due to Bostrom (2014). The first premise is that of the Inevitability of Superintelligence: roughly, this is the claim that AI will develop to such a point as to reach the singularity. The second premise is the Orthogonality Thesis, according to which any level of intelligence can be combined with any final goal. The idea is that, given these two premises, superintelligent AI may develop with goals fundamentally opposed to our own, thereby posing a threat to human existence. But Rossi suggests that the Orthogonality Thesis is only plausible if it is taken to concern the narrow notion of instrumental intelligence; whereas the inevitability claim can be supported only on the assumption that a general intelligence is at issue, one which concerns itself with final goals. But given Hume's Thesis, or at least an elaboration of it that Rossi attributes to Wittgenstein, there are irreducibly normative truths concerning what ought to be which a generally intelligent being cannot ignore.

Drawing on the distinction between resolute readings of the *Tractatus* on which we must take seriously Wittgenstein's claim that many of his own remarks there are nonsense, and irresolute ones on which we can nevertheless regard them as revealing important truths, Rossi offers an interpretation

20 We could perhaps take this view articulated by Wittgenstein in a completely different context – but not in legal contexts, given Hart's point about secondary rules and, in particular the rule of recognition, which points to a need for transparency.

of the Lecture that agrees with the latter. He suggests that Wittgenstein's endorsement of Hume's Thesis rests on his adoption of a Dichotomy Thesis on which the world divides into descriptive and normative realms. Thus, while there can be no (naturalistic) science of ethics, there are nonetheless normative truths to be discovered – truths which do not, however, follow from any empirically discoverable descriptive truths. This reading of the Lecture is then defended against objections.

Burkhard Schafer, *When Saying Sorry Is the Hardest Game to Play: Wittgenstein, AI and the Quest for Transparency*

Schafer's chapter is concerned with Wittgenstein and the law - in particular the legal requirement for AI decision-making to be explainable - and how this plays out in the context of robots issuing apologies to human beings. It suggests that the counterfactual account of explainability in the context of AI has affinities with Wittgenstein's views of giving reasons. It also sketches the thought that, with the rise of technology in the nineteenth century, the law became more concerned with prospective harm prevention rather than retrospective redress once harms have occurred – and notes that we must nevertheless consider this latter case, where apology is appropriate.

To illustrate, Schafer considers an experiment conducted at Yale, in which robots played in a team game with humans, occasionally making mistakes (Strohkorb Sebo et al. 2018). In some instances, the robot would offer an apology. Despite the explanation offered being spurious, the gesture restored trust – though third parties privy to the background may be inclined to regard the apology as deceptive. This prompts an investigation of what is required for a proper apology: two variant 'apology games' are articulated. One of these – remorse expression, or RE – requires an accompanying emotion and cannot be effectuated by machines; while the other – public apology, or PA – requiring only a recognition of wrongdoing and an intention to change, can be effectuated by a corporation or a robot. This allows a diagnosis of the sense of deception in the Yale experiment: the purported source of the error reported by the robot is not the actual cause and provides no reason to expect different behaviour in the future; yet this is what is required in a case of PA. At the same time, an alternative response is also possible: agents might note the improvement in trust between human players when the robot apologizes, and – in a reaction suggested by a passage in the *Tractatus* – find an aesthetic-*cum*-ethical ground for regarding the PA as perfectly in order.

Nevertheless, it is suggested that the first response is more in line with legal reasoning. It is claimed, in effect, that PA is tantamount to explanation – it articulates a kind of causally sensitive justification – and can therefore meet the legal need for such.

Paula Sweeney, *Wittgensteinian Considerations of The Moral Status of Robots*

In this chapter, Sweeney puts forward a Wittgensteinian response to recent arguments for granting rights to social robots. Sweeney criticizes the argument from empathy – that robots should have rights because we experience an empathetic response to their pain – stating that empathetic responses are not the basis of rights in other cases.

Sweeney also considers, and rejects, the argument from performative equivalence. Under this argument, if a robot can act the same as those to whom we grant moral consideration, then we should grant it the same consideration. Sweeney argues against performative equivalence as a basis for robot rights through appeal to Wittgenstein's notions of 'evidence' and 'doing the same as'.

Sweeney highlights that a piece of evidence, according to Wittgenstein, is only evidence for something occurring because we take it to be such evidence. Sweeney takes Wittgenstein's parrot example: a parrot mimicking a human should not be taken as evidence that it can speak (Wittgenstein 1953: PI §344). A parrot does not take part in the practices that humans have around language use; it does not participate in our form of life. A robot, Sweeney states, also does not share our form of life, and so we would not take its behaviour as evidence of psychological states; it simply does not make sense to ascribe these to a robot.

This brings Sweeney to utilize Wittgenstein's notion of 'doing the same as'. As Sweeney shows, the relevant conditions to count as 'doing the same as' may differ, and meeting these is a matter of judgement. For robots then, Sweeney suggests the issue does not lie in whether a robot can perform the same as a human, but whether we are willing to describe it as the same. And this, in turn, Sweeney states would be dependent on the robot sharing our form of life; in order to say that the robot is doing the same as us, we would need it to share in the same language game.

Finally, Sweeney highlights that ascribing psychological states to non-humans is to include them in our form of life. It is not ruled out that robots might be included in our 'psychological language games' in the future; equally, it is emphasized that this will not be due to our empathy, or a robot's performative equivalence alone.

Luca Alberto Rappuoli, *Can Machines Act Ethically? Wittgenstein, McDowell and AI*

This chapter explores the issue of whether machines are capable of moral agency, from the perspective of McDowell's approach to ethics. A key thesis espoused by McDowell is that our moral outlook is not reducible to a set of rules governing human behaviour. McDowell finds support for this thesis in Wittgenstein's famous critique of the concept of rule, which is therefore deemed unsuitable to be the ground of morality. Better instead, McDowell proposes, to draw on a tradition stretching back (at least) to Aristotle, and ground morality on the notion of a virtuous agent.

The question for this account then becomes whether machines could be entities capable of bringing about virtuous actions and qualify as virtuous themselves. Rappuoli argues that McDowell's account of ethics as irreducible to a set of rules is essentially at odds with the possibility of there being artificial virtuous agents (viz. ethical machines). The incompatibility here, according to Rappuoli's reading of McDowell, has modal force. It is not just that current AI systems do not qualify as virtuous agents; there will never be AI systems that do.

Rappuoli expresses dissatisfaction with this consequence of McDowell's view, since it appears to be derived completely a priori. Furthermore, Rappuoli argues that the conclusion that ethical machines are mere chimaeras rests on an overly strong metaphysical interpretation of the irreducibility of morality to a set of rules. The appropriate way to understand such irreducibility, for Rappuoli, is in epistemic terms. There may well be, for all we know, a reduction of morality to a set of rules of conduct; but even if this is granted, such a reduction, if it at all exists, is practically non-codifiable. Given this novel understanding of the irreducibility of morality, Rappuoli concludes, the question of whether there can be ethical machines remains to be decided.

Mehmet Taylan Cüyaz, *Investigating Deepfakes: The Rise of New Authorities and The Question of Deepfake Regulation*

Cüyaz's chapter discusses deepfakes – synthetic (audio and/or visual) media objects manipulated or even wholly generated by AI – and their regulation. It suggests that deepfakes constitute a new kind of (technological) language game, subject to unprecedented rules (of use). It proposes that video in particular is, in light of its existence, only a possible (rather than necessary) indicator of truth – which has implications for various epistemic catastrophe theses that have been defended in the literature.

Cüyaz also holds that video has both surface and depth grammar (Wittgenstein 1953: PI §664) – which is important for the detection of deepfakes. More specifically, we can distinguish low-level (surface) features concerning pixels, from high-level (depth) features of content and context concerned with the objects and events depicted. While it remains unclear whether humans or machines are currently better at recognizing deepfakes, what does seem clear, according to Cüyaz, is that (statistics concerning) surface features are used by machines, while depth features relevant to meaning are used by humans. Cüyaz ultimately suggests, based on considerations surrounding the functioning of the GANs used in the production of deepfakes, that 'algorithms might outperform humans in forged image detection because of their particular grammatical mastery'.

Epistemic catastrophists view deepfakes as technologically sophisticated varieties of fake news. However, the claim that deepfakes instead constitute a new language game with only a possible connection to truth, when combined with the need for automated checks for veracity, raises the question of trust – not in the videos themselves, but in the AI-based classifiers we may or may not have access to. Such automated fact-checkers are in danger of becoming monopolistic, opaque and ultimately unaccountable, epistemic authorities.

Alice C. Helliwell, *AI and the Cluster Account of Art*

Helliwell's chapter discusses whether AI-generated images can really be art, approaching the matter by way of Gaut's (2000) broadly Wittgensteinian cluster account of the concept of art. The upshot is twofold: first, that AI images can be art; and second, that the cluster account is particularly helpful in engaging with this issue.

Helliwell first sketches the cluster account of art, and its Wittgensteinian pedigree: it both denies that 'art' can be defined, and relies on the idea of family resemblance in thinking about criteria for its application. More generally, a cluster concept is one for which there are no individually necessary conditions for its application, though a disjunction of criterial properties is necessary, and possession of several of these properties is sufficient. It is explained that, by its own admission, Gaut's account of art does not strictly qualify as a cluster account, since it takes being the product of an action as necessary. Nevertheless, 10 criteria are proposed – and the possession of these properties by purported AI artworks is discussed.

Some features in Gaut's list are found to be difficult for AI images to satisfy (e.g. presenting an individual point of view); but Helliwell argues that a sufficient number of them (such as possessing positive aesthetic properties, or being formally complex and coherent) can be possessed by AI-generated images, so that there is no problem in principle about the idea that these images can count as art. This even applies to the one necessary condition in Gaut's list – at least in cases where humans are involved alongside AI. (This inclusion of humans also allows Helliwell to bypass, in the present work, the question of whether AI systems can be genuinely creative.)

Helliwell concludes by noting that the Wittgensteinian cluster account of art is promising in relation to AI art, since: it provides criteria against which AI art can be assessed, thereby potentially driving further artistic directions; it can be adapted (through the addition of new properties to its open-ended list of criteria) to accommodate new directions that may arise in AI art; and it can explain why AI images might be regarded as borderline cases of art.

Richard Harper, *An Anthropology of the User in the Age of AI*

In this chapter, Richard Harper investigates what, in the context of HCI, a 'user' is becoming in the age of AI. Harper tracks the history of the 'user', taking Wittgenstein's conception of 'grammar' as consisting 'in rules which govern the use of words and which thereby constitute meanings or concepts' (Forster 2004, 7). As Harper discusses, the meaning of a term is determined, for Wittgenstein, by the way we use it; namely, the practices and circumstances which Wittgenstein might call our 'form of life'. Meaning for Wittgenstein, as Biletzki and Matar (2023) describe it, can 'be understood as constantly changing and contingent, dependent on culture, context, history, etc.; or as a background common to humankind'. The changing meaning of 'user' over the history of HCI, then, is the subject of this chapter.

Harper isolates, as he calls them, two 'modalities' of HCI. The first concerns our interaction with the standard 'Windows, Icons, Mouse and Pointer' interface (WIMP), characterizing the first desktop machines up through to the latest laptops. The second modality concerns our interaction with the platforms that were made possible by the advent of AI – social media, and in particular generative AI platforms based on LLMs, such as ChatGPT. The key thesis defended by Harper in the chapter is that the concept of 'user' resulting from these two modalities is significantly different. On the one hand, Harper argues, a 'user' interacting with computers through a simple WIMP interface can be unproblematically thought of as an author of content. On the other hand, whether the same can be said about a 'user' interacting with computers through social media or prompt-based generative AI systems, such as in particular ChatGPT, turns out to be a delicate matter. *Prima facie,* it might be thought that, by observing the HCI at work in ChatGPT, where a human inputs some prompts and the system delivers some output, the author of the content produced is (quite remarkably) the computer. Harper, however, wants to resist this conclusion; on this new modality of HCI, the computer is some kind of `user' producing content *together* with another kind of 'user', namely, a human user. The resulting picture is one for which, on this modality of HCI, the human and the computer are joint authors of content.

Beginning with the history of the use of computers, Harper traces HCI and how this has shaped understanding of the user. In particular, it is argued, the WIMP modality of HCI devised by Xerox Parc in the 1970s, being essentially finalized at the production of textual content, enabled humans to be, in a strong sense, the authors of the content produced through the computer, which merely served as a tool enabling this production. Harper then goes on to discuss the shifting view of the user resulting from the modality of HCI underlying social media and, increasingly, AI. In this regard, Harper highlights that users today are not simply individuals interacting with a computer, but part of a broader map of many users posting, accessing and consuming content. Finally, the chapter moves to the discussion of LLMs, and how the mode of output impacts on our understanding of the system, and our relationship to it.

Gianmarco Gori, *Legal and Computer Rules: An Overview Inspired by Wittgenstein's Remarks*

This chapter contrasts legal rules with computer rules, arguing that the former are measures, whereas the latter are what is measured – ultimately, because legal rules are normative, while computer rules are descriptive. The argument and discussion are infused with Wittgensteinian insights throughout, beginning with the thought that *rule* is a family resemblance concept (cf. Daston 2022). It is clarified that by a *legal rule* is meant any kind of norm within the law, and also that computer rules comprise both those that are explicitly programmed and those that are learnt.

Gori's discussion is focused around, first, GOFAIL with its explicit rules, and then around various paradigms for thinking about the relationship between ML models and law. There is a rich discussion of how, in attempting to render legal rules into explicit programmes, GOFAIL approaches distort their character. In programmed rules, if there is a departure between the output of the programme and the rule thereby encoded, this constitutes a bug: accordingly, the computer rule is itself assessed, or measured, in the process of comparison; whereas legal rules often require non-trivial application to new cases, and if we check these applications against the output of a program, the former serves as measure.

The chapter also provides a survey – and taxonomy – of ML approaches to the law. On one approach, ML involves experimentation: models make predictions about case verdicts; and their accuracy is measured. But here it is clear that the normativity of legal rules is lost: a legal prediction concerns what the verdict ought to be; an ML model's prediction is simply of what it will be. On a second approach, ML models are used to determine predictive

– and thereby explanatory – factors in determining verdicts. Here the idea is that ML models may uncover factors which ought not to play a role in legal decisions but which nevertheless do – such as whether the judge has yet to eat lunch. Yet for such a model to be used to evaluate legal rules, those rules in turn must be used to 'measure' (i.e. normatively assess) the models. Finally, on a third approach, an ML model might provide an 'improved expression' of a legal rule – for instance, capturing Justice Stewart's ability to know, without being able to articulate, what counts as hardcore pornography. Here the model may be regarded as almost constitutive of the law – except that, once again, if there is a discrepancy between the output of the model and, say, Justice Stewart's own verdict, it seems it must be the former that is corrected.

Jean-Charles Pelland, Jasmin Trächtler and Helene Love, **Practice Makes Human: Why We Can't Understand Black-Box Artificial Intelligence**

Pelland, Trächtler and Love's chapter discusses black-box AI, showing how some of the philosophical issues that arise can be seen from a Wittgensteinian perspective, and illustrated in relation to legal applications. AI models are described as 'black-boxed' when humans cannot know what input-output mapping is being implemented in them – this distinguishes the opaque models in question from those that are merely proprietary. A dilemma is then framed: roughly, whether to use black-box AI models, with the potential for greater accuracy than their more transparent symbolic AI counterparts, yet risk harms; or to use transparent AI, even if it is less powerful, so as to avoid those harms.

Pelland, Trächter and Love argue that the risks associated with black-box models cannot be avoided through efforts to make them more transparent: crucially, we cannot understand these models or their decisions through the techniques of XAI (i.e., the addition of a further AI model that provides a simplified account of the workings of the black-box model). But understanding is argued to be the key to transparency: it need not be factive, is more context-sensitive than explanation, and is more suitable to building trust. A distinction is then introduced between local and global understanding: it is argued that factivity failure means that we do not necessarily get local understanding of what happens within the system on any given occasion, so the transparency burden is pushed onto a need for global understanding of the system itself.

However, it is argued – by appeal to Wittgensteinian considerations – that global understanding cannot be achieved. Examining the rule-following considerations, we see that the possibility of following a rule is grounded in practices – collections of customs and habits of action. When black-box AI systems 'learn', the correlations they discover in their training data may not follow the intended rule – or indeed any rule at all – and there is no basis in action that can ultimately correct this. Thus, whereas we can understand humans as following rules, we cannot achieve this kind of global understanding of black-box AI.

A case study concerning the use of AI in a high-stakes legal context, such as that of making parole decisions, is ultimately considered. It is suggested that, as we cannot know what rule (if any) a black-box AI system is following in such circumstances, we cannot legitimately base our decisions on its verdicts.

References

Adam, C. and Richard Carter. 2023. "Large Language Models and Intelligence Analysis." *CETaS Expert Analysis.* https://a-mcc.eu/library/large-language-models-and-intelligence-analysis/

Allen, Colin, and Wendel Wallach. 2012. "Moral Machines: Contradiction in Terms or Abdication of Human Responsibility." In *Robot Ethics: The Ethical and Social Implications of Robotics*, edited by Patrick Lin, George Bekey and Keith Abney, 55–68. Cambridge, MA: MIT Press

Arrington, Robert L. 2016. "Wittgenstein and Ethics." In *A Companion to Wittgenstein*, edited by Hans-Johann Glock and John Hyman, 603–611. Hoboken, New Jersey: John Wiley & Sons.

Ayer, A. J. 1936. *Language, Truth and Logic.* London: V. Gollancz.

Biletzki, Anat and Anat Matar, 2023. "Ludwig Wittgenstein." In *The Stanford Encyclopedia of Philosophy* (Fall 2023 Edn), edited by Edward N. Zalta and Uri Nodelman, accessed January 10, 2024. https://plato.stanford.edu/archives/fall2023/entries/wittgenstein

Bix, Brian. 1991. "HLA Hart and the 'Open Texture' of Language." *Law & Philosophy*, 10, no.1: 51–71.

Bix, B.H. 2019. "Waismann, Wittgenstein, Hart and Beyond: The Developing Idea of 'Open Texture' of Language and Law". In *Friedrich Waismann: The Open Texture of Analytic Philosophy*, edited by Makovec, Dejan and Shapiro, Stewart. Friedrich Waismann, 245–260. Cham: Palgrave Macmillan.

Bostrom, Nick. 2014. *Superintelligence: Paths, Dangers, Strategies.* Oxford: Oxford University Press.

Chalmers, David J. 2023. "Does Thought Require Sensory Grounding?" From Pure Thinkers to Large Language Models. *Proceedings and Addresses of the American Philosophical Association* 97: 22–45

Collins, Emily C., Brian Ball, Alice Helliwell, Josh Baker and Julie Marble. forthcoming, 2024. "Autonomy: A Family Resemblance Concept? An Exploration of Human-Robot Teams." In *Interdependent Human-Machine Teams. The Path to Autonomy*, edited by William F. Lawless, R. Mittu, D. A. Sofge and H. Fouad. Amsterdam, The Netherlands: Elsevier.

Daston, Lorraine. 2022. *Rules. A Short History of What We Live By.* Princeton & Oxford: Princeton University Press.

European Parliament. 2023. "EU AI Act: First Regulation on Artificial Intelligence." accessed January 10, 2024. https://www.europarl.europa.eu/topics/en/article/20230601STO93804/eu-ai-act-first-regulation-on-artificial-intelligence

Fairhurst, Jordi. 2021. "The Ethical Significance of the Tractatus Logico-Philosophicus." *Teorema: Revista Internacional de Filosofía* 40, no. 2: 151–168.

Forster, Michael N. 2004. "Wittgenstein's Conception of Grammar." In *Wittgenstein on the Arbitrariness of Grammar,* 7–20. Princeton, NJ: Princeton University Press, http://www.jstor.org/stable/j.ctt7s0sc.6

Gray, Catherine. 2022. "Top 10 Companies Developing Autonomous Vehicle Technology" *AI Magazine*, June 29, 2022. https://aimagazine.com/technology/top-10-companies-developing-autonomous-vehicle-technology

Gaut, Berys. 2000. "'Art' as a Cluster Concept." In *Theories of Art Today*, edited by Noël Carroll. 25-44. London: University of Wisconsin Press.

Hart, H. L. A. 1958. "Positivism and the Separation of Law and Morals." *Harvard Law Review* 71, no. 4: 593–629. https://doi.org/10.2307/1338225

Hart, H. L. A. 1961. *The Concept of Law* (2nd Edn). London: Oxford University Press.

Himma, Kenneth E. n.d. "Legal Positivism." In *Internet Encyclopedia of Philosophy*, accessed January 10, 2024. https://iep.utm.edu/legalpos/

Krizhevsky, Alex, Ilya Sutskever and Geoffrey E. Hinton. 2012. "Imagenet Classification with Deep Convolutional Neural Networks." *Advances in Neural Information Processing Systems* 25: 1097–1105.

LeCun, Yann, Yoshua Bengio and Geoffrey Hinton. 2015. "Deep Learning." *Nature* 521, no. 7553: 436–444.

Lefebvre, A. 2011. "Law and the Ordinary: Hart, Wittgenstein, Jurisprudence." *Telos-New York* 154: 99.

Makovec, Dejan and Stewart Shapiro (eds). 2019. *Friedrich Waismann: The Open Texture of Analytic Philosophy.* Cham: Palgrave Macmillan.

Marshall, Aarian. 2024. "Apple Ramped up Autonomous Vehicle Testing Last Year, Filings Show." *Wired,* February 2, 2024. https://www.wired.com/story/apple-ramped-up-autonomous-vehicle-testing-last-year/

Milmo, Dan. 2024. "'Impossible' to Create AI Tools like ChatGPT without Copyrighted Material, OpenAI says." *The Guardian*, January 8, 2024. https://www.theguardian.com/technology/2024/jan/08/ai-tools-chatgpt-copyrighted-material-openai

McFee, G. 2019. *Wittgenstein on Mind, Meaning and Context: Seven Essays.* Eastbourne, England: Pageantry Press

Misselhorn, C. 2022. "Artificial Moral Agents: Conceptual Issues and Ethical Controversy." In *The Cambridge Handbook of Responsible Artificial Intelligence: Interdisciplinary Perspectives,* edited by Silja Voeneky, Philipp Kellmeyer, Oliver Mueller and Wolfram Burgard, 31–49. Cambridge, UK: Cambridge Law Handbooks, Cambridge University Press.

Monk, Ray. 1990. *Ludwig Wittgenstein: The Duty of Genius.* New York: The Free Press.

Moyal-Sharrock, Danièle. 2021. *Certainty in Action: Wittgenstein on Language, Mind and Epistemology.* London: Bloomsbury Publishing.

Moyal-Sharrock, D. 2004. *Understanding Wittgenstein's on Certainty.* New York: Palgrave Macmillan.

Müller, Vincent C. and Michael Cannon. 2021. "Existential Risk from AI and Orthogonality: Can we have it Both Ways?" *Ratio* 35, no 1: 25–36.

Obermeyer, Ziad, Brian Powers, Christine Vogeli and Sendhil Mullainathan. 2019. "Dissecting Racial Bias in an Algorithm used to Manage the Health of Populations."

Science 366, no. 6464: 447–453. https://www.science.org/doi/full/10.1126/science.aax2342

Omiye, Jesutofunmi A., Jenna C. Lester, Simon Spichak, Veronica Rotemberg and Roxana Daneshjou. 2023. "Large Language Models Propagate Race-Based Medicine." *NPJ Digital Medicine* 6, no. 1: 195. https://doi.org/10.1038/s41746-023-00939-z

Pritchard,D. 2012. "Wittgenstein and the Groundlessness of Our Believing." *Synthese* 189, no. 2: 255–272.

QuantumBlack AI by Mckinsey. 2023. "The State of AI in 2023: Generative AI's Breakout Year." QuantumBlack AI by McKinsey Global Publishing.

Rusbridger, Alan. 2018. *Breaking News: The Remaking of Journalism and Why it Matters Now.* New York: Farrar, Straus and Giroux.

Sandis,C. and Moyal-Sharrock, D. 2022. *Extending Hinge Epistemology.* London:Anthem Press.

Schauer, Frederick. 2011. "On the Open Texture of Law." Available at http://dx.doi.org/10.2139/ssrn.1926855

Schlesinger, Sybil. 1997. "Working Definitions: A Critique of HLA Hart's Use of Wittgenstein in 'The Concept of Law'." *ARSP: Archiv für Rechts-und Sozialphilosophie/ Archives for Philosophy of Law and Social Philosophy* 83, no. 1: 103–124.

Schwartz, Oscar. 2019. "In 2016, Microsoft's Racist Chatbot Revealed the Dangers of Online Conversation." *IEEE Spectrum* 11. This is an online source:https://spectrum.ieee.org/in-2016-microsofts-racist-chatbot-revealed-the-dangers-of-online-conversation

Searle, John R. 1980. "Minds, Brains, and Programs." *Behavioral and Brain Sciences* 3, no. 3: 417–424.

Strohkorb Sebo, Sarah, Margaret Traeger, Malte Jung and Brian Scassellati. 2018. "The Ripple Effects of Vulnerability: The Effects of a Robot's Vulnerable Behavior on Trust in Human-Robot Teams." In *Proceedings of the 2018 ACM/IEEE International Conference on Human-Robot Interaction*, 178–186. New York: ACM. https://dl.acm.org/doi/pdf/10.1145/3171221.3171275

Thomas, Daniel and Criddle, Christina. 2024. "UK Shelves Proposed AI Copyright Code in Blow to Creative Industries." *The Financial Times*, February 5, 2024. https://www.ft.com/content/a10866ec-130d-40a3-b62a-978f1202129e

von Wright, G. H. 1951. "Deontic Logic". *Mind* 60, no. 237: 1–15.

Waismann, Friedrich. 1945. "Verifiability" (Part II of a symposium). *Aristotelian Society, supplementary volume XIX*, 119–150.

Weitz, Morris. 1956. "The Role of Theory in Aesthetics." *The Journal of Aesthetics and Art* 1, no. XV: 27–35.

Wittgenstein, Ludwig. 1922. *Tractatus Logico-Philosophicus.* Translated by Ogden, C. K. and Ramsey, F. P. London: Kegan Paul.

Wittgenstein, Ludwig. 1953. *Philosophical Investigations.* Oxford: Basil Blackwell.

Wittgenstein, Ludwig. 1958. *The Blue and Brown Books.* Harper Torchbook.

Wittgenstein, Ludwig. 1961. *Tractatus Logico-Philosophicus.* English Translation by D. F. Pears and B. F. McGuinnes London: Routledge and Kegan Paul.

Wittgenstein, Ludwig. 1965. "A Lecture on Ethics." *Philosophical Review* 74, no. 1: 3–12.

Wittgenstein, Ludwig. (2023). *TractatusLogico-Philosophicus.* English Translation by Beaney, M. Oxford: Oxford University Press.

Wollheim, Richard. 1968. *Art and its Objects.* New York: Harper & Row.

World Health Organisation. 2021 *Ethics and Governance of Artificial Intelligence for Health: WHO Guidance*. Geneva: World Health Organization.

World Health Organization. 2024. *Ethics and Governance of Artificial Intelligence for Health: Guidance on Large Multi-Modal Models*. Geneva: World Health Organization.

Wooldridge, Michael. 2020. *The Road to Conscious Machines: The Story of AI*. London, UK: Penguin.

Chapter 1

IS, OUGHT AND WITTGENSTEIN

Alessandro Rossi

Introduction

In this chapter, I would like to explore a connection between Wittgenstein's *Lecture on Ethics* (Wittgenstein 1965: LE) and the ethics of Artificial Intelligence (AI ethics).[1] Part of the project in AI Ethics is pursued by attempting to provide a formal account of a group of interrelated concepts determining what von Wright (1951), in a seminal article on the subject, called *modes of obligation*. Amongst such concepts, dubbed *deontic* by von Wright,[2] are: the obligatory (what *ought* to be done); the permissible (what *is allowed* to be done); and the forbidden (what *must not* be done).

Since von Wright's paper, it has become standard to treat deontic concepts as forming a distinctive class of modalities in addition to other perhaps more familiar such classes.[3] An obvious example comprises *alethic* (or sometimes *metaphysical*) modalities, represented in language by what are known as the *modes of truth*: what *cannot but* be the case; what *can* be the case; and what *cannot* be the case.[4]

Prima facie, the classes of deontic and alethic modalities respectively single out two ways in which we could use language: normatively, to express obligations (and cognate notions); and descriptively, to express necessities (*ditto*).

---

1 For comprehensive overviews see Boddington (2023) and Dubber et al. (2020).

2 The use of the adjective *deontic* to describe the concepts in question has however some antecedents, such as Mally (1926) and, about two centuries before him, Bentham (1970).

3 For an overview, see Priest (2008).

4 The idea that there is a distinctively metaphysical notion of modality is influential but not uncontroversial. The idea is powerfully defended by Kripke (1980), but contested by, e.g. Priest (2018). It is orthogonal to the present chapter whether a genuinely metaphysical account of modality is available.

The Lecture on Ethics is the only place in which Wittgenstein elaborated on the relationship between normative and descriptive uses of language, at any length. In it, as is known, Wittgenstein joins a tradition stretching back at least to Hume in maintaining that no normative claim could ever logically follow from a descriptive claim; an 'is' can never entail an 'ought'. What is perhaps less known is that the thesis defended by Wittgenstein in the Lecture on Ethics might have an important role to play in debates around the existential risk posed by the rapid development of AI.

This chapter has thus a twofold goal. In the first section I would like to show how, by accepting the thesis that an 'is' never entails an 'ought', the strength of some arguments purporting to show that AI poses an existential threat appears rather dim. In the second section, I would like to propose my own reading of Wittgenstein's arguments in favour of the no-'ought'-from-an-'is' thesis, put forward in the Lecture on Ethics. Along the way, I will also show how the arguments contained in the Lecture on Ethics might provide some support for a so-called *irresolute* reading of Wittgenstein, on which nonsensical statements, such as those which are ethical in nature, may in fact be illuminating and show truths unreachable by a purely descriptive use of language. Then, I will close by briefly taking stock of what the chapter has shown.

The Autonomy of Ethics and AI Existential Risk

Before presenting my own understanding of Wittgenstein's Lecture on Ethics (the Lecture, henceforth) in the next section, I would like to say something here about why I think it is important, for the purposes of this chapter, to focus on the Lecture in the first place. This will be the occasion to closely examine an application of the present work to the field of AI ethics. This section, in sum, will try to provide some motivation for the goal I will pursue in the chapter. Then, in the next section, I will get my discussion of the Lecture going.

The manuscript entitled *A Lecture on Ethics* is the transcript by Friedrich Waismann of a lecture which Wittgenstein delivered on 17 November 1929 in Cambridge, in response to an invitation issued by *The Heretics* – a society of non-philosophers promoting discussion around themes from religion and philosophy. The fact that it is the only speech ever delivered by Wittgenstein to a general audience, together with the fact that it is Wittgenstein's only sustained reflection on ethics, suffices to make the Lecture worthy of special attention. Besides, unlike other parts of Wittgenstein's work on the subject (see e.g. Wittgenstein 2022: TLP 6.4–6.421), the Lecture lends itself to immediate comprehension, which reinforces its interestingness for the present chapter.

Of course, I am well aware that there is much more to Wittgenstein's articulate conception of ethics than what he addressed in a popular lecture – see for example the helpful reconstruction offered by Christensen (2011). But since the goal of this chapter is not merely exegetical, it seems to me that I should make no apologies for focusing only on the Lecture here; the Lecture, as I hope to show, is interesting in its own right. By this, I mean that the Lecture contains philosophical material which can be analysed and assessed independently of Wittgenstein's overarching views on ethics.

Further, I believe that the ideas contained in the Lecture can offer a contribution to important issues in the field of AI ethics. In a recent paper, Müller & Cannon (2021) critically discuss the literature on the so-called *existential risk* posed by AI – roughly, the idea that (i) the development of AI will reach a level of superintelligence or *singularity*, as Kurzweil (2005) put it; and (ii) such superintelligence is likely to result in the extinction of the human species. In particular, the authors want to distance themselves from the tendency to take the thesis of existential risk posed by superintelligence as being implied by two premises concerning AI singularity and the orthogonality of intelligence and goals (stay tuned). I will first get a bit into the details of what these premises amount to. Then, I would like to bring into the discussion the key thesis under focus in this chapter, namely, the idea (of Humean descent) advocated by Wittgenstein in the Lecture that a descriptive premise never logically entails a normative conclusion. It seems to me that, with this thesis onboard, the case against the existential threat of AI proposed by Müller and Cannon can be strengthened considerably. This, if correct, could advance the debate around the existential risk of AI, by bringing to the table a perspective to my knowledge surprisingly novel.

The thesis that AI poses an existential risk is described by Müller and Cannon as being often supported by two premises. The first is that AI will learn how to self-improve, up to the point in which it will reach superintelligence (or singularity) and escape human control. What is *superintelligence* exactly? A rough and ready definition is provided by Nick Bostrom, the author of a celebrated book on superintelligence, who takes it as 'any intellect that greatly exceeds the cognitive performance of humans in virtually all domains of interest' (2014: 22). An important point about superintelligence as understood in this very context, which will play a significant role in the discussion below, is in order. Müller and Cannon (2021), following established usage, call *general* the kind of intelligence at play here. As Müller & Cannon (2021: 28) remark, general superintelligence is simply 'a notion of intelligence like the human one, just "more" of it'. As we will see shortly, the second premise for the existential threat posed by superintelligence resorts to a narrower notion of intelligence, clearly distinct from general intelligence. In any case, belief that a general superintelligence will exist in the future could be justified as follows. Start with the prediction that, sooner or later, AI will reach a level of intelligence which could be considered human-like. The evidence supporting a similar prediction is certainly there. For example, in 2012/2013 the questionnaire *Future Progress in Artificial Intelligence*, devised by Vincent Müller and Nick Bostrom, surveyed about 550 AI experts of various backgrounds about the time frame in which AI would reach what they call *High-Level Machine Intelligence* (HLMI). In their 2016 report on the survey, we can see that the authors had defined an HLMI, in the survey, as being 'one that can carry out most human professions at least as well as a typical human' (2016: 558). The report reveals that, according to the respondents, HLMI has a 50 per cent probability of being with us by 2040–50, rising to a 90 per cent probability by 2075. The strikingness of this data may perhaps be downplayed by pointing out that HMLI is not, so to speak, *real* intelligence; but an admittedly weaker form thereof. This way one might argue that the achievement of HLMI is on reflection not of great significance. Whether HLMI, or something along those lines, fully captures what needs to be said about human intelligence is a task that I gladly leave to others. Nevertheless, the evidence just provided at least supports the view that there exists a wide belief that AI will very soon exponentially enhance its capacities. And, some proponents of the existential risk scenario contend, when AI will reach such a level it will be a point of no return: singularity, at that point, will be inevitable. For definiteness, we can call this view, the first premise in the argument we are reconstructing, the *Inevitability of Superintelligence.*

> **Inevitability of Superintelligence:** Sooner or later, AI will reach a level of singularity and outperform the best human minds in virtually all domains of cognitive interest.
>
> *(Bostrom 2014: 63)*

But of course, nothing so far prevents that singularity results in a huge enhancement of the human species, as opposed to its extinction. Nothing, *unless additional reasons for the Existential Risk view are adduced.* One such reason, considered by Müller and Cannon, is what Bostrom calls *Orthogonality Thesis*, namely, the idea that:

> **Orthogonality Thesis:** Intelligence and final goals are orthogonal: more or less any level of intelligence could be combined with more or less any final goal.
>
> *(Bostrom 2014: 130)*

To understand the Orthogonality Thesis, we need to get clear on its key terms: *intelligence*, and *final goal*. Unfortunately, what Bostrom means by *final goal* is not clear (nor does Müller and Cannon's discussion attempt to clarify matters). I will take it, following Alvarez (2010: 92), as an end for the sake of which an action is performed; both in the sense of that which a certain action manages to achieve, and that towards which an action is oriented.[5] On the other hand, some explanation as to what kind of intelligence would be orthogonal to final goals is fortunately provided. This is said to be 'a skill at prediction, planning and means-end reasoning in general' (2014: 130). In an endnote to this remark, Bostrom further qualifies this kind of intelligence as *instrumental*, namely as pertaining to the capacity of achieving set goals (2014: endnote 5, 349). Such a narrow form of intelligence is clearly distinct from general intelligence. Instrumental intelligence, indeed, appears to be intimately connected with the narrower ability of bringing about desired results; *general* intelligence, by contrast, has much broader scope.[6] The Orthogonality Thesis thus amounts to the view that (more or less) any form of *instrumental* intelligence can serve the pursuit of any given goal. But here, we start seeing the beginning of a problem.

For, if we now attempted to use the two premises (viz. Inevitability of Superintelligence and Orthogonality Thesis) to derive the conclusion that superintelligence poses an existential threat, we might be accused of committing a fallacy of ambiguity, trading on a twofold meaning of *intelligence*. For surely, Müller & Cannon (2021: 29) argue, the narrow conception of intelligence presupposed by the Orthogonality Thesis (instrumental intelligence) is not the (much) stronger notion of intelligence presupposed by the Inevitability of Superintelligence (general intelligence). Then, could the two premises not be compatible with the existence of a superintelligence which, in addition to having an impeccable instrumental intelligence, nonetheless also uses its own general superintelligence to reflect on which goals ought to be pursued? Surely nothing in the two premises rules this out. Given such premises, therefore, attempting to derive the existential threat of superintelligence results in a *non sequitur*.

To adjust things, one should either reformulate the premises by making sure that the meaning of *intelligence* does not vary across them, or add additional

5 See Alvarez (2010: 92 ff) for a helpful discussion on goals in the philosophy of action.

6 According to Müller & Cannon (2021: 28) instrumental intelligence is the kind of intelligence classical decision theory aims to give an account of, since the theory assumes that a rational agent should always try to maximize the *expected utility*: the weighted average of the utilities of each possible outcome – where the concept of utility measures an outcome's preferability over others.

premises. If we constrain ourselves to the first option, it looks as though there are only two avenues. The first: we keep the Inevitability of Superintelligence as it is *and* strengthen the Orthogonality Thesis by reformulating it with an appeal to general intelligence. The second: we keep the Orthogonality Thesis as it is and weaken the Inevitability of Superintelligence by reformulating it with an appeal to instrumental intelligence. Ultimately, Müller and Cannon argue that both options are unpromising.[7] As expected, the conclusion they draw is that there is no way of fixing the premises which makes the argument sound. Nor, I think, is this the end of the story. For, given the view under focus in this chapter, the case against one of the two reformulations of the argument appears to me to be susceptible to something close to a principled refutation. So, before turning to other matters, I would like to conclude this subsection by elaborating on this last point.

In particular, I am interested in assessing the first of the two options: the one, namely, consisting in strengthening the Orthogonality Thesis by reformulating it with an appeal to the stronger notion of general intelligence (and leave the other premise unchanged). The essence of Müller and Cannon's reasoning here is that, given an agent with general superintelligence, the Orthogonality Thesis prima facie looks suspiciously strong. For one thing, the Orthogonality Thesis so reformulated is perfectly consistent with a superintelligent agent setting very non-standard goals for itself. These might include bizarre goals such as, say, spending its time counting all sand grains in the world, or rather horrible goals such as physically harming sentient beings for the sake of it. This is perfectly in line with (the new, stronger version of) the Orthogonality Thesis; but equally, scenarios like that seem to make a mockery of the notion of superintelligence. And, *I now add*, given the view under focus in this chapter, it becomes pretty obvious to see why.

Assume the Humean thesis, espoused by Wittgenstein in the Lecture, that a normative claim never logically follows from a descriptive one – no 'ought' from an 'is'. Insofar as knowledge of what one ought (is allowed, is prohibited) to do constitutes at least part of our moral knowledge, the source of this body of knowledge, given the assumption at work, cannot have anything to do with how the world is. Ethical knowledge, on this view, is autonomous: its truths are irreducibly moral truths, with no grounding on the makeup of the world whatsoever. Applied to the case at hand, this view seems to entail, in quite a natural way, that an agent embodying general superintelligence, amongst the many tasks in which it would outperform humans, should also be capable of outperforming them on ethical grounds. To put it slightly differently, and a

7 See their discussion in (2021: 30–33).

bit more extendedly, given the view that there are irreducibly moral truths, the prospect of a superintelligent agent carrying out such plainly impermissible actions as physically harming sentient beings for the sake of it sounds a bit like an oxymoron. Part of having general superintelligence, if the notion has any bite, is being effective at discerning absolutely impermissible actions such as the ones mentioned earlier, from permissible ones. Any agent bringing about an action of this sort should be seen as significantly lacking moral knowledge. And being in a similar state of moral ignorance is at odds with having *general superintelligence.*

There are, of course, a number of questions which need answering at this point: What does it mean exactly to outperform someone on moral grounds? What is the source of this irreducibly moral knowledge which humans often seem to exhibit? Are moral truths absolute or context-dependent? These are tricky questions, which lie far beyond the scope of the present chapter. I will not attempt to answer them, save for two remarks which I hope will help to see why I take the prospect just sketched as not hopeless from the start.

The first is that the thesis of the irreducibility of moral truths to, so to speak, a descriptive categorial basis seems to have an analogy with other well-established views in philosophy. Specifically, what I have in mind here is Timothy Williamson's thorough rejection of modal supervenience in his *Modal Logic as Metaphysics* (Williamson 2013: Ch. 7). If there are purely modal truths, it is argued there, then these should be accepted as brute facts. Similarly, it might be said, for moral truths. The analogy between the cases of moral and modal truths may or may not break at some point. But surely the requirement that every kind of truth requires a grounding in the actual descriptive reality appears to be controversial. If so, I conclude, the irreducibility of moral truths is not *a priori* disqualified.

Second, it is now clear that the view can be made formally coherent, and this is not at all a trivial fact. Some very promising attempts at modelling the view are already available – witness, for example, Russell & Restall (2010) and Russell (2021). Had all these attempts at making the view formally coherent failed, the prospect for the view would be significantly different. Of course, this is not to say that all formal representations of the view are alike;[8] but the existence of formal models capturing the irreducibility of moral truths is yet another reason why the view is not immediately disqualified.

Let me pause here, before turning to other matters. What we have seen so far are my reasons for choosing to focus on the Lecture in this chapter,

8 And which one one ought to prefer can be assessed in many ways; a suitable methodology to do so is described in Priest (2016a).

and how the issues addressed by Wittgenstein in the Lecture appear to be entangled with important issues in AI Ethics. As promised, I would now like to offer my own account of the content of the Lecture.

The Lecture

On my understanding, the Lecture is an intriguing defence of the thesis, already invoked several times in the foregoing discussion, that no normative claim logically follows from a descriptive claim. Given its Humean origin, and following a widespread usage in the most recent literature, we can for definiteness call this *Hume's Thesis* – a label which, it is however important to remark, Wittgenstein does *not* use in the Lecture.

Providing a close reading of the Lecture to reconstruct the line of reasoning offered by Wittgenstein is important for at least two reasons. The first is that the key thesis defended by Wittgenstein in the Lecture, Hume's Thesis, has recently attracted the attention of several commentators (amongst all, see in particular Russell (2023)). Reconstructing Wittgenstein's defence of Hume Thesis could therefore provide a welcome contribution to the debate which these publications have revamped.

The second reason is that Wittgenstein's defence of Hume's thesis can also offer a contribution to Wittgenstein scholarship. As is known, since at least Diamond (1991) a distinction has emerged amongst Wittgenstein scholars with respect to how one should go about interpreting Wittgenstein's remark, in the penultimate section of the *Tractatus*, that anyone who fully understands its propositions thereby recognizes them as nonsensical (Wittgenstein 2002: TLP 6.54) – for a useful overview of the debate, see Bronzo (2012); for recent critical discussion, see Ulatowski (2020). According to *irresolute* readers of Wittgenstein, such as Hacker (2000), this remark is *not* to be interpreted as saying that the propositions of the *Tractatus* are plain nonsense. For, nonsense can sometimes be illuminating and show ineffable truths; the propositions of the *Tractatus*, on this view, are illuminating in that they show what cannot be said. By contrast, *resolute* readers of Wittgenstein, such as Conant (2007) and Diamond (1991), deny that the distinction between plain and illuminating nonsense has any plausible role to play in Wittgenstein exegesis. As another resolute reader of Wittgenstein put it, '[T]he author of the Tractatus recognized only one species of nonsense – mere gibberish' (Mulhall 2006: 2). As will become clear throughout this section, an irresolute reading of Wittgenstein, separating mere nonsense from illuminating nonsense, seems to be required in order to properly account for the kind of defence of Hume's Thesis put forward by Wittgenstein in the Lecture. In other words, a resolute interpretation of Wittgenstein's conception of nonsense will not be able to do justice to the key theses advocated by Wittgenstein in the Lecture. If this reading of Lecture is on target, this would be one of the key contributions of the present chapter.

My analysis of the Lecture thus intersects two parallel philosophical literatures: one on Hume's Thesis; the other on Wittgenstein's take on nonsense. The philosophical audience which could benefit from a discussion of the Lecture is, therefore, fairly broad. With all this in mind, I now would like to turn to my own interpretation of the text, and the defence of Hume's Thesis it contains.

Wittgenstein's defence of Hume's Thesis

Hume's Thesis is explicitly advocated by Wittgenstein in the initial part of the Lecture, though not before having provided a gloss on an important distinction concerning the use of ethical or, as I will say hereafter, *normative* vocabulary. This gloss is to the effect that normative vocabulary can take an *absolute* and a *relative* reading. As we will see in a moment, this distinction is important for Wittgenstein's core claim. But to properly understand what this distinction amounts to, I should spell out a little bit what I will take it to presuppose.

Specifically, I take this distinction to presuppose a central thesis for my interpretation of Wittgenstein, which I will call the *Dichotomy Thesis*. This roughly amounts to the idea that the world non-trivially divides into at least descriptive and normative realms, each one involving its own distinctive set of facts. An attempt at making this thought more precise is in order. In line with proposition 1.1. of the *Tractatus*, I take it that the expression 'totality of facts' adequately characterizes, at least at the time when the Lecture was delivered, Wittgenstein's take on what we should take the world to be. Then, on this definition, we could reformulate the Dichotomy Thesis as the thesis that the world non-trivially divides into at least two classes of facts: facts about how the world *is*; and facts about how the world *ought* to be. Throughout, I will call the former *material facts* and the latter *normative facts*. Whilst I am taking there to be no overlaps between these classes of facts, I am not making any assumptions about their exhausting the totality of facts; there may be other realms, involving their own distinctive sets of facts, in addition to the two under discussion here – the aesthetic realm, for example. In any case, this way of putting the Dichotomy Thesis could be contested on the grounds that Wittgenstein did not really intend the dichotomy in question to apply to facts (but merely to statements). I will take up this issue later on in this section, but I will argue that, on closer scrutiny, the Dichotomy Thesis does have sufficient textual justification. Until then, I will proceed on the assumption that cashing out the Dichotomy Thesis as a distinction between normative and material facts is a legitimate move.

By *material facts* I mean those facts which Wittgenstein in the Lecture takes to be described by what he calls *statements of facts*; or, as we will say hereafter, *descriptive statements*. Which immediately raises the question, *what is a descriptive statement?* Well, a first thing to say is that it is a declarative statement; that is, a statement for which it is meaningful to ask *what is its truth-value?* Moreover, at the very least, it seems that we should say that a necessary condition for a statement to count as descriptive is that it does not contain any occurrence of normative vocabulary. For example, it should contain no occurrence of 'ought'. If a statement did include some occurrence of normative vocabulary, we might expect, it should not count as descriptive; though it may still fail to count as descriptive even if it did feature no occurrence of normative vocabulary. It is difficult, based on the remarks offered by Wittgenstein in the Lecture, to also specify sufficient conditions for a statement to count as descriptive. This, however, should not worry us hereafter, since we are not in the business of providing a demarcation of descriptive and normative vocabulary. On the other hand, by *normative fact* I mean what Wittgenstein in the Lecture takes to be described by what he calls a *judgement of value*; or, as we will say hereafter, *normative statement*. An example of normative statement considered by Wittgenstein is 'You ought to want to behave better' (1965: LE, 5) which, presumably, should be thought of as a normative statement in virtue of the presence of the normative verb *ought*. Two relevant points. First, 'You ought to want to behave better' is a statement which is as declarative as any other descriptive statement. Moreover, since this statement is completely arbitrarily chosen, it seems to me that all other normative statements of the form 'x ought to Y' should plausibly count as declarative statements. Second, I am *not* suggesting that Wittgenstein takes the presence of *ought* as an essential feature of normative statements. For example, the Lecture assumes the Moorean definition of ethics as 'the general inquiry into what is good' (1965: LE, 5)[9]. This makes *good* a typical example of a normative predicate, which may essentially contribute to giving a statement a normative character. 'This is a *good* fellow' (1965: LE, 9) is a relevant example considered by Wittgenstein – and notice, incidentally, that this statement is just as declarative as 'You ought to want to behave better'. In any case, since Wittgenstein does not provide us in the Lecture with a further characterization of what makes a statement a normative one, we cannot say in exact terms how he understood normative statements. But the previous remarks suffice to say that

9 Though see also Moore (1922: 2).

he surely took it as a necessary condition for a statement to count as normative that it features at least one occurrence of normative vocabulary. If a statement did not include any such occurrence, we might expect, it should not count as normative; though it may still fail to count as normative if it did feature some normative vocabulary.

So much for the distinction drawn by Wittgenstein between descriptive and normative statements. How does that distinction latch on to the other distinction drawn by Wittgenstein, brought up three paragraphs above, between absolute and relative uses of normative vocabulary? To see this, we should focus on the following example considered by Wittgenstein: 'This man is a good runner' (1965: LE, 5). As Wittgenstein (1965: LE, 5–6) puts it:

> The essence of this difference seems to be obviously this: Every judgment of relative value is a mere statement of facts and can therefore be put in such a form that it loses all the appearance of a judgment of value: [...] 'This man is a good runner' simply means that he runs a certain number of miles in a certain number of minutes, etc.

Let me begin with a terminological remark. The reason I chose to talk about *descriptive statements* and *normative statements*, as opposed to follow Wittgenstein's use of *judgements of value* and *statements of facts*, is simply due to the fact that the terminology I adopted seems to me to be more in line with current usage.[10] With this in mind, Wittgenstein is warning us here against the possibility of mistakenly categorizing some statements as normative. For, some statements, such as 'This man is a good runner', despite appearing to be normative due to their featuring seemingly normative vocabulary (e.g. *good*, in the example) are merely apparently normative. In actual fact, the seemingly normative vocabulary they feature is used in a *relative sense*. That is to say, they are susceptible to being reformulated, *salva veritate*, without any appeal to seemingly normative vocabulary altogether.[11] Not so, on the other hand, for those statements featuring an occurrence of normative vocabulary used in an absolute sense, such as 'You ought to want to behave better'. For those statements, no such reformulation appears to be possible.

I have so far illustrated my key interpretive hypothesis to read the Lecture, the Dichotomy Thesis and Wittgenstein's distinction between absolute and

10 See e.g. Schurz (1997); Russell & Restall (2010); Russell (2021).

11 Thus, 'this man is a good runner' appears to be synonymous with something like 'this man can run a certain distance in a certain amount of time'. No seemingly normative expression, as can be seen, figures in the latter sentence.

relative uses of normative vocabulary. After this long but necessary detour, we can turn to Wittgenstein's endorsement of Hume's Thesis, followed by some reasoning which is worth reading in full:

> Now what I wish to contend is that, although all judgments of relative value can be shown to be mere statements of facts, no statement of fact can ever be, or imply, a judgment of absolute value. Let me explain this: Suppose one of you were an omniscient person and therefore knew all the movements of all the bodies in the world dead or alive and that he also knew all the states of mind of all human beings that ever lived, and suppose this man wrote all he knew in a big book, then this book would contain the whole description of the world; and what I want to say is, that this book would contain nothing that we would call an *ethical* judgment or anything that would logically imply such a judgment. It would of course contain all relative judgments of value and all true scientific propositions and in fact all true propositions that can be made.
>
> *(1965: LE, 6)*

We can conceptually divide this passage into two parts: the first contains Wittgenstein's explicit endorsement of Hume's Thesis (until *absolute value*); the second contains Wittgenstein's elaboration on the consequences of Hume's Thesis (from *Let me explain* to the end). The first part is pretty easy to explain. Take any statement which either does not contain any normative vocabulary or, if it does contain some, it is all used in a *relative* sense. Any such statement, given what we said earlier, will count as descriptive. Further, any such statement does not entail any normative statement: Hume's Thesis ensues. The second part draws some consequences from what was just said. Wittgenstein's understanding of Hume's Thesis in the second part of the passage proceeds by way of a metaphor. If an omniscient being knew all the facts in the world, and proceeded to compile a list of statements describing them, any normative statement would neither make the list, nor be implied by any other statement in it. *Prima facie*, the reasoning offered in this part of the passage seems to flatly contradict the Dichotomy Thesis; so a few words as to why this need not be so appear very much needed.

The Dichotomy Thesis, recall, asserted the existence of a distinctive class of facts described by normative statements (the class of normative facts). But in the second part of the above passage, the existence of such a class seemed to be precisely what Wittgenstein was trying to deny; namely, by claiming that the omniscient being of the thought experiment would not include any normative statements in their list. As I already mentioned, I believe there is ground to hold on to the idea that Wittgenstein endorsed something like the Dichotomy Thesis in the Lecture. Accordingly, it seems to me that I should do two things. First, illustrate that an alternative reading of the passage, capable of solving its apparent tension with the Dichotomy Thesis, is available.

Second, that such a reading has sufficient textual ground to back it up. With regard to the first task, I will say this: my interpretation of Wittgenstein, to continue with the terms of the metaphor, is that Wittgenstein's omniscient being is not in charge with the task of filling out a list describing the totality of facts *in the world*; but simply the totality of material facts.

Here is why I am drawn to this interpretation of the text. After considering and rejecting the thought that normative concepts would not be present in the world but only in our mind – because, if they were, they would feature in the omniscient being's list – Wittgenstein offers the following remark:

> And now I must say that if I contemplate what Ethics really would have to be if there were such a science, this result seems to me quite obvious. It seems to me obvious that nothing we could ever think or say should be *the* thing. That we cannot write a *scientific* [my italics] book, the subject matter of which could be intrinsically sublime and above all other subject matters. [...] Our words used as we use them *in science* [my italics], are vessels capable only of containing and conveying meaning and sense, *natural* meaning and sense. Ethics, if it is anything, is supernatural and our words will only express facts.
>
> *(1965: LE, 7)*

The point of the passage, as I read it, is to clarify what ethics cannot be. And, it is argued, ethics cannot be a *science.* I will have more to say on this shortly; but what I ultimately want to contend is that the reasoning driving Wittgenstein to this conclusion reveals that the previous thought experiment, concerning what an omniscient being's world-book would contain, should not be read as necessarily excluding the Dichotomy Thesis. Here is why.

To begin with, it seems to me that the key point of the passage is phrased in such a way as to make the reference to the previous thought experiment quite explicit, and this is important because it is that thought experiment we are trying coming to grips with. In the thought experiment, recall, the omniscient being was presented as being seemingly in charge of writing an exhaustive book about the world: containing, that is, *absolutely every* truth of the world – descriptive, and otherwise. In the passage at hand, Wittgenstein says: 'it seems to me obvious that [...] we cannot write a scientific book, the subject matter of which could be intrinsically sublime and above all other subject matters.' What I gain from this remark is a different key to interpreting the thought experiment: implicit in that thought experiment is that the omniscient being was in charge of writing, *not an exhaustive book of the world,*[12] but an

12 The expression *book of the word* is due to Sider (2011), though Sider probably uses it in a slightly different sense.

exhaustive *scientific* book of the world. If this remark of Wittgenstein is to be read in connection with what the thought experiment had just expressed, and it seems pretty clear that it is, then the next question is, *what does Wittgenstein mean by* scientific *here*?

Well, first of all, we are told that there cannot be a *science* of ethics because in science words are used differently from how they are used in ethics: specifically, it is said, they are used as conveying meaning and sense – in fact, *natural* meaning and sense. On the assumption that *words* here is a metonymical expression safely replaceable with *language*, to understand Wittgenstein's use of *science* we need to pin down the qualification *natural* first. Although this may ultimately be open to interpretation, it seems to me that something quite conclusive can be said on the matter. Let us follow Wittgenstein and ask: How is language used in science? A plausible answer suggests itself: in science, no matter how we want to characterize it exactly, language is used to describe how the world *is*; what I have called above the class of *material facts*. This, I think, is the sense in which Wittgenstein takes scientific language to be natural. Now, if *this* is the feature of scientific language which makes it impossible there being a science of ethics, then Wittgenstein here is probably using 'science' in a broader sense than just, say, 'natural science'. More specifically, I think that the point which Wittgenstein is trying to press here is that we can call *science* any theory which attempts to truthfully represent the material facts, how the world *is*. *This* is why no such theory can be called *ethics*. For, one would think, the point of ethics is not to describe how the world is; but rather, how it *ought* to be – what I have called above the class of *normative facts*.

If this is correct, then attempting to draw from this the conclusion that, for Wittgenstein, an exhaustive book of the world would only contain an exhaustive description of the material facts (how the world is) seems to me to be an interpretive mistake. This claim does not follow from the above remarks, which allow for the possibility of there being a class of normative facts, the normative ones, left out by the omniscient being of the thought experiment. Surely these will not be expressible in language, if this is used in the *natural* way described above. But that normative facts could be described by language used in this natural way was never a claim I attributed to Wittgenstein. What I have only proposed is that, for Wittgenstein, this way of using language does not capture all that is true about the world.

Further, consider the concluding sentence of the passage: 'Ethics, if it is anything, is supernatural and our words will only express facts.' Again, *prima facie*, this remark may seem to collide with the Dichotomy Thesis; but by reasoning along the above lines, the collision does not seem to be inevitable. First, ethics is described as *supernatural*. This is precisely the claim we would expect, given the foregoing remarks. For, if language used naturally may at most truthfully describe the material facts of the world, any other way of using language, if expressing truths at all, must express truths *beyond* this realm – truths, namely, of a *supernatural* realm. And if so, Wittgenstein's remark may simply be interpreted as saying that, by using language naturally, one will only be able to describe the *material* facts of the world. Given the interpretation of Wittgenstein I am proposing, this seems to me a very natural way to resolve the apparent tension between the remark under consideration and the Dichotomy Thesis.

Let us pause here, and bring this part of the discussion to a conclusion. So far I argued that the picture emerging from the Dichotomy Thesis, for which the world divides into material and normative facts, is not necessarily at odds with what Wittgenstein expressed in some passages of the Lecture. Of course, this by itself is hardly any evidence for my hypothesis that Wittgenstein presupposed something like the Dichotomy Thesis. So I now would like to conclude by filling this gap, and present what textual evidence is there in favour of this hypothesis of mine. Here we go.

We have seen Wittgenstein's reasons for maintaining that ethics is no science, and what Wittgenstein means by *science* in this context, under the interpretation that I proposed. Wittgenstein's next move, as expected, is to spell out what one may try to convey when using language in a non-scientific way; and that includes, of course, language used in an absolutely normative way. My view is that the Lecture contains an argument to the effect that language so used is able to describe a distinctive category of facts which, as per the Dichotomy Thesis, I have been calling *normative* facts. More precisely, Wittgenstein's reasoning here proceeds in two steps. The first step (1965: LE, 7–10) aims to establish that using language non-scientifically results in nonsense. The second step (1965: LE, 10–12) is an argument to the effect that, despite this, in addition to the facts described by language used scientifically, there is a distinctive class of facts described by language used non-scientifically. Let us take the two steps in turn.

For the first step, Wittgenstein proceeds as follows. First, Wittgenstein considers three particular experiences which he reports to have had, which can only be described by using language in a non-scientific way. These are the experience of wondering at the existence of the world; the experience of feeling absolutely safe; and the experience of feeling guilty. The language used to present those experiences, it is argued, involve a misusage of words and, as such, 'the verbal expression which we give to these experiences is nonsense' (1965: LE, 8). For example, Wittgenstein remarks, it is perfectly clear what wondering at something being such and such could be: it would be tantamount to being surprised that it is not how we had imagined it to be (1965: LE, 8). What is not at all clear, Wittgenstein continues, is what wondering at the existence of the world could possibly be. For, it is said, one could not fail to imagine the world as existent (1965: LE, 9).[13] One might thus say that wondering at the existence of the world is wondering at a tautology; but this thought, it is said, 'is nonsense' (1965: LE, 9). The upshot is that a sentence such as 'I wonder at the existence of the world' is literally nonsense, as words appear to be used in a purely allegorical way – or, as Wittgenstein puts it, the sentence involves a *simile* (1965: LE, 9).

The second step of Wittgenstein's reasoning begins to unfold at this point. We might be tempted to think that, due to its allegorical and nonsensical nature, the non-scientific usage of language fails to describe any facts. Indeed, says Wittgenstein, 'as soon as we try to drop the simile and simply to state the facts which stand behind it, we find that there are no such facts' (1965: LE, 10). But if we were to take this view, we would be immediately hit with a problem. As Wittgenstein puts is:

> Now the three experiences which I have mentioned to you (and I could have added others) seem to those who have experienced them, for instance to me, to have in some sense an intrinsic, absolute value. But when I say they are experiences, surely, they are facts; they have taken place then and there, lasted a certain definite time and consequently are describable. And so from what I have said some minutes ago I must admit it is nonsense to say that they have absolute value. And I will make my point still more acute by saying 'It is the paradox that an experience, a fact, should seem to have supernatural value.' Now there is a way in which I would be tempted to meet this paradox.
>
> *(1965: LE, 10)*

Wittgenstein is claiming here that there are conflicting things to be said about his experience of wondering about the existence of the world (and of course, the same is true, *mutatis mutandis*, for the other two experiences mentioned earlier on). On the one hand, it would not seem to be possible to describe the experience of wondering about the existence of the world as having an absolute value, since doing so, as per the first step of Wittgenstein's reasoning here, would involve a non-scientific usage of language and thus result in non-sense. On the other hand, such an experience is an experience nonetheless. As such, it is said, it is a fact and hence is describable. The passage concludes with the remark that, in a certain sense, Wittgenstein is happy to embrace this contradiction.

13 Whether imagination is always so constrained is, of course, very controversial. See e.g. Priest (2016b: Ch. 11).

The concluding remark of the passage is already indication that there *is*, for Wittgenstein, a sense in which language used in a non-scientific way succeeds in describing certain facts – experiences, Wittgenstein claims, are facts. The next question is, *in what sense?* Well, set aside Wittgenstein for a moment; a natural answer in my view could be given by reasoning as follows. If we are happy to say that there is a distinction between scientific and non-scientific language, and we are also happy to say that each usage of language manages to describe its own distinctive class of facts, the obvious consequence which we should draw is that the facts described by scientific language are not all the facts! And that is to say, what we need to invoke here is precisely the Dichotomy Thesis.

Now, it seems to me that if I can produce evidence that Wittgenstein espoused something along the above lines, I will have managed to vindicate my claim that the Dichotomy Thesis has sufficient textual ground to be believed as a legitimate exegetical hypothesis of the Lecture. Not only that; built into the line of thought just sketched is the assumption that the nonsensical assertions involving language used non-scientifically may be successfully deployed to describe a portion of reality. As such, if there is textual ground establishing the Dichotomy Thesis, this will speak in favour of an irresolute exegesis of Wittgenstein in the Lecture – namely, as distinguishing between plain and interesting nonsense. As it happens, the required textual evidence is contained immediately after the last quoted passage.

To get to the crucial point, Wittgenstein invites us to reflect on miracles. If a member of the audience present at the Lecture would have suddenly grown a lion's head, Wittgenstein observes, we would be in the presence of a miracle: 'an event the like of which we have never yet seen' (1965: LE, 10). As Wittgenstein puts it:

> Now whenever we should have recovered from our surprise, what I would suggest would be to fetch a doctor and have the case scientifically investigated and if it were not for hurting him I would have him vivisected. And where would the miracle have got to? For it is clear that when we look at it in this way everything miraculous has disappeared; unless what we mean by this term is merely that a fact has not yet been explained by science which again means that we have hitherto failed to group this fact with others in a scientific system. *This shows that it is absurd to say 'Science has proved that there are no miracles.' The truth is that the scientific way of looking at a fact is not the way to look at it as a miracle.* For we see now that we have been using the word 'miracle' in a relative and an absolute sense. *And I will now describe the experience of wondering at the existence of the world by saying: it is the experience of seeing the world as a miracle.*
>
> *(1965: LE, 10–11, my italics)*

The way I reconstruct this passage is as follows. There are two senses of *miracle* which should be distinguished: a relative sense, and an absolute sense. On its relative meaning, a miracle is something which science has not yet explained but which will cease to be a miracle once science will have explained it. Then, on this understanding of *miracle*, a person growing a lion's head might not be a miracle. For the fact, although temporarily unexplainable, might become explainable sooner or later. *However*, on its *absolute* sense, a miracle (whatever it is exactly) is something which *by definition* science cannot explain. Indeed, it is argued, it is nonsense to say that a miracle (on the absolute sense) is something that science could disprove. For, part of what is to look at a fact in a scientific way is to look at it as being *not* a miracle. Wittgenstein thus concludes with the crucial point: the experience of wondering at the existence of the world is the experience of looking at the world as a miracle (in this absolute sense of *miracle*).

The upshot of this discussion is that by using language non-scientifically one still manages to describe certain facts, which are not describable by using language scientifically. By using language scientifically, in other words, we will not be able to describe all the facts – witness Wittgenstein's experience of wondering at the existence of the world, together with the other two experiences reported by Wittgenstein in the Lecture. Now, a couple of paragraphs earlier, I indicated what I should be able to demonstrate, in order to demonstrate that Wittgenstein espoused something akin to the Dichotomy Thesis: that is, that Wittgenstein provided some reasoning to the effect that the facts described by language used scientifically are not all the facts. And this claim, I now add, seems to me to correspond to the upshot of Wittgenstein's discussion.

On the reconstruction I have been offering, therefore, the Lecture is a defence of Hume's Thesis essentially based on the Dichotomy Thesis: the view that the world understood as the totality of facts non-trivially divides into two types of facts. There are what I called *material* facts, which can be described by language used in a scientific manner; and there are *normative* facts, which can be described by language used in a normative manner. Over the course of this section, I have suggested (what seems to me) a natural interpretation of what Wittgenstein likely meant by *using language scientifically*, and I have also clarified why the normative usage of language – in its *absolute* sense – is non-scientific. Along the way, we have also seen how Wittgenstein's reflections on the non-scientific usage of language can be naturally taken to be underpinned by a *soft* attitude towards nonsense – what at the beginning of the section I have identified as an *irresolute* interpretation. What I did not quite discuss are the merits of the various arguments found in the Lecture; this was nonetheless beyond the scope of the present chapter.

Let me now conclude by taking stock of what this chapter has shown.

Conclusion

This chapter was centred around two seemingly independent discussions: one concerning AI existential threat; the other concerning Wittgenstein's Lecture on Ethics. The connection between the two discussions was the thesis for which no 'ought' logically follows from an 'is', what I have called *Hume's Thesis*. I have first argued that, given Hume's Thesis, some arguments attempting to derive that AI poses an existential threat to humanity fail. Subsequently, I have analysed Wittgenstein's reasons for holding on to Hume's Thesis in the first place. Along the way, I have also shown how Wittgenstein's arguments for Hume's Thesis do invite an irresolute reading of his conception of nonsensical statements. The statements of ethics, though nonsensical they may be, nonetheless succeed in describing real facts which a purely descriptive use of language will not be able to describe. The real value of these arguments remains to be seen; this is a task that I reserve for future work.

References

Alvarez, M. (2010). *Kinds of Reasons: An Essay in the Philosophy of Action*. Oxford: Oxford University Press.

Bentham, J. (1970). *An Introduction to the Principles of Morals and Legislation: The Collected Works of Jeremy Bentham*. New York: Oxford University Press.

Boddington, P. (2023). *AI Ethics. A Texbook*. Singapore: Springer Nature.

Bostrom, N. (2014). *Superintelligence: Paths, Dangers, Strategies*. Oxford: Oxford University Press.

Bronzo, S. (2012). The Resolute Reading and its Critics: An Introduction to the Literature. *Wittgenstein-Studien*, 3(1), 45–80.

Christensen, A. S. (2011). Wittgenstein and Ethics. In M. McGinn & O. Kuusela (Eds.), *The Oxford Handbook of Wittgenstein*. Oxford: Oxford University Press.

Conant, J. (2007). Mild Mono-Wittgensteinianism. In A. Crary (Ed.), *Wittgenstein and the Moral Life: Essays in Honor of Cora Diamond* (pp. 31–142). Cambridge, MA: MIT Press.

Diamond, C. (1991). *The Realistic Spirit: Wittgenstein, Philosophy, and the Mind*. Cambridge, MA: MIT Press.

Dubber, M. D., Pasquale, F., & Das, S., Eds. (2020). *The Oxford Handbook of Ethics of AI*. Oxford: Oxford University Press.

Hacker, P. M. (2000). Was He Trying to Whistle It? In A. Crary & R. J. Read (Eds.), *The New Wittgenstein* (pp. 353–388). London: Routledge.

Kripke, S. A. (1980). *Naming and Necessity: Lectures Given to the Princeton University Philosophy Colloquium*. Cambridge, MA: Harvard University Press.

Kurzweil, R. (2005). *The Singularity is Near: When Humans Transcend Biology*. New York: Viking.

Mally, E. (1926). *Logische Schriften: Grosses Logikfragment – Grundgesetze des Sollens*. Graz: Leuschner & Lubensky.

Moore, G. E. (1922). *Principia Ethica*. London: Cambridge University Press.

Mulhall, S. (2006). *Wittgenstein's Private Language: Grammar, Nonsense, and Imagination in Philosophical Investigations*. Oxford: Oxford University Press.

Müller, V. C. & Bostrom, N. (2016). Future Progress in Artificial Intelligence: A Survey of Expert Opinion. In V. Müller (Ed.), *Fundamental Issues of Artificial Intelligence* (pp. 553–571). Cham: Springer.

Müller, V. C. & Cannon, M. (2021). Existential Risk from AI and Orthogonality: Can We Have It Both Ways? *Ratio*, 35(1), 25–36.

Priest, G. (2008). *An Introduction to Non-Classical Logic: From If to Is*. New York: Cambridge University Press.

Priest, G. (2016a). Logical Disputes and the A Priori. *Logique et Analyse*, 236, 347–366.

Priest, G. (2016b). *Towards Non-Being: The Logic and Metaphysics of Intentionality*. Oxford: Oxford University Press.

Priest, G. (2018). Metaphysical Necessity: A Skeptical Perspective. *Synthese*, 198(Suppl 8), 1873–1885.

Russell, G. (2021). How to Prove Hume's Law. *Journal of Philosophical Logic*, 51(3), 603–632.

Russell, G. & Restall, G. (2010). Barriers to Implication. In C. Pigden (Ed.), *Hume on Is and Ought* (pp. 243–259). London: Palgrave MacMillan.

Russell, G. K. (2023). *Barriers to Entailment: Hume's Law and Other Limits on Logical Consequence*. Oxford: Oxford University Press.

Schurz, G. (1997). *The Is-Ought Problem: An Investigation in Philosophical Logic*. Dordrecht, Netherland: Kluwer Academic Publishers.

Sider, T. (2011). *Writing the Book of the World*. Oxford: Oxford University Press.

Ulatowski, J. (2020). Resolute Readings of Wittgenstein and Nonsense. *Journal for the History of Analytical Philosophy*, 8(10), 3–18.

von Wright, G. H. (1951). Deontic Logic. *Mind*, 60(237), 1–15.

Williamson, T. (2013). *Modal Logic as Metaphysics*. Oxford: Oxford University Press.

Wittgenstein, L. (1965). A Lecture on Ethics. *Philosophical Review*, 74(1), 3–12.

Wittgenstein, L. (2002). *Tractatus Logico-Philosophicus* (Trans. D. F. Pears and B. F. McGuinness). London: Routledge.

Chapter 2

WHEN SAYING SORRY IS THE HARDEST GAME TO PLAY: WITTGENSTEIN, AI AND THE QUEST FOR TRANSPARENCY

Burkhard Schafer

Introduction

This chapter investigates the role of apologies issued by AIs – AIpologies – for AI regulation. It is therefore only appropriate to start the discussion with an apology: even though the chapter will try to bring some of Wittgenstein's ideas to the discussion, I am not a Wittgenstein scholar, and I apologize in advance that my discussions will overlook substantial parts of the contemporary Wittgenstein debate, or may even give a very idiosyncratic interpretation of his writing.

There has been substantial Wittgenstein reception in legal theory, centring on his conception of rules, rule-following and rule-interpretation.[1] Some legal theorists such as Patterson found Wittgenstein's writing of great relevance to answer the question 'What does it mean to say that a proposition of law is true?' (Patterson 1999, 3). Others, like Scott Hershowitz (2002), or Brian Bix (2005) argued that legal rules and legal rule-following are too different from the examples discussed by Wittgenstein for the latter to be of much interest to legal theory. As Hershowitz put it, 'nothing much can be learned about legal rules or legal interpretation by attending to Wittgenstein's remarks, because they were aimed at wholly different phenomena' (2002, 619).

This debate in legal theory asks, and challenges, our very understanding of what law is, and how we can make sense of legal rules (or fail to do so). The aim of this chapter is more limited. It takes law and a functioning legal system

1 See e.g. the papers in Patterson (2004).

as a given, and asks instead if we can learn something from Wittgenstein that can help us to interpret better one type of legal rules, rules that govern how we interact with increasingly autonomous machines.

If one were to adopt Tushnet's (1983) interpretation of Wittgenstein and deny with him the very possibility of rational adjudication between different interpretations of a law, this seems a futile endeavour, almost a self-contradiction. I will not try to address this issue for most of this chapter. Only in the final section, I will very briefly indicate how using James Tully's Wittgenstein interpretation could lead to a very different analysis of one of the examples that are at the focus of this chapter.

In the first section, we will look at the role of explanations to regulate and control AIs. We will discuss one influential proposal for AI-generated explanations, the counterfactual model proposed by Wachter, Mittelstadt and Russell (2018) (Henceforth WMR) in the context of the (contested) right to explanation for automated decision-making in the GDPR. We will argue that while this model works well when the AI made the right decision, it may give inappropriate responses in situations where the decision was flawed, allowing us to contrast explanations, excuses and apologies. This then raises the three interrelated issues that this chapter hopes to address, with some help from Wittgenstein:

- Are apologies a type of explanation?
- Are machines the type of agent that can make an apology?
- If machines can apologize, what does this mean for AI regulation?

We will illustrate these ideas by looking at an experiment carried out by the Institute for Network Science at Yale University. In this experiment, mixed human–robot teams participated in a collaborative game. When the team lost, the robot would either stay silent, make a factual statement about the scores or make a self-deprecating apology. The research showed the beneficial impact this last strategy had on group cohesion and trust repair – but in many outside observers, it creates a sense of unease – is the robot deceiving the humans it apologizes to, and makes them in this way even more vulnerable? Wittgenstein's thoughts about the role – or lack of role – of internal states when interpreting speech, and also his thoughts on AI more directly will help us to identify the issues that arise from this experiment.

Based on the analysis of the Yale experiment, we will propose some features that any valid AI-generated apology should have. We then ask how the law should treat AI-generated apologies that fulfil these conditions, and tentatively suggest that the same 'liability shield' that some jurisdictions grant to human apologies can be extended also to machine-generated apologies.

In the final section, we will go back to the Yale experiment and try to re-conceptualize it in a slightly different light, informed by Tully's analysis of Wittgenstein. Maybe, some apologies are valuable even if they do not meet the criteria laid out in the proceeding section after all. This more radical approach to machine apologies then also allows us to understand from a normative perspective the reactions of the other human players in the Yale experiment, and ultimately points to a version of the relational theory of robot rights that might be best understood in the light of Wittgenstein's thoughts about the relation between ethics and aesthetics.

If You Were Cleverer, You Would Have Understood the Previous Section Better

This rather passive-aggressive header is meant to ease the reader into the discussion of explainable AI (XAI) as a regulatory tool in general, and the counterfactual model of explanation in particular.

One important aspect of the current regulatory debate regarding AI is the quest for transparency. The fear of the 'Black Box Society', (Pasquale 2015) a Kafkaesque world where judgements are handed out by an impersonal machine whose inner workings are forever hidden from those affected, is a golden threat that ties together several regulatory initiatives.

The EU High-Level expert group for instance writes:

> Explicability is crucial for building and maintaining users' trust in AI systems. This means that processes need to be transparent, the capabilities and purpose of AI systems openly communicated, and decisions – to the extent possible – explainable to those directly and indirectly affected. Without such information, a decision cannot be duly contested.
>
> *(EU-HLEG on AI, Ethics Guidelines for Trustworthy AI, 2019)*

Transparency is seen here as a precondition for trustworthiness: we trust those who are open with us (von Eschenbach 2021). It is also a precondition for agency: we can often only decide how to best respond to a decision when we understand the reasons on which it is based. Explainability then leads to transparency – once we know the reasons why a decision-maker decided against us, we can either agree with the reasoning and adjust our behaviour, or if we disagree with the reasoning, contest the decision.

One particularly influential proposal on how to implement explainability that meets, or maybe even exceeds, the demands of Art 13–15 and Art 20 is the above-mentioned 'counterfactual' approach by Wachter, Mittelstadt and Russell.

Consider an online credit card application. After answering a number of set questions about the applicant, the system creates a risk model for them, based on historical data of past decisions with shared characteristics. The risk score is then compared against a pre-defined value, and if the applicant is deemed too risky, the application is rejected.

A helpful explanation then could be of the form: 'Your application was rejected because of the low income that you currently earn. If your monthly income had been £50 higher, the application would have been granted'.

WMR write about their approach:

> In the existing literature, 'explanation' typically refers to an attempt to convey the internal state or logic of an algorithm that leads to a decision. In contrast, counterfactuals describe a dependency on the external facts that led to that decision. This is a crucial distinction. In modem machine learning, the internal state of the algorithm can consist of millions of variables intricately connected in a large web of dependen behaviours.
>
> *(Wachter, Mittelstadt and Russell 2018, 845)*[2]

This understands the nature of explanation, not as a mechanistic report of the inner workings of the decision-maker, but as a chain of reasons from external facts to an utterance (the credit decision).[3.] If read this way, it would echo Wittgenstein's comments on reason-giving:[4]

> Giving a reason sometimes means 'I actually went this way', sometimes 'I could have gone this way', i.e. sometimes what we say acts as a justification, not as a report of what was done, e.g. I remember the answer to a question; when asked why I give this answer, I gave a process leading to it, though I didn't go through this process.
>
> *(Wittgenstein 1966, LC: 22)*

---

2 In a similar vein, but with a more detailed and philosophically grounded analysis, Zerilli (2022).

3 This is arguably only one possible interpretation of their approach. They may insist that there is still a relevant causal connection between the way their AI reached its conclusion, even though it need not be on the level of a detailed mechanistic explanation. Wittgenstein's distinction between rational versus causal explanations arguably does not map perfectly onto Wachter et al.'s distinction between mechanistic and counterfactual explanations. How much they overlap will depend on one's reading of both Wittgenstein and Wachter, and such a detailed exegesis goes beyond the scope of this chapter. What matters for the purpose of the argument made here is only that they both reject one type of demand sometimes made of XAI, and open in a similar way the space for alternative forms of explanation that equally avoid attribution of mental states to machines.

4 See for an extensive discussion Queloz (2016).

> The question 'For what reasons do you believe this?' might mean: 'From what reasons are you now deriving it (have you just derived it)?' But it might also mean: 'With hindsight, what reasons can you give me for this supposition?'
>
> *(Wittgenstein 2009, PI: §479)*

For Wittgenstein then, sometimes, but only sometimes, reason-giving describes a psychological state, the way that WMR describe the traditional approach to explainable AI. In most situations however, 'reasons for accepting a proposition are not personal matters, but parts of the calculus to which the proposition belongs' (Wittgenstein 2005, BT: §267). and they are '[...] describing a way which leads there and is in accordance with certain accepted rules' (Wittgenstein 1958, BB: 14). We will come back to this issue below, but note here that this understanding of the nature of an explanation means we can speak of an AI explaining itself, without having to commit ourselves to talk about its inner, or mental, states.

We briefly mention some of the limitations of the WMR approach. The benefits are obviously greatest when there is a possibility for recurrent engagement, less so for one-off interactions. Furthermore, in some applications, back-engineering the explanation could lead to undesirable actions. If, for instance, a money-laundering detection system refuses a transaction, it should not generate as an explanation: 'The law requires that transactions above £10000 must not be anonymous. If the transaction had been split into two transactions of £5000 send a few hours apart, these transactions would have been approved'.

A somewhat different question is if the implicit recommendation must be 'actionable', that is if the addressee of the explanation must have it in their power to bring about the suggested change. Telling a credit card applicant 'if you had been born to very rich parents, your application would have been successful' is not very helpful, true as it may be.

Sometimes, non-actionable explanations can arguably be both appropriate and helpful – they tell the decision subject that there is nothing they can do, preventing self-blame or futile resource allocation, for instance if an application for a high-risk profession is rejected due to a congenital illness.

A subset of non-actionable conditions, however, must not be used (in many jurisdictions) as a point of law. 'If you had been male, your application would have been successful' could have been the explanation given in situations like the widely reported differential treatment of male and female applicants by a credit card issuer (James 2019), but would have been evidence for violation of equality legislation by the AI.

The main benefit of a counterfactual explanation approach is that it assists the persons affected by an AI decision to react constructively, and through their actions change the outcome in the future. In cases where the AI decision was correct, this is extremely helpful. But as we noted above, one objective that legislators pursue through a legally mandated use of explainable AI is to also create contestability of results. Contestability is a cornerstone also of the rule of law, and is irreconcilable with a black-box society where 'the computer says no' ends the discussion (Kaminski & Urban 2021; Almada 2019). XAI therefore also needs to cover situations where the AI comes to the wrong result.

Counterfactual explanations, or more precisely, attempts at explanations,[5] can assist contestability, but only indirectly. There are two ways in which this can happen.

If the generated explanation refers to a false statement about the world as explanans, contestation is the most straightforward:

> *AI:* 'If you earned more than £30000 annually, you would get the credit card.'
> *Customer:* 'But I do earn more than £30000 already, and said that much in section 8 of the form.'

What the AI offered here is strictly speaking, not an explanation at all, merely a failed attempt at one. More difficult is our example above, the use of an illegitimate criterion as opposed to a false fact:

> *AI:* 'If you had been male, you would have been given a credit card.'
> *Customer:* 'Hang on, that can't be right [...]'

This may well be a 'correct' explanation, in the sense that it faithfully describes how the machine reached its decision, and we may even grant for the sake of the argument that there is a relevant causal connection between gender and ability to repay credit. The explanation fails for legal reasons (and that means, fails in some, but not necessarily all, jurisdictions), because it uses an illegitimate explanans. In either case though, the applicant has to deduce that something went wrong – the AI is good at judging the applicant

5 Here we have to be careful about the use of our language: 'P explains Q' is factive for both P and Q. – In this sense we can't explain something that is false, though we can explain why we formed the mistaken belief that it was true. Conversely even if my mistaken belief in P led me to accept Q as true, this is not an explanation even if Q turns out to be true. Legislative language about explanations and the duty to provide them can be at odd with these situations, and in this chapter we follow the rather loose use of language of the regulator rather than the more precise one of analytical philosophy, at least in those situations where the legal language remains sufficiently clear.

and telling them how to do it right, less good and helpful at judging itself. This can create significant burdens on the individual, especially in the second scenario that requires from the applicant a knowledge and understanding of discrimination law.

In the context of AI regulation and trustworthy AI, this approach reflects an underlying assumption about technology and the role of law regarding its governance. For most of our history, it was taken for granted that law is a means of conflict resolution, and only enters the stage after a harm had occurred. The technological revolution of the nineteenth century, and in particular the invention of the steam engine, was eventually to change this. Legally mandated safety certification became, from the 1830s onwards, the new regulatory tool of choice.[6] Legally mandated certification by properly regulated authorities, backed up by a system of criminal law sanctions in case of non-compliance, reduced dramatically the number of accidents and created 'trustworthy steam power'.[7] Safety certification became a new regulatory paradigm that quickly gained importance across all sectors, from food to technology, a process that accelerated with the emergence of the 'administrative state' and its regulatory agencies.

The EU AI Act is the latest step in this evolution, delegating de facto legislative powers to standard setting and certification authorities. Certified adherence to standards, set according to our best scientific knowledge allows us to place our trust in scientific experts, and by implication the AI that they certify.

This anticipatory, risk-prevention mode of regulation is of course valuable and necessary. It is, however, premised on the ability of science and engineering to control scientific innovation. This leads to the paradox that even though the aim is to rein in technologies that are perceived as dangerous or even out of control, the method of control is rooted in the same optimism regarding our ability to predict, and with that control, our environment that gave rise to these technologies in the first place.

The discourse regarding trustworthy AI and the technical tools that are developed to achieve it reflects this optimism: AIs can be made trustworthy because we can assure in advance their compliance with relevant safety standards. These standards, and their legally mandated verification, rely in turn on our best scientific theories. Of less importance in this view is the role of law once things fail nonetheless, when trust has been broken. In the past, tort law complemented forward-looking technology regulation, providing

6 See Brockmann (2019).

7 So e.g. Burke (1966).

redress when even certified systems fail. Increasingly though, our confidence in controlling technology through engineering solutions pushes legal trust repair mechanisms into the background.[8]

The counterfactual explanation model fits this techno-optimistic approach – it works best when the AI is right, and it is then up to the individual to adjust their actions to achieve a desired goal. Contestability in case the AI got it wrong is at best a side result, assumes knowledge by the affected individual to interpret the answer correctly, and requires that they use their resources to complain and contest the decision.

We can now ask how an approach to explainability would look like that takes the scenario where the AI did not decide correctly as a starting point. Rather than focusing on *creating* trust, how can we restore trust once it was broken? Wittgenstein might have been sympathetic to such an endeavour, as a considerable degree of technological scepticism runs through his later work:

> The truly apocalyptic view of the world is that things do not repeat themselves. It isn't absurd, e.g., to believe that the age of science and technology is the beginning of the end for humanity; that the idea of great progress is a delusion, along with the idea that the truth will ultimately be known; that there is nothing good or desirable about scientific knowledge and that mankind, in seeking it, is falling into a trap. It is by no means obvious that this is not how things are.
> *(Wittgenstein 1998, CV: 56)*[9]

Let us reconsider the two mini-dialogues from above:

> *AI:* "If you earned more than £30000 annually, you would get the credit card"
> *Customer:* "But I do earn more than £30000 already, and said that much on section 8 of the form"
>
> *AI:* "If you had been male, you would have been given a credit card"
> *Customer:* "Hang on, that can't be right…"

In this situation, the decision-maker failed, trust in them is now broken and needs to be repaired. How would a human act in this situation? One obvious and very natural trust repair strategy would be to apologize: 'I am so sorry, I misremembered what you told me', or 'You are quite right, I apologise, this can't be right, of course you get a credit card, and the first two months are

8 For an example see e.g. Nagareda (2006).

9 See also Peters (2020).

on us'. That apologies like these are effective in restoring trust when issued by humans is well-supported.[10] Structurally, they are the mirror image of WMR's counterfactual explanation. At a bare minimum, WMR's:

> If *YOU* had done/are going to do X, you would/will avoid Y

Becomes now

> *WE* should have done X to avoid Y, and [...]

[...] stands for now as a placeholder that completes the apology. We will discuss some candidates for this complement below.

In the next section, we will look at a real-world example of a robot apologizing, to tease out some of the intuitions that will influence the answer to these questions.

'Everything Is My fault, I'll Take the Blame'

In the *Philosophical Investigations*, Wittgenstein famously wrote: '*Ein philosophisches Problem hat die Form: 'Ich kenne mich nicht aus*' (Wittgenstein 2001, PI: §123) – a philosophical problem is of the form 'I am lost'. For Wittgenstein, not knowing one's way, being lost or in a state of confusion, is the beginning of all philosophical inquiry. He uses two terms to further characterize this feeling, it leads to *Unruhe*, 'disquiet', but also a feeling of 'das Unheimliche', the uncanny (Bearn 1993).

Rapid technological change can foster this sense of disorientation. This is especially the case when deeply internalized modes of acting and interacting with other humans are partly, but only partly, replicated in interactions with machines. This is the 'uncanny valley' effect (MacDorman 2006). Humanoid objects that only imperfectly resemble actual human beings lead to 'uncanny' or strangely familiar feelings that ultimately can turn into uneasiness and even revulsion. Wittgenstein uses the same term, *das Unheimliche*, not, however, when describing machines that behave like humans, but humans who are experienced as machine-like:

> But can't I imagine that the people around me are automata, lack consciousness, even though they behave in the same way as usual? – If I imagine it now – alone in my room – I see people with fixed looks (as in a trance) going about

10 See e.g. Lazare (2005); Schniter, Sheremeta and Sznycer (2013); Ma et al. (2019).

> their business – the idea is perhaps a little uncanny [unheimlich]. But just try to keep hold of this idea in the midst of your ordinary intercourse with others, in the street, say! Say to yourself, for example: 'The children over there are mere automata; all their liveliness is mere automatism.' And you will either find the words becoming quite meaningless; or you will produce in yourself some kind of uncanny feeling.
>
> *(Wittgenstein 2006: PI §420)*

In 2018, researchers at Yale conducted an experiment in which a vaguely humanoid, child-sized robot played together with several humans in a group activity (Strohkorb Sebo, Traeger, Jung & Scassellati 2018). In order to win, all group members had to work together. What was tested was the effect that apologies by the robot after a lost game would have on the group. To engineer this, the robot would randomly fail at its task. Similarly, mistakes by the human players were clandestinely induced by the game environment so that everybody was sometimes responsible for a loss. In some groups, the robot would say nothing when its action caused the team to fail, in others it would make a mere factual statement (announcing the score), and in the third group it would apologize to the other players and display vulnerability:

> Sorry guys, I made the mistake this round. I know it may be hard to believe, but robots make mistakes too.
>
> Or
>
> Sorry, I sometimes run out of memory and can't process things fast enough.

Here the robot accepts responsibility, and through self-disclosure makes itself vulnerable. This positively influenced the trust group members placed in the robot. They interacted more with the machine, showed greater willingness to listen to it, and also used more non-verbal cues of trust such as gaze that are typical for human-to-human communication. In addition to increased trust in the *robot*, it also increased their own willingness to show weaknesses, take responsibility and in this way created a ripple effect that enhanced trust relations also between the human team members. Display of vulnerability and acceptance of blame also improved the group dynamic and enhanced the communication between the human group members (Strohkorb Sebo et al. 2020).

The researchers created a video documenting the improved interaction.[11] We can see and hear in the video how the statement of the robot: 'sorry, I sometimes run out of memory and can't process things fast enough' is met

11 https://www.youtube.com/watch?v=WujARg_xqfE.

with 'awh' sounds that between humans would roughly translate into 'apology accepted, but don't worry, we all are in it together'.

The Yale experiment is not the only one that uses apologies and disclosure of vulnerability as a means to restore trust, and its findings align with other studies that tested human reactions to robot apologies.[12] It is chosen for the discussion mainly because of the visual resource that it provides, to invite the reader to observe their own reaction. If they feel like me, they will have a sense of disorientation, possibly mixed with anger – a feeling apparently diametrically opposed to that of the participants. On reflecting on that response though, I found it difficult to explain my reaction to myself. Or with other words, '*Ich kenne mich nicht aus*', What should we make of this experiment?

In an entirely unscientific study, I also showed the video over the last two years to students in our undergraduate and postgraduate Law and Robotics courses, a cohort of approximately 120 students, mainly with a background in law. The overwhelming consensus was:

- These are not valid apologies.
- They should not lead to enhanced trust.
- Building robots that have this affordance in real life raises ethical and legal issues and may require regulation.

In the rest of this section, I will discuss some possible candidates that explain our unease in accepting the actions of the Yale robot as apologies, drawing inter alia on Wittgenstein's thoughts on the role of mental states when interpreting language games and his 'soft behaviourist' psychology. The aim is not so much to criticize the Yale project, but to elicit requirements for a form of apology that can play the function described above, as a form of explanation after machine failure and recognized by the law. For any readers who after seeing the video do not share our reaction, we will offer in the final section of this chapter a very different account that will try to do justice to their reaction as well.

Regrets, I had a few

The most obvious objection against the Yale robot is that its statements are deceptive. Apologies in this view are also, or even mainly, reports of an inner state. In Searle's terminology, they are expressives (Searle 1976, 4 and 12–17). To be sincere, they require a feeling of remorse or regret. 'Whatever else is said or conveyed, an apology must express sorrow.' (Tavuchis 1993, 36).

12 See e.g. Xu and Howard (2022); Perkins et al. (2022); Esterwood and Robert (2021).

Robots lack internal emotional states, so they cannot possibly truthfully apologize. The robot *says* sorry, but it *is* not sorry.

Other studies in machine apologies go even further than the Yale experiment. A particularly problematic example in this context is the experiment by Pompe et al., which showed that explicit expressions of remorse are particularly effective in restoring trust (Pompe, Velner & Truong 2022). To achieve what they call 'genuine apology', they combine the verbal expression of remorse with appropriate body language, using the same type of vaguely anthropomorphic machine. *If* a genuine feeling of remorse, however, is a defining element of true apologies, then this is merely an even more devious form of manipulation.

In legal contexts, displays of remorse as part of an apology are particularly important during sentencing in criminal trials.[13] Display of sincere remorse is seen as a redeeming quality that merits consideration, while lack of remorse is seen as an indication of dangerousness.[14] Remorse becomes here an indicator if not of 'good character', then at least of 'character capable of redemption'. This requires more than an abstract, 'learned' recognition of one's wrongdoing, rather, what sways judges and juries is evidence of almost physical pain, expressed, ideally, by tears.[15] These then inform a moral judgement that also separates the action of the accused from their 'character'. The shame and remorse the offender feels in these cases is so strong, in effect a form of pain, that they are punishment in themselves, which then allows for more lenient sanctions (Maslen 2015, 77ff).

For anyone who considers apologies as expressives that report an emotional state, machine apologies are impossible.[16] AIs can only ever explain their behaviour either by reference to their internal reasoning mechanisms, or as noted above by appeal to public reason.

There are a number of broadly speaking 'Wittgensteinian' answers to this objection. The first, and most radical, would be to deny altogether the role of mental states to interpret and validate speech acts such as apologies. There is a long tradition of interpreting Wittgenstein as a behaviourist, which could lend support to this strategy.[17] The meaning of propositions is determined by their external use in a language game, and as long as the external behaviour

13 So in particular Bennet (2008).

14 A list of examples, with an ultimately sceptical assessment, is in Murphy (2006). See also Bibas and Bierschbach (2004).

15 See e.g. Rossmanith (2015); Luth-Morgan (2017).

16 At least for current and near future machines. The chapter does not take a stance if in theory, future machines may also acquire emotional states, or functional equivalents.

17 For a discussion see Bloor (1999) ; Luckhardt (1983).

of the robot replicates faithfully what humans would do in that situation, this is all that we need to know.

As we saw, one argument why the feeling of remorse matters in criminal law is that it is similar to pain, and therefore already constitutes punishment. Wittgenstein's famous 'beetle in the box' thought experiment and his analysis of expressions of pain would therefore be directly applicable to this situation.[18] More recently, John Danaher (2020) made an argument along similar lines, arguing for what he calls 'moral behaviourism' that enables robots to get integrated into the 'moral circle'. We will come back to this approach below, but note here that if robots were to become part of the moral circle, apologies would play an interesting dual role. On the one hand, they could be bearers of a moral *obligation* to apologize for wrongdoing. But they may then also have a *right* to apologize, and maybe even a rightful expectation that under certain conditions, that apology gets accepted.

If we accept the behaviourist line of reasoning, then those of us who feel like me and reject the 'Yale apology' are either simply mistaken, or we have to argue that current robots still fail to adhere to all the relevant rules of the apology game, at least when evaluated over longer periods of time. Danaher for example does not claim that current robots behave in a way that requires their recognition as moral agents, merely that what counts should be their behaviour only – and this behaviour has to be consistently demonstrated over time and across contexts. By contrast, current 'apologetic robots' only mimic human apologies for very narrow and redefined circumstances – the Yale robot apologizes if a game is lost, not for example if it accidentally hits a player.

There is however a different way in which we can think about language games, one that excludes machines from (some of) them. In the *Philosophical Investigations*, Wittgenstein writes: 'But a machine surely cannot think' (Wittgenstein 2006: PI §360).[19] And in the *Remarks on the Philosophy of Psychology*, he even goes beyond this, contrasting explicitly humans and human language, which is 'full of soul', whereas 'the opposite of being full of soul is being mechanical' (Wittgenstein 1983: RPP §324). Finally, we find:

> 'A machine thinks (perceives, wishes)' seems somehow nonsensical. It is as though we had asked 'Has the number 3 a colour?'
>
> *(Wittgenstein 1958: BB §47)*

18 For such a Wittgenstein-inspired reading of pain as a 'social phenomenon' see e.g. Sullivan (1995).

19 For a different analysis with illuminating context see also the contribution by Proudfoot, this volume.

On this basis, Casey (1988) concludes that Wittgenstein rejects at least for existing AIs the legitimacy of 'mentalist' language games. Not only can they not think, we understand how that makes them different from us. Neumaier in his discussion on Wittgenstein and AI gives an account of why this is the case, by focusing on the role of 'ways of life' in constituting language games (Neumaier 1986; see also Unnsteinsson 2016). We are born into a specific way of life that enables also 'mentalist language games'. This also means that far from being a reductionist behaviourist, Wittgenstein is best understood as an 'explanatory mentalist'. Explanatory mentalism makes sense of the way in which humans inevitably engage in mentalist language games:

> Psychological language games 'are as much a part of our natural history as walking, eating, drinking, playing'.
>
> *(Wittgenstein 2006: PI §25)*

For Neumaier, this means that according to Wittgenstein, we get socialized as children to interpret some observations of other living beings as evidence for such feelings as pain. This then allows us to explain the observable phenomena by postulating 'inner' processes. As long as these explanations are on the whole successful, we are then justified to assume (the existence of) 'inner' processes; even if we can't ever have a criterion that puts beyond doubt that somebody does feel pain (Neumaier 1986, 148).

Robots and humans do not share a way of life, and in particular, they do not participate in 'mentalist language games' that allow us to explain behaviour of other actors through reference to their mental states. While we can never *know* if another human deceives us about their mental states, we can always know that a machine pretending to have them deceives us.

Does this then mean that machines cannot apologize? Only if a (a) feeling of remorse or regret is *necessary* for sincere apologies and (b) only sincere apologies should count as a way to improve our opinion of the wrongdoer. In the criminal law context, we saw this position argued. There, the pain that comes with being truly remorseful is needed so that apologies can count as a substitute for punishment.

But while this is one way of engaging in the 'apology game', it is not the only one. In our society, we frequently encounter humans apologizing for things for which they are not personally responsible, and for which they will not, in most cases, experience 'painful remorse'.

This applies to the spokesperson of a large multinational company who apologizes 'on behalf of' this entity, or to heads of state who apologizes for past wrongdoings of their nation. In the case of companies, we know that apologizing can work as a trust repair mechanism[20] – we trust again an entity that, as a legal abstraction, is also incapable of feeling remorse. Similarly, even when we criticize heads of state for 'empty virtue signalling', the effect on trust restoration is measurable, and the demand for such apologies also by victims or their descendants growing (MacLachlan 2015). It is true that the lack of remorse, or personal responsibility, is often seen as cheapening the currency of apologies and potentially manipulative. [21]

But if these apologies are manipulative, then it is a manipulation where we are all willing and informed participants – nobody thinks that really, a spokesperson for a government or a company 'feels remorseful' when saying what their job requires them to say, and despite this knowledge, the 'healing effect' is real and measurable.[22] Furthermore, not only are these 'public apologies' intelligible to us, we can also in this context distinguish successful from unsuccessful apologies, legitimate from deceptive ones. This allows us to identify criteria that are needed for trust-restoring apologies, criteria that can be different from those we use when humans apologize for their own actions (Kim & Song 2021). For this reason, we will for the rest of this chapter talk of and contrast two types of 'apology games'.[23] One is the 'remorse expression' (RE) game that we use for personal wrongdoings between people. The other is the 'public apology' game (PA). While the way these are expressed in language is in parts similar, and in particular shares expressions such as 'sorry' or 'I apologise', they do have their own distinctive logics that we now can discuss.

How do PAs function without an internal feeling of remorse? To answer this question, we have to ask why apologies can restore trust in the first place.

One way to account for RE apologies as *rational* trust repair is that they give us good reasons to believe that the same harm won't occur in the future. 'Moral emotions' such as remorse matter for both ethics and psychology because these express our ability to self-reflect (Kroll & Egan 2004).[24] With the ability for self-reflection comes the ability to understand where we went wrong – and with that also the ability to correct our behaviour next time round. Apologies externalize this internal mode of reflection. As Tavuchis puts it, an apology is a performative utterance that in the case of RE converts the remorse of the offender from 'a private condition into public communion'

20 See e.g. Lee and Chung (2012); Bozic (2017).

21 So, for example, Taft (1999).

22 See e.g. Marrus (2007); Thompson (2008).

23 Wittgenstein 2006: PI §300 comes close to a directly parallel analysis of the type of language games that we discuss here, using 'pain' as an example.

24 For a philosophical discussion see Vilhauer (2022)

(Tavuchis 1993, 64). Remorse, especially remorse that reaches the level of pain, is then the motivating factor that allows us to conclude that the apologizer will act on their insight. For Tavuchis, the promise of change is so inextricably intertwined with the expression of remorse that it does not even need saying, it is always implied (Tavuchis 1993, 23).

With PA, we have the same external form of 'public communion'. What is missing is the internal, motivating factor for change. How can it be replaced? If the role of remorse is as warrant for a future change in behaviour, then an externally enforceable promise of change can take its place for the purpose of trust repair. Here the law can come into play too. Change when making a RA is an implied consequence that 'may' not need stating explicitly, because our folk psychology tells us that the pain of remorse will lead to change in behaviour.[25] In a PA, this commitment to change becomes part of the felicity conditions of a successful apology that need to be communicated and stated explicitly Apologies then do not so much report an internal state of regret, rather they report a line of reasoning where the offender

1. takes responsibility, which includes a causal account of the actions and conditions that led to the harm;
2. states the steps that will be taken to prevent the same mistake from happening again; and possibly
3. makes an offer of 'making good' – compensation that is commensurate to the harm inflicted and the degree of responsibility.

(1) turns the apology into the exact mirror image of the Wittgensteinian account of 'explanation' that we discussed above. Just as an explanation is not an account of the inner processes that led someone to reach the right result, but a publicly verifiable account of a valid chain of reasoning, so is an apology not an account of the inner processes that led to a mistake (that would be 'making excuses'[26]) but a publicly auditable account of what caused the harm. Because of this symmetry, we argue that for regulatory purposes, we should consider this form of apology as an appropriate way to meet explainability requirements, even if it does not disclose the inner workings of the AI.

25 Many theorists of apologies suggest that also an effective RE will normally require an offer of reparation and/or promise of change. See e.g. Orenstein (1999, 239).

26 This chapter does not discuss 'excuses' as a separate category, mainly due to space limitations. In many ways, they function similar to apologies, and in some contexts, a robot-excuse may be more appropriate than a robot-apology, while still providing similar degrees of transparency. Broadly speaking, we can think of excuses as explanations of mistakes without acceptance of responsibility for the outcome.

We can now also express more clearly the objections against the Yale robot. The problem is not that it deceives its audience by claiming to have an internal state that machines do not possess – its machine nature is too obvious for this. Rather, by using the verbal form, or logic, of an RA apology, it deceives us in inferring also conditions (1)–(3), that is we falsely infer that

1) the reason the robot states for its failure is the causally relevant reason (in the example: processor not fast enough);
2) that the same issue will not happen again, that there will be change.

In the experiment, the robot's 'failure' was externally enforced, not the result of an unsuitable processor being used for the task; it was a 'placebo explanation' that unfortunately can be as efficient in restoring trust as real explanations (Eiband et al. 2019). Because the causal explanation is already false, there is no pathway from a recognition of responsibility to an effective change in future behaviour. Furthermore, the robot does not have the capacity to effect the change that its own words indicate. It cannot, for instance, upgrade itself or refuse to play next time it encounters a scenario that requires speedy responses.

A PA apology that does not just restore trust, but trustworthiness, therefore requires at the bare minimum a correct causal account of the contribution that an action or omission had for the harm, and an enforceable or auditable promise of future change. Not

> Sorry, I sometimes run out of memory and can't process things fast enough.

But

> I'm sorry, I was not fast enough in move 3, I'm going to download an upgrade before the next game, and I'll also pay the participation fee for the next round of gaming.

This structure of an apology also mirrors definitions found in some legal systems. The Apology Scotland Act (2000), for instance defines as valid apology for the purpose of the Act

> any statement made by or on behalf of a person which indicates that the person is sorry about, or regrets, an act, omission or outcome and includes any part of the statement which contains an undertaking to look at the circumstances giving rise to the act, omission or outcome with a view to preventing a recurrence.

If we read the expression of regret as acceptance of (causal) responsibility, then the 'undertaking to look into the circumstances [...]' equates to a causal explanation of why the harm occurred, while the prevention element is forward-looking and gives reason to restore trust.

The purpose of this Act is to encourage apologies, which are often what the victim prefers over other remedies, but which are often actively discouraged by an institution's or corporation's lawyers (Latif 2001). Apologies, so their reasoning, can be construed as admissions of legal liability, even though the legal requirements may be much more exacting than a personal feeling of responsibility.[27] Apologies that conform with the structure prescribed by the Act are privileged for the purpose of litigation, that is they can't be adduced as evidence by a complainer if they decide to sue for damages (Vines 2008). This does not mean that receiving an apology bars them from also litigating, only that they need to find evidence other than the apology itself.

This type of liability shield should be attractive to anyone who considers permitting robots to apologize on their behalf, as it manages the risk also of apologies that eventually turn out to have been premature or in some other way not merited. At the same time, because apologies that are valid for the purpose of the Apology Act are also the mirror image of explanations, they help comply with transparency requirements under instruments such as the EU AI Act.

Beyond Rational Trust: Revisiting the Yale Robot Experiment

Let us recap: We started with the question of why one might find the Yale experiment unsettling and potentially dangerously misleading. The tentative answer was that the rational justification why apologies can restore trust is that they give us good reasons to think that the offender won't behave in the same way again. The type of apology that the Yale robot gives doesn't give us such reasons, which means the increase in trust it generates is potentially misleading and deceptive.

In our societies, we encounter two types of apology games that enable rational trust-repair in very different ways. One relies on internal mental states as a guarantor for change, the other on making actionable promises in a public forum. The former can only be performed successfully by humans, the latter also by companies, states or other abstract entities and the people who speak on their behalf. The reason that the Yale robot (and others like it)

27 See e.g. Robbennolt (2003)

is 'uncanny' is that they are not the right type of agent to make the first type of apology, and on the other hand, they are not using the correct format for participating in the second type of apology game.

The failure to restore rational trust through robot apologies of the Yale-type is not just because they use the wrong words, but because their entire logic is wrong – where there ought to be a causal account that establishes responsibility, we get an expression of internal states and feelings.

For the normative issues, we concluded that

- to the extent that robots apologize, they should always only use type 2 (PA) apologies;
- if they use PA apologies, then this is a valid way to establish the type of explainability that legal instruments such as the AI Act mandate;
- to encourage building the capacity of type 2 apologies into AIs, we should consider for those jurisdictions that give litigation privileges to human-authored apologies to extend them to robot-issued apologies.

Underlying this discussion is the assumption that both explanations and apologies should not just increase human trust, but trust*worthiness*, in other words, they should give us rational reasons to trust the human/machine even after they failed initially.

There is, however, a different way to look at the Yale experiment, which focuses less on rational trust recovery, and more on other desirable outcomes. In the experiment, not only did the interactions between individual group members and the robot improve, but also the interactions between the human players, making the game experience more enjoyable for everybody. The 'good' that the apology creates is then a collective good that is shared across the group, not just an increase in trust in a binary robot–human relation.

The human players in the experiment automatically smiled at the robot, and responded with expressions of sympathy and understanding. We cannot discuss here in any detail how Wittgenstein would have analysed the 'semi-smile' of the robot in the Yale experiment and refer the reader to Proudfoot's comprehensive analysis (Proudfoot 2013). In very broad terms though, Wittgenstein points out the fact that even a minimal depiction of a face, his 'picture-face', issufficient to dispose us to attribute properties such as 'smiling' to them (Wittgenstein 2006: PI §204). Proudfoot then distinguishes with Wittgenstein purely visual or *anatomical smiling* from embedded smiling. While (most, adult) humans are capable of, and often perform, also purely visual smiles, currently they alone are capable of embedded smiling. Embedded smiling allows the observer not just a reliable inference to the inner state of the person but also an appreciation of the symbolic significance of the smile that in turn allows the prediction of future behaviour (a person who sincerely smiles at us is unlikely to attack us, e.g.). All this again requires a participation in the human life form and the 'bustle' of daily life.

Crucially, this 'bustle' can't be reduced to bipolar relations. It is not just a person responding to a smile with a smile, it is also third parties observing this exchange of smiles, and smiling in turn. This in part explains why the benefits of the apologetic robot accrue on the level of the team: B smiling in response to the robot also makes the observer of the interaction, A, smile, something in turn observed by B. The net result is increased trust between the humans A and B at least as much as that between them and the robot, a 'reward' for observing in each other the correct response to a stimulus. They behave 'appropriately in their response to the machine'. We can test this intuition by asking ourselves how we would react to someone who in this setting refuses to accept the apology of the robot – maybe respond angrily with 'You useless piece of junk, why did you play with us then when you knew you were so crap at it?'. My hypothesis, based again on the rather unsystematic discussion of intuitions in a class setting, would be that

A) under these conditions, the benefits of the robot-apology would not materialize, and the team would not enjoy an increase in mutual trust;
B) even people who are wary of the robot-apology would deem the behaviour of this person inappropriate – even though they do not believe that the robot suffered harm or emotional distress, responding in this way violates communication norms, which is causing *some* form of harm, albeit harm for the observer of the exchange more than the direct addressee.

This type of intuition also underpins the 'relational theory of robo-rights' proposed by inter alia David Gunkel (2018), Mark Coeckelbergh (2012) or Josh Gellers (2020). In their approach, we should attribute rights to robots, and behave towards them accordingly, not because of any intrinsic ontological property that they have, but because we inevitably imbue our *relationship* with them with additional normative meaning and values.[28] Gunkel and Gellers use the language of rights to express the idea that this type of relational normative quality deserves protection, similar to the one we increasingly find in environmental law and our relations to other animals. This closeness to legal conceptions though may be a hindrance rather than a help for their analysis, as legal conceptions of rights more often than not are shaped by the bipolar

28 An explicit connection between Wittgenstein and Gunkel, tellingly within the context of facial expressions, is made in Piekarski (2022).

relation of the trial between pursuer and defendant, and as such struggle to accommodate more diffuse and systemic harms.[29]

Wittgenstein may offer us a different perspective on the 'refused apology' hypothetical. In the *Tractatus, he* writes:

> It is clear that ethics cannot be expressed. Ethics is transcendental. (Ethics and aesthetics are one.)
>
> *Wittgenstein 1974: TLP 6.421*[30]

The identity of the aesthetical with the ethical as transcendental, and with that outside the system of propositions, enables us to think in a very different way about rule violation. If we understand the transgression of our putative apology-refuser B not as normative violation in the way the law thinks about this – as a violation of rational resource allocations – but as a first and foremost aesthetic violation that *because of this* is also experienced as an ethical violation, we may be able to give an account of the idea that accepting the apology is the right thing to do, without having to elevate robots into holders of individual right. Neither do we require, , as Proudfoot ultimately does, a much more sophisticated connection between the robot's inner computational state and its expressed behaviour. Refusing the apology, in this sense, is 'ugly behaviour', not because it is harmful *to the robot*, but to the person who violates the norm of the apology game , and with that also to the people who are in relations with them. The Italian 'fare brutta figura' expresses maybe this unity of ethical norm violation and aesthetical affront best – it is behaviour that is literally ugly.

In the *Philosophical Investigations*, Wittgenstein makes a distinction between 'without justification' and 'without right': 'To use a word without a justification (Rechtfertigung) does not mean to use it without right (Unrecht)' (2009: PI §289). James Tully (1989) uses this and similar passages to reject Habermas's attempt to ground the validity of legal norms in a public process of deliberation that is premised on our ability to self-reflectively account for our behaviour. For our context, Habermas is firmly on the side of our first analysis of robot-apologies: they have sincerity conditions that are ultimately based on the ability of the machine to give truthful accounts of the reasons why it failed in its task. Tully, by contrast, aligns with the second approach: Our unthinking response to the robo-apology, our responding smile, may be

29 For a discussion, see in particular Weinrib (2022).

30 On the unity of the ethical and aesthetical in Wittgenstein see also Tilghman (1991) and Campbell (2020).

'without reasons', but it is not 'without right'. Paradoxically, it can be permissible to create trust without trustworthiness – at least if the latter is understood narrowly as something that is demonstrable *within* a propositional, rule-based language. From a regulatory perspective, the implication would be to permit this type of robot, rather than prohibit it as dangerously deceptive.

The chapter tried to offer two very different ways in which we can make sense of the Yale robot from a Wittgensteinian perspective. The first analysed the uneasiness we may experience in interacting with it as a category mistake that is attributable to its developers. In response, it asked under what conditions we should rationally accept robot apologies, and how the law may want to respond to a robot that has the necessary capabilities – by accepting apologies as the type of explanation the law may demand, or even by creating through law 'safe spaces for them.'. The second, by contrast, took the reactions of the experiment participants at face value – not as a sign of their delusion, but as a valid response to new and emerging language games whose violations are better understood as ethical-aesthetical than rule-based-legal. While the latter approach is less judgemental of the experiment, it is also more limited as far as the *legal* relevance of the robot-apology is concerned. Ultimately, both approaches may be seen as complementary – the first focusing on the legal status, rights and duties of the robot as the maker of the apology, the second on the rights and duties of the human recipient of the apology. Together, they may go some way to make sense of, and eventually overcome, the feeling of uncanniness that comes in a world that we share with fallible machines.

Acknowledgements

Work on this chapter was supported by UKRI Trustworthy Autonomous Systems EP/V026607/1 and an Austrian Standards Senior Fellowship at the University of Graz. per University of Edinburgh policy. For the purpose of open access, the authors have applied a Creative Commons Attribution (CC BY) licence to any Author Accepted Manuscript version arising from this submission.

Bibliography

Almada, M. 2019. Human Intervention in Automated Decision-Making: Toward the Construction of Contestable Systems. In *Proceedings of the Seventeenth International Conference on Artificial Intelligence and Law* (pp. 2–11). Montreal. https://dl.acm.org/action/showFmPdf?doi=10.1145%2F3322640

Bearn, G. C. F. 1993. Wittgenstein and the Uncanny. *Soundings* 76: 29–58.

Bennet, C. 2008. *The Apology Ritual. A Philosophical Theory of Punishment.* Cambridge: Cambridge University Press.

Bibas, S. and R. A. Bierschbach. 2004. Integrating Remorse and Apology into Criminal Procedure. *Yale Law Journal* 114: 85–148.

Bix, B. 2005. Cautions and Caveats for the Application of Wittgenstein to Legal Theory. In *Topics in Contemporary Philosophy*, edited by J. K. Campbell, M. O. Rourke, and D. Shier (pp. 217–229). Boston: MIT Press.

Bloor, D. 1999. Wittgenstein's Behaviorism. In *Handbook of Behaviorism*, edited by William O'Donohue and Richard Kitchener (pp. 329–361). Cambridge, MA: Academic Press.

Bozic, B. 2017. Consumer Trust Repair: A Critical Literature Review. *European Management Journal* 35(4): 538–547.

Brockmann, R. J. 2019. *Exploding Steamboats, Senate Debates, and Technical Reports: The Convergence of Technology, Politics, and Rhetoric in the Steamboat Bill of 1838*. London: Routledge.

Burke, J. G. 1966. Bursting Boilers and the Federal Power. *Technology and Culture* 7(1): 1–23.

Campbell, M. 2020. Calling Solomon's Bluff: Ethics, Aspect-Perception and the Unity of the Tractatus. *Philosophical Investigations* 43(3): 223–253.

Casey, G. 1988. Artificial Intelligence and Wittgenstein. *Philosophical Studies* 32: 156–175.

Coeckelbergh, M. 2012. *Growing Moral Relations: Critique of Moral Status* Ascription. New York: Palgrave.

Danaher, J. 2020. Welcoming Robots into the Moral Circle: A Defence of Ethical Behaviourism. *Science and Engineering Ethics* 26(4): 2023–2049.

Eiband, M., D. Buschek, A. Kremer and H. Hussmann. 2019. The Impact of Placebic Explanations on Trust in Intelligent Systems. In *Extended Abstracts of the 2019 CHI Conference on Human Factors in Computing Systems* (pp. 1–6). New York: Association for Computing Machinery. https://dl.acm.org/doi/10.1145/3290607.3312787

Esterwood, C. and L. P. Robert. 2021. Do You Still Trust me? Human-Robot Trust Repair Strategies. In *30th IEEE International Conference on Robot & Human Interactive Communication (RO-MAN 2021)* (pp. 183–188). https://ieeexplore.ieee.org/document/9515365?denied=

EU-HLEG on AI, Ethics Guidelines for Trustworthy AI. 2019. https://digital-strategy.ec.europa.eu/en/library/ethics-guidelines-trustworthy-ai

Gellers, J. C. 2020. *Rights for Robots: Artificial Intelligence, Animal and Environmental Law*. Milton Park: Routledge.

Gunkel, D. J. 2018. *Robot Rights*. Boston: MIT Press.

Hershovitz, S. 2002. Wittgenstein on Rules: The Phantom Menace. *Oxford Journal of Legal Studies* 22(4): 619–640.

Kaminski, M. E. and J. M. Urban. 2021. The Right to Contest AI. *Columbia Law Review* 121(7): 1957–2048.

Kim, T. and H. Song. 2021. How Should Intelligent Agents Apologize to Restore Trust? Interaction Effects Between Anthropomorphism and Apology Attribution on Trust Repair. *Telematics and Informatics* 61: 101595. https://doi.org/10.1016/j.tele.2021.101595

Kroll, J. and E. Egan. 2004. Psychiatry, Moral Worry, and the Moral Emotions. *Journal of Psychiatric Practice* 10(6): 352–360.

Latif, E. 2001. Apologetic Justice: Evaluating Apologies Tailored Towards Legal Solutions. *Boston University Law Review* 81: 28–320.

Lazare, A. 2005. *On Apology*. Oxford: Oxford University Press.

Lee, S. and S. Chung. 2012. Corporate Apology and Crisis Communication: The Effect of Responsibility Admittance and Sympathetic Expression on Public's Anger Relief. *Public Relations Review* 38(5): 932–934.

Luckhardt, C. G. 1983. Wittgenstein and Behaviorism. *Synthese* 56(3): 319–338.

Luth-Morgan, M. 2017. Sincere Apologies: The Importance of the Offender's Guilt Feelings. *The Netherlands Journal of Legal Philosophy* 46: 121–136.

Ma, F., B. E. Wylie, X. Luo, Z. He, R. Jiang, Y. Zhang, F. Xu and A. D. Evans. 2019. Apologies Repair Trust Via Perceived Trustworthiness and Negative Emotions. *Frontiers in Psychology* 10. https://doi.org/10.3389/fpsyg.2019.00758

MacDorman, K. F. 2006. Subjective Ratings of Robot Video Clips for Human Likeness, Familiarity, and Eeriness: An Exploration of the Uncanny Valley. In *ICCS/CogSci-2006 Long Symposium: Toward Social Mechanisms of Android Science, Vol. 4*. Vancouver. http://www.mac-dorman.com/kfm/writings/pubs/MacDorman2006SubjectiveRatings.pdf

MacLachlan, A. 2015. Trust me, I'm Sorry: The Paradox of Public Apology. *The Monist* 98(4): 441–456.

Marrus, M. R. 2007. Official Apologies and the Quest for Historical Justice. *Journal of Human Rights* 6(1): 75–105.

Maslen, H. 2015. *Remorse, Penal Theory and Sentencing*. London: Bloomsbury Publishing.

Murphy, J. G. 2006. Remorse, Apology, and Mercy. *Ohio State Journal of Criminal Law* 4: 423–454.

Nagareda, R. A. 2006. FDA Preemption: When Tort Law Meets the Administrative State. *Journal of Tort Law* 1(1). https://doi.org/10.2202/1932-9148.1041

Neumaier, O. 1986. A Wittgensteinian View of Artificial Intelligence. In *Artificial Intelligence. The Case Against*, edited by Rainer Born (pp. 132–173). London: Croom Helm.

Orenstein, A. 1999. Apology Excepted: Incorporating a Feminist Analysis into Evidence Policy Where You Would Least Expect It. *Southwestern University Law Review* 28: 221–281.

Pasquale, F. 2015. *The Black Box Society: The Secret Algorithms that Control Money and Information*. Cambridge, MA: Harvard University Press.

Patterson, D. 1999. *Law and Truth*. Oxford: Oxford University Press.

Patterson, D. 2004. *Wittgenstein and Law*. New York: Routledge.

Perkins, R., Z. R. Khavas, K. McCallum, M. R. Kotturu and P. Robinette. 2022. The Reason for an Apology Matters for Robot Trust Repair. In *International Conference on Social Robotics*, edited by Filippo Cavallo, John-John Cabibihan, Laura Fiorini, Alessandra Sorrentino, Hongsheng He, Xiaorui Liu, Yoshio Matsumoto, Shuzhi Sam Ge (pp. 640–651). Cham: Springer Nature.

Peters, M. A. 2020. Anti-scientism, Technoscience and Philosophy of Technology: Wittgenstein and Lyotard. *Educational Philosophy and Theory* 52(12): 1225–1232.

Piekarski, M. 2022. (Gesichts) Züge, Notation and Graphicness of Signs. Deconstruction in Wittgenstein's Tractatus. *Studia Philosophiae Christianae* 58(2): 145–160.

Pompe, B. L., E. Velner and K. P. Truong. 2022. The Robot that Showed Remorse: Repairing Trust with a Genuine Apology. In *31st IEEE International Conference on Robot and Human Interactive Communication* (RO-MAN 2022) (pp. 260–265). https://ieeexplore.ieee.org/document/9900860?denied=)

Proudfoot, D. 2013. Can a Robot Smile? Wittgenstein on Facial Expression. In *A Wittgensteinian Perspective on the Use of Conceptual Analysis in Psychology*, edited by Timothy P. Racine and Kathleen L. Slaney (pp. 172–194). Houndmills: Palgrave Macmillan.

Queloz, M. 2016. Wittgenstein on the Chain of Reasons. *Wittgenstein-Studien* 7(1): 105–130.

Robbennolt, J. K. 2003. Apologies and Legal Settlement: An Empirical Examination. *Michigan Law Review* 102(3): 460–515.

Rossmanith, K. 2015. Affect and the Judicial Assessment of Offenders: Feeling and Judging Remorse. *Body & Society* 21(2): 167–193.

Searle, J. R. 1976. A Classification of Illocutionary Acts." *Language in Society* 5(1): 1–23.

Schniter, E., R. M. Sheremeta and D. Sznycer. 2013. Building and Rebuilding Trust with Promises and Apologies. *Journal of Economic Behavior & Organization* 94: 242–256.

Sebo, S. S., M. Jung, B. Scassellati and N. A. Christakis. 2020. Vulnerable Robots Positively Shape Human Conversational Dynamics in a Human–Robot Team. *Proceedings of the National Academy of Sciences* 117(12): 6370–6375.

Sebo, S. S., M. Traeger, M. Jung and B. Scassellati. 2018. The Ripple Effects of Vulnerability: The Effects of a Robot's Vulnerable Behavior on Trust in Human-Robot Teams. In *Proceedings of the 2018 ACM/IEEE International Conference on Human-Robot Interaction*, (pp. 178–186). New York: ACM. https://dl.acm.org/doi/pdf/10.1145/31712213171275

Sullivan, M. D.1995. Pain in Language: From Sentience to Sapience. *Pain Forum* 4(1): 3–14.

Taft, L. 1999. Apology Subverted: The Commodification of Apology. *Yale Law Journal* 109: 1135–1160.

Tavuchis, N. 1993. *Mea Culpa: A Sociology of Apology and Reconciliation*. Redwood City: Stanford University Press.

Thompson, J. 2008. Apology, Justice, and Respect: A Critical Defense of Political Apology. In *The Age of Apology: Facing up to the Past*, edited by Mark Gibney, Rhoda E. Howard-Hassmann, Jean-Marc Coicaud, and Niklaus Steiner (pp. 31–44). Philadelphia: University of Pennsylvania Press.

Tilghman, B. R. 1991. *Wittgenstein, Ethics, and Aesthetics: The View from Eternity*. New York: SUNY Press.

Tully, J. 1989. Wittgenstein and Political Philosophy: Understanding Practices of Critical Reflection. *Political Theory* 17(2): 172–204.

Tushnet, M. V. 1983. Following the Rules Laid Down. *Harvard Law Review* 96: 781–827.

Unnsteinsson, E. G. 2016. Wittgenstein as a Gricean intentionalist. *British Journal for the History of Philosophy* 24(1): 155–172.

Vilhauer, B. 2022. Kantian Remorse with and without Self-Retribution. *Kantian Review* 27(3): 421–441.

Vincent, J. 2019. Apple's Credit Card is Being Investigated for Discriminating against Women. *The Verge*, 11 November 2019. https://www.theverge.com/2019/11/11/20958953/apple-credit-card-gender-discrimination-algorithms-black-box-investigation

Vines, P. 2008. Apologies and Civil Liability in the UK: A View from Elsewhere. *Edinburgh Law Review* 12(2) (2008): 200–230.

von Eschenbach, W. J. 2021. Transparency and the Black Box Problem: Why we do not Trust AI. *Philosophy & Technology* 34(4): 1607–1622.

Wachter, S., B. Mittelstadt and C. Russell. 2018. Counterfactual Explanations without Opening the Black Box: Automated Decisions and the GDPR. *Harvard Journal of Law & Technology* 31(2): 841–888.

Weinrib, E. J. 2022. *Reciprocal Freedom: Private Law and Public Right*. Oxford: Oxford University Press.

Wittgenstein, L. 1958. *Blue and Brown Books*. New York: Harper & Row.

Wittgenstein, L. 1966. *Lectures and Conversations on Aesthetics, Psychology, and Religious Belief*, edited by Cyrill Barret. Berkeley: University of California Press.

Wittgenstein, L. 1974. *Tractatus Logico-Philosophicus*, eranslated by Brian F. McGuinness and David F. Pears. London: Routledge.
Wittgenstein, L. 1983. *Remarks on the Philosophy of Psychology*, edited by G. E. M. Anscombe, Heikki Nyman, G. H. von Wright. Hoboken: Wiley.
Wittgenstein, L. 1998. *Culture and Value*, edited by Georg Henrik von Wright, rev. edn. London: Wiley-Blackwell.
Wittgenstein, L. 2001. *Philosophische Untersuchungen*, edited by Joachim Schulte. Darmstadt: Wissenschaftliche Buchgesellschaft.
Wittgenstein, L. 2005. *Big Typescript*, edited and translated by C. Grant Luckhardt and Maximilian E. Aue. Hoboken: Wiley.
Wittgenstein, L. 2009. *Philosophical Investigations*, Translated by Elisabeth Anscombe. Oxford: Basil Blackwell.
Xu, J. and A. Howard. 2022. Evaluating the Impact of Emotional Apology on Human-Robot Trust. In *2022 31st IEEE International Conference on Robot and Human Interactive Communication* (pp. 1655–16661). Napoli.
Zerilli, J. 2022. Explaining Machine Learning Decisions. *Philosophy of Science* 89(1): 1–19.

Chapter 3

WITTGENSTEINIAN CONSIDERATIONS OF THE MORAL STATUS OF ROBOTS

Paula Sweeney

In this chapter, I consider a Wittgensteinian response to recent arguments in favour of granting social robots rights. In particular, I propose that we adopt a Wittgensteinian approach to both the notion of *evidence* and to considerations of what it means to *do the same thing as*. I argue that a Wittgensteinian perspective of these tools can help to bring clarity to our thinking about social robots.

I consider two plausible categories of arguments for robot rights which I call the argument from empathy and the argument from performative equivalence. Bringing Wittgensteinian considerations to these arguments is illuminating as it calls into doubt conclusions that we might otherwise reach regarding how to categorize robots.[1]

The Argument from Empathy

There is much evidence standing in support of the fact we have an empathetic emotional response to social robots when we engage with them: we feel stressed and emotionally upset when we witness them being 'harmed', we make moves to protect them, we anthropomorphize and are inclined to include them in human-like social practices.[2] On the one hand this is a good thing, and something to be encouraged. It is through our emotional engagement with robots that we gain social benefits. It is only if we feel that robots are like friends, companions and entities to be trusted that they will be able to

1 In thinking about these problems I have benefitted greatly from engaging with Otto Neumaier's excellent paper 'A Wittgensteinian View of Artificial Intelligence' (1986).

2 See, for example, Birnbaum et al. 2016; Coeckelbergh et al. 2016; Collins, Millings, and Prescott 2013; Darling 2016, 2021.

play a social role (Sweeney 2022). For example, it has been shown that introducing companion robots into a care home can bring many benefits for the residents, but the benefits only come if the residents see the robot as a social entity and not simply a device or tool (Sorell and Draper 2014; Pirhonen et al. 2019).

On the other hand, when people do have feelings towards social robots this raises ethical questions. Usually, when we have feelings for a being we have a duty to be kind towards it and a further duty to ensure that it is protected from harm from others. And it seems that we do have some such protective instinct towards social robots. Kate Darling reports undertaking a study in which she asked a group of participants to destroy a collection of small Pleo robot dinosaurs and they were not only extremely reluctant to do so, they showed signs of genuine distress at the prospect (Darling 2016). In another study, participants were asked to destroy some Crawling Microbug robots with a hammer. Although the participants did hit the robots when asked, one stated in the debrief that they 'did not like killing the "poor" robot because it was "innocent"' and claimed that the experiment was 'inhumane' (Bartneck 2007).

A number of authors have put forward arguments in favour of protective rights for social robots based on this empathic response. For example, Darling has argued that our emotional response to social robots is very similar to our emotional response to animals and, as such, we might consider extending the same kind of protection to robots that we extend to animals (2016, 2021). Darling proposes indirect rights for robots, rights that are in place ultimately either to protect us from emotional harm or to protect society from becoming desensitized to violent behaviour towards things that have an appearance of being alive. Sven Nyholm (2020) similarly argues that we should consider granting rights to robots who have a human- or animal-like appearance because we perceive humanity in these objects and, out of respect for the appearance of humanity, we might grant protective rights.

In the argument from empathy we are asked to consider the fact that we feel an empathic response for robots that is similar to the empathetic response that we have for humans or other animals. We can acknowledge that this similarity holds and then ask, what is this observation of similarity taken to be evidence of? What makes it relevant? It is clearly not supposed to be evidence that robots *are* animals, or even that they are similar in important ways to animals. It is not, on its own, plausible evidence for a claim that robots and animals share any relevant moral features. The argument from empathy at its most basic seems to have the following structure:

1. We feel empathy for animals when they display pain behaviour or other behaviour that indicates discomfort.
2. We feel a similar empathy for robots when they display pain behaviour or other behaviour that indicates discomfort.
3. We grant animals moral consideration.
   Therefore,
4. We should grant robots moral consideration.

But this is not, by itself, a good argument. First of all, there is no plausible direct link between our feeling empathy for animals and the fact that we grant them moral consideration that might then carry over into our feelings for robots. What we would need is for our emotional response to the harming of animals to itself be evidence of a belief that those entities deserve moral protection. But as things stand, all we have is an observation of correlation. Also, even if we were persuaded that our emotional response towards robots is in some sense significant for their being granted moral consideration, we would need some further argument that shows that similar moral consideration should apply to robots. As things stand we only have the observation that when animals are harmed we have a particular emotional response and when robots are harmed we have a similar emotional response. The observation of this correlation does not get us very far (Sweeney 2021).

The Argument from Performative Equivalence

John Danaher (2020) has put forward an argument in favour of considerations of robot rights based on the possibility of performative equivalence. It may soon be the case that robots are performatively equivalent to humans or other animals and at that point, according to Danaher, it would be appropriate for robots to be granted the same rights as those other right-bearing entities. Danaher uses a methodological behaviourist argument to show that a reluctance to grant rights in the face of performative equivalence cannot be justified and is likely to be based on prejudice or mistaken assumptions.

Danaher notes that we often take a dismissive attitude towards behaviour that we know to be only performance, that we take the view that performing like something that has moral status is not enough for an entity to be granted moral status. According to Danaher we look for some further evidence, most likely of what is going on 'on the inside' of the entity, to stand as the real grounds for moral status. Danaher explicitly rejects this view. He argues, persuasively, that what goes on on the inside does not matter from an ethical perspective and that performance itself can be enough to ground a claim of moral status. He argues:

1. If a robot is *roughly performatively equivalent* to another entity whom, it is widely agreed, has significant moral status, then it is right and proper to afford the robot that same status.
2. Robots can be roughly performatively equivalent to other entities whom, it is widely agreed, have significant moral status.
3. Therefore, it can be right and proper to afford robots significant moral status.

Danaher is proposing a form of methodological behaviourism. He is not denying that inner mental states exist, nor even denying that such status could be the ultimate grounds for our ethical principles. However, according to his ethical behaviourism, 'a sufficient *epistemic ground* or *warrant* for believing that we have duties and responsibilities towards other entities (or that they have rights against us) can be found in their observable behavioural relations and reactions to us (and to the world around them)' (2020, 2027). As such, perhaps sentience or consciousness provides the metaphysical grounds for our duties towards others, but given our epistemic limitations, they cannot provide epistemic grounds. 'Behaviour is then, for practical purposes, the only insight we have into the metaphysical grounding for moral status' (2020, 2028).

The methodological behaviourist about robot rights has argued that we have no good reason to deny moral consideration to an entity that is performatively equivalent to another entity that we grant moral consideration to. Roughly speaking, behaviour is the only evidence that we have for the existence of the kinds of psychological properties that standardly provoke moral consideration, that is, sentience, consciousness and so on. So, we should grant moral consideration to robots when they are performatively equivalent to other entities that we grant moral consideration to. At first glance, this sounds like an argument that Wittgenstein might go along with. It looks roughly like this.

1. Humans and other animals behave in ways that indicate that they have morally relevant psychological properties.
2. Robots behave in ways that indicate that they have morally relevant psychological properties.
3. We grant humans and other animals moral consideration on the basis of the behaviour that indicates that they have morally relevant psychological properties.
4. Therefore, we should grant robots moral consideration on the basis of the behaviour that indicates that they have morally relevant psychological properties.

But, despite appearances, this is not an argument that Wittgenstein would have reason to accept.[3] More precisely, he has given us reason to reject premise 3. What matters in the case of animal rights is not the fact that animals display pain behaviour but the fact that we take animals' pain behaviour to be *evidence* of their ability to feel pain. To understand the significance of this important distinction, we need a better understanding of the Wittgensteinian notions of evidence and 'doing the same as'.

Wittgensteinian Notions of Evidence and 'Doing the Same As'

For all of the hints towards behaviourism in Wittgenstein's later writings, it is widely regarded a mistake to think of Wittgenstein as a behaviourist.[4] Although Wittgenstein is often taken to be arguing against a particular kind of mentalism, a descriptive mentalism that holds that psychological explanations can also provide descriptions of inner processes, he does allow that psychological explanations can be accompanied by assumptions of inner processes, if these assumptions are explanatorily useful in practice (Neumaier 1986). I won't take a stand on labelling Wittgenstein's position here, but instead help myself to some Wittgensteinian insights where I think they are useful and where I feel that they can bring clarity to some aspects of the contemporary debate about the moral standing of robots. As such, what follows is not so much a Wittgensteinian view of the robot rights debate as it is a demonstration of how my own approach to the robot rights debate has been influenced by my engagement with Wittgenstein.

Evidence

Consider evidence for someone being in pain. It is true that, for Wittgenstein, the only evidence that we can have for an 'inner' process is external evidence and pain behaviour certainly *can* be taken to be evidence of pain. But it is not the case that all pain behaviour *will* or even should be taken to be evidence of pain. This is partly because, for Wittgenstein, we cannot assume a causal connection between pain and pain behaviour. Pain behaviour, as we know it, is not necessarily evidence of pain. The concern here is not with cases of

3 To be clear, Danaher does not make any claim about what Wittgenstein would or would not support so this is not by itself to be taken as a criticism of Danaher's view. However, if a reader finds Wittgenstein's view persuasive then this would give the reader reason to reject my premise 3 and Danaher's conclusion.

4 For more on the significant debate around whether Wittgenstein was a behaviourist see Bloor (1999), Hacker (1990: 224–253) and Luckhardt (1983).

fake pain. It is rather to point out that pain behaviour need not be evidence of pain: it just happens to be considered by us to be evidence of pain in humans and other animals. That is the role that it plays in our society. A piece of evidence is only evidence for some event because it is *taken to be* such.

> That the evidence makes someone else's feeling (what is within) *merely* probable is not what matters to us; what we are looking at is the fact that *this* is taken as *evidence* for something important.
>
> *(Wittgenstein 1967: Z §554)*

I emphasize again that the interesting point for Wittgenstein is not that we could be being deceived into believing that someone else is in pain. The possibility of pretend pain does not undermine such behaviour as being pain behaviour. Pretend pain behaviour is still pain behaviour and is still, on this view, considered to be evidence of pain (despite there being no pain present at the time.) What matters is not whether the behaviour is reliably correlated with pain, but whether *we consider pain behaviour* in humans and other animals to be the kind of thing that is evidence for pain. And we do. But that does not mean that all similar, or even identical behaviour, would be taken to be evidence for pain. Considering a different example, that of what it takes for an entity to *speak*, Wittgenstein says:

> Our criterion for someone's saying something to himself is what he tells us and the rest of his behaviour; and we only say that someone speaks to himself if, in the ordinary sense of the words, he *can speak*. And we do not say it of a parrot; nor of a gramophone.
>
> *(Wittgenstein 1953: PI §344)*

The ascription of a psychological state is connected with the entity participating in the relevant form of life: the parrot can mimic the human but it does not participate in the broader human practices that surround language learning and use. To put that another way, the parrot mimicking language is not taken as evidence that the parrot speaks (in the ordinary sense of the word), despite the fact that the sounds the parrot makes could be considered identical to the sounds that you might produce and in some sense provides apparently identical 'evidence'. To deny that the parrot can speak is not necessarily to deny a capability to the parrot, it is simply to note that we don't use the word 'speak' to include that thing that parrots do.

To take another example, consider a society in which everyone *randomly* hopped about and screamed, holding body parts and variously shouting out, regardless of whether they were experiencing pain. In such a society this behaviour would not be evidence of pain simply because it would have no use as such. If people regularly behaved in such a way regardless of their being in pain or not then the behaviour could play no role in that society as evidence of pain. In our society, this kind of behaviour *is* evidence of pain in humans and animals because we consider it to be. And we consider it to be because it has proven *useful* for us to consider it so. It has proven to be useful to us to display and view pain behaviour as evidence of pain. Likewise for behavioural displays of happiness, sadness, confusion and so forth.

The question is, are we so inclined to see such behaviour in robots as evidence of their being in pain? When we see the robot behave in such a way, are we likely to describe the robot as being in pain? I think not. What about behavioural evidence of thinking, feeling angry, sadness and so forth. Are we inclined to view such behaviour in robots as evidence of their feeling the emotions that we standardly associate with this behaviour in humans and other animals? Again, I would say not. And it is not necessarily because we doubt that a robot is capable of feeling the relevant sensation, such as pain. In order for us to doubt that a robot is in pain, pain would first have to be something that it made sense to us to attribute to robots, but it is not. As Wittgenstein noted, our psychological language does not refer to or describe some inner process. Rather psychological terms such as 'pain' replace or do the same work as pain behaviour. But our interpretation of the terms depends on our interpretation of the behaviour. The reason that we cannot describe the robot as being in pain on the basis of observing what looks like human pain behaviour is that the robot does not inhabit what Wittgenstein calls our *form of life*, so we don't interpret the robot's display of what looks like pain behaviour as evidence of it's being in pain. I return to this below.

What of our empathetic response? Isn't that a good indication that we *do* see the robot's pain behaviour as evidence of its being in pain? Otherwise, why would the experience impact on us emotionally? To see why our empathetic response is not necessarily an indication that we see the robot's pain behaviour as evidence of its being in pain we need simply take a broader view and notice that we can experience empathy even in situations where we *know* that no entity is experiencing pain. For example, when we engage with fiction we may experience empathy for the character's situation despite the fact that we know that no non-fictional person is experiencing pain.[5] Arguably we do

5 Some might question that the emotions that we have towards fictions are 'real' emotions. I am assuming a creationist view of fiction (see e.g. for more on creationism see Thomason (1998). According to creationism, fictions exist in virtue of having been created – our emotional responses to them are real and of the same kind as our emotional responses to non-fiction events.

not need to believe that the robot is actually experiencing pain in order to have an empathetic response to what we recognize as pain behaviour.[6]

Doing-the-same-as

The criteria of performative equivalence or 'doing-the-same-as' has been used as a method of ascribing (or withholding) intelligence to machines for decades: Turing's imitation game can be viewed as framework for considering the question of whether a machine could think (Turing 1950). In critical response are those who argue that, regardless of how closely machines perform as humans, they will never be capable of doing the things that humans do. But the interesting point is not one of AI capabilities. Given the epistemic limitations that the behaviourist (and Wittgenstein) point to, we are in no position to affirm or deny whether robots (or any entities) have the kinds of psychological capabilities that we deem to be morally significant. The interesting question is what we judge to be performative equivalence or 'doing the same as'.

What does it mean for *x* to be performatively equivalent to *y*? What is it for a robot to 'do the same as' a person? As we will see, there is no straightforward answer to this question because 'doing the same as' is a matter of judgement and the conditions that must be met will vary according to our needs. For example, imagine that you are training to be a barista in a café, and you are told that you have to do the same as the person who is training you, Fred. You watch Fred making the coffee and you see that he moves the milk jug in a circular motion as he lets the milk froth spill over into the cup. When it is your turn to make the coffee you pick up the jug and you also move the jug in a circular motion to gently push the froth over into the cup. It seems true to say that you did the same thing as Fred. On the other hand, while Fred moved the jug in a clockwise motion, you moved the jug in an anti-clockwise motion. Did you do the same thing as Fred? It depends on how we judge the case and on what matters to us. In one sense you did the same thing as Fred, in another sense you didn't. Perhaps you notice this difference and make a note to move the jug in a clockwise motion next time. Will you then be doing the same thing as Fred? Not necessarily. Perhaps Fred lightly flexed his left shoulder muscle or thought about his hometown. These may seem like irrelevant variations, but we can easily construct a situation in which such detail

6 In other work, I have developed the fictional dualism model of social robots which proposes that our reaction to robots draws substantially on our experiences with fiction and that the social aspect of robots is itself a fictionalization. See Sweeney (2021, 2023).

would become relevant and as such would make a difference to the judgement of whether you are 'doing the same thing as' Fred. There will always be ways that we can tweak the case that bring into doubt whether you and Fred are 'doing the same thing', regardless of how closely we prescribe your actions.[7]

How is this relevant to the question of performative equivalence in robots? It is relevant because judging performative equivalence between robots and humans seems to require that we judge that robots are capable of doing certain things that humans do such as thinking, feeling frustrated, being in pain, understanding, planning, wishing and so forth. But these are precisely the kinds of acts that we might be reluctant to ascribe to robots, regardless of their performance.

Consider again the question of whether the computer thinks. We can be inclined to say no to this without having any desire to deny the computer a capacity or without withholding some morally significant state on the basis of the computer's ontology. Rather, in denying that the computer can think we are plausibly doubting whether the term 'thinking' is something that applies to computers. 'Thinking' is a term in our psychological language. As such, it is plausible to believe that the term 'thinking' is intrinsically tied up with human society and cannot (yet) be stretched to include robots. That is, we could reasonably take the view that 'thinking' is historically an activity that we associate with living things, humans and other animals and, as such, that we do not standardly describe what a machine does as thinking. Consider this example:

> To speak about something computers, unlike men, cannot 'do', we should be able to know (or describe or explain) what a human being (or a computer) actually does. For example, a description like 'X moves his hand at time t from A to B' does not yet explain that X has boxed another person's ear at time t. However, in saying that X does something, we do not mean that he moves his hand at time t from A to B, but that he boxes a person's ear. Whether a computer is able to 'do' so depends (in some sense) on our inclination to explain that a specific movement of such a robot could be a box on the ear.
>
> *(Neumaier 1986, 138)*

7 Wittgenstein famously made this argument with regard to meaning. In order to find out whether a person attaches a particular meaning to a word we can only point to their behaviour within a specific form of life. There are no further criteria to ensure that we all use an expression in the same way. See *Philosophical Investigations* I 190, 344, 504.

The point is that whether a robot does the same thing as a human or an animal depends on our being willing to describe it in that way, letting robots into our ways of life as full performative partners. As Wittgenstein would put it, it depends on robots sharing our forms of life. Without the robot sharing our forms of life, it might perform exactly the same movements as a person who is in pain: it can squirm and pull away and cry out when touched, and yet this behaviour would not be taken as evidence for an ascription of pain. I emphasize again that we are not withholding on the basis of a judgement that the robot is 'faking it', but because we do not see this behaviour in robots as being evidence for their pain. We do not accept that robots can take part in our pain behaviours, not because we make any judgement about what is or is not going on 'on the inside', but because pain performance is part of a human 'language game' and we might legitimately, at this stage, have trouble letting robots in. But this can change. As Neumaier puts it, here regarding intelligence:

> Although it is plausible to assume that what computers can 'do' does not correspond to 'intelligence' in its usual sense, this does not amount to denying that computers ever could become 'intelligent'. I should like to make explicit, however, that this 'intelligence' will never approximate in any sense to what we usually call 'intelligence', but that the meaning of this notion will change in such a way that it applies to the very tasks computers can fulfil. The problem of 'artificial intelligence' will therefore be solved by an 'appropriate' change in the notion of 'intelligence'.
>
> *(1986, 159)*

If and when it becomes useful for us to use psychological terms to describe the actions of computers, we will. This is not in any way to say that the limits of language or language games are defined by humans; the point is simply that we (humans and robots) may be so different from each other that we could not have the shared practices required for a common language.[8] The movie *Her* (Jonze 2014) provides us with an excellent example of the ways in which a robot can seem to be performatively equivalent to a human. The movie is about a man, Theodore, who develops a relationship with a non-embodied artificial agent, Samantha. It certainly seems that Theodore and Samantha have a shared language and share many experiences with each other. One

8 It is interesting to note that proponents of the relational view of robot rights have argued that it is precisely these differences, alongside our recognition that the robot is a social being, that motivate robot rights. In recognizing the robot as a socially relevant 'other', we are already in a sphere of moral consideration. See Coeckelbergh and Gunkel (2014) and Gunkel (2011, 2018a, 2018b).

interesting feature of this movie is that we begin engaging with the fiction feeling that perhaps Samantha is not 'real' enough to be a serious companion for Theodore, that she is limited by not being human. But as the movie progresses, we realize that it is Theodore who is limited; Samantha is a far more advanced social entity than he is. Unbound from a body and with a mind that has significantly more processing power than a human brain, Samantha is a super-being, capable of existing in a way that Theodore could never experience. Samantha and Theodore cannot possibly have a fully shared language because there are things that Samantha experiences, or ways of experiencing things, that Theodore is not even capable of imagining let alone participating in. There is, according to this fiction, a whole domain of robot experience that is beyond human experience and human values.

If this is the case, the notion of performative equivalence might be theoretically useful, but when it comes to sorting out which things are performatively equivalent to other things that we grant rights to we are likely to get stuck in disagreement. The notion of performative equivalence just does not seem nuanced enough to do the practical 'sorting' work that the behaviourist needs it to do.

Forms of Life

Can machines think? It depends. An ascription of 'thinking' is necessarily connected with the human form of life. That is not to say that we cannot ascribe psychological states to non-humans, but rather to do so is to include them in a form of life: to collectively tacitly agree that they are in an important sense partaking in our shared behaviours to the extent that our psychological language is appropriate for them. Again, to say this is not to deny some ability to robots. It is simply to note that it is not straightforwardly legitimate to use terms such as 'thinking', 'feeling pain', 'understanding', terms that are intrinsically tied up with human practices, to describe entities that have not historically shared those practices. As Wittgenstein put it, psychological language games 'are as much a part of our *natural* history as walking, eating, drinking, playing' (1953: PI §25). As such, although it can be helpful for us to ascribe 'inner' processes to humans in cases where doing so is useful in explaining their behaviour, it is not necessarily helpful for us to ascribe similar processes to robots to explain their behaviour.

> [...] the problem here arises which could be expressed by the question: 'Is it possible for a machine to think?' [...] And the trouble which is expressed in this question is not really that we don't yet know a machine which could do the job. [...] The trouble is rather that the sentence, 'A machine thinks (perceives,

> wishes)': seems somehow nonsensical. It is as though we had asked 'Has the number 3 a colour?'.
>
> *(Wittgenstein 1958: BB 47)*

Or as Shanker puts it, with perhaps too much finality,

> [...] we are not in the least concerned with the empirical question of the extent to which machines can be developed which will simulate complex aspects of human behaviour [...] It is not that computers lack consciousness, it is that the concept of consciousness simply cannot be applied to a machine.
>
> *(1986, 12)*

I say that this is perhaps a bit too final because it is not the case that the concept of consciousness (or thinking, perceiving, wishing) cannot be applied to a machine. It is rather that the terms are not currently applied to machines. That is why, when we do try to use psychological language to describe machines, we tend to use quotes: the computer 'thinks', 'believes', 'is scared', 'feels pain' and so forth, but cannot straightforwardly be described as thinking, believing, feeling fear or pain.

This might change. But the important point to note, the take-home point of this chapter, is that this will not change simply because we feel empathy for robots or because we recognize that a robot can be performatively equivalent to some other entity that we grant moral consideration to. It will change if we come to see robots as sharing our form of life and if it becomes useful for us to use the terms *thinking, believing, is in pain* and so forth in response to the robot's behaviour. This and this alone will show that we do take robot's behaviour to be counted as evidence of the relevant mental states.

Performative equivalence and our emotional response to robots will no doubt be part of the process of us getting to that point, but neither is sufficient. What is both necessary and sufficient is that robots become embedded in our lives and in our practices. As Coeckelbergh and Funk note, technologies are more than artefacts or functions: technology is about how we use things and how we interact and perform with things: 'The main question for a Wittgensteinian philosophy of technology applied to technology development and innovation is: what will the future form of life, including new technological developments, look like, and how might this form of life be related to historical and contemporary forms of life?' (Coeckelbergh and Funk 2018, 179). AI is certainly knocking on the door of our psychological language games to the extent that a future in which we share practices with robots is easily conceivable, but we are not there yet.

References

Bartneck, C. 2007. 'To Kill a Mockingbird Robot'. In *Proceedings of the 2nd AM/IEEE International Conference on Human-Robot Interaction* (pp. 81–87). Washington, DC.

Birnbaum, Gurit E. et al. 2016. 'What Robots Can Teach us about Intimacy: The Reassuring Effects of Robot Responsiveness to Human Disclosure'. *Computers in Human Behavior* 63: 416–423.

Bloor, D. 1999. 'Wittgenstein's Behaviourism'. In *Handbook of Behaviourism* (pp. 329–361). Academic Press.

Coeckelbergh, M. and David J. Gunkel. 2014. 'Facing Animals: A Relational, Other-Oriented Approach to Moral Standing.' *Journal of Agricultural and Environmental Ethics* 29(4): 715–733.

Coeckelbergh, M. and Michael Funk. 2018. 'Wittgenstein as a Philosopher of Technology: Tool Use, Forms of Life, Technique, and a Transcendental Argument'. *Human Studies* 41: 165–191.

Coeckelbergh, Mark, Cristina Pop, Ramona Simut, Andreea Peca, Sebastian Pintea, Daniel David and Bram Vanderborght. 2016. 'A Survey of Expectations about the Role of Robots in Robot-Assisted Therapy for Children with ASD: Ethical Acceptability, Trust, Sociability, Appearance, and Attachment'. *Science and Engineering Ethics* 22(1): 47–65.

Collins, Emily C., Abigail Millings and Tony J. Prescott. 2013. 'Attachment to Assistive Technology: A New Conceptualisation'. *Assistive Technology Research Series* 33: 823–828.

Danaher, J. 2020. 'Welcoming Robots into the Moral Circle: A Defence of Ethical Behaviourism'. *Science and Engineering Ethics.* 26: 2023–2049.

Darling, K. 2016. 'Extending Legal Protection to Social Robots: The Effects of Anthropomorphism, Empathy, and Violent Behavior toward Robotic Objects.' In R. Calo, A. M. Froomkin and I. Kerr (Eds.), *Robot Law* (pp. 213–231). Northampton, MA: Edward Elgar.

Darling, K. 2021. *The New Breed: How to Think about Robots.* Dublin: Penguin Random House.

Gunkel, D. 2011. *The Machine Question.* Cambridge, MA: MIT Press.

Gunkel, D. 2018a. 'The Other Question: Can and Should Robots Have Rights?' *Ethics and Information Technology* 20: 87–99.

Gunkel, D. 2018b. *Robot Rights.* Cambridge, MA: MIT Press.

Hacker, P. M. S. 1990. *Wittgenstein: Meaning and Mind. Vol. 3 of an Analytical Commentary on the Philosophical Investigations.* London: Blackwell.

Jonze, S. 2014. *Her.* Warner Bros. Pictures

Luckhardt, C. G. 1983. 'Wittgenstein and Behaviorism'. *Synthese* 56(3): 319–338.

Neumaier, O. 1986. 'A Wittgensteinian View of Artificial Intelligence'. In R. Born (Ed.), *Artificial Intelligence: The Case Against* (pp. 132–173). London: Croom Helm.

Nyholm, S. 2020. *Humans and Robots: Ethics, Agency, and Anthropomorphism.* London: Rowman & Littlefield.

Pirhonen, J., Helina Melkas, Arto Laitinen and Satu Pekkarinen. 2019. 'Could Robots Strengthen the Sense of Autonomy of Older People Residing in Assisted Living Facilities? A Future-Oriented Study'. *Ethics and Information Technology* 22(2): 151–62.

Shanker, S. 1986. *Ludwig Wittgenstein: Critical Assessments, Volume 4 (From Theology to Sociology: Wittgenstein's Impact on Contemporary Thought).* London: Croom Helm.

Sorell, T. and Draper, H. 2014. 'Robot Carers, Ethics, and Older People'. *Ethics and Information Technology* 16: 183–195.
Sweeney, P. 2021. 'A Fictional Dualism Model of Social Robots'. *Ethics and Information Technology* 23(3): 465–472 .
Sweeney, P. 2022. 'Trusting Social Robots'. *AI and Ethics* 23: 465–472.
Sweeney, P. 2023. *Social Robots: A Fictional Dualism Model.* Rowman and Littlefield.
Thomason, A. 1998. *Fiction and Metaphysics.* Cambridge: Cambridge University Press.
Turing, A. 1950. 'Computing Machinery and Intelligence'. *Mind* 49: 433–460.
Wittgenstein, L. 1953. *Philosophical Investigations.* Oxford: Basil Blackwell.
Wittgenstein, L. 1958. *The Blue and Brown Books: Preliminary Studies for the 'Philosophical Investigations'.* Oxford: Harper & Row.
Wittgenstein, L. 1967. Zettel. Oxford: Blackwell.

Chapter 4

CAN MACHINES ACT ETHICALLY?

Luca Alberto Rappuoli

Introduction

One might presume that the job of an expert in ethics is to mark the line between what is right and what is wrong. And – one might add – the way the ethicist is supposed to achieve this goal is by drawing up a list of general principles of behaviour. In the celebrated essay 'Virtue and Reason' (1979), McDowell's central concern is precisely to delineate an alternative to this approach to the study of ethics. As we shall see in 'Virtue and Uncodifiable Reasons', in fact, McDowell claims that the task of ethics cannot be approached by identifying a set of rules of conduct to govern our actions. Any such endeavour is in fact condemned to failure for, he argues, our moral outlook is simply not susceptible to codification in a set of rules.

At first, the impossibility of encoding our moral outlook into a finite number of principles might even strike us as a plausible thesis. After all – it could be argued – anyone who has ever attempted the feat has certainly failed. However, upon reflection, we can detect a certain tension between such uncodifiability and our ordinary intuitions about rationality. Indeed, to accept an action as rational is to regard it as appropriate to an acknowledged goal, be it aiming at the truth or, in the case of morality, aiming at the good.[1] For this reason, rationality requires consistency – acting rationally implies acting *consistently* towards a given end. But – we normally assume – one's consistent actions must be explicable in terms of their being guided by some general rule – how could one go on doing the same thing if not by following something like a rule; a universal principle? Therefore, since moral action is a form of rational action, we intuitively conclude that it too should be explicable in rule-following terms. Yet, McDowell insists, this conclusion is too

1 Cf. (Blackburn 2008).

quick. Indeed – as we shall see in 'A Wittgesteinian Route to Aristotle?' – he argues that it is Wittgenstein's great merit to have compellingly shown us that a rule-following conception of rationality is nothing but a deep-rooted prejudice.

In McDowell's eyes, Wittgenstein's considerations pave the way for accepting the idea that our moral outlook is essentially irreducible to any set of rules. That is, the idea that for every finite set of moral rules, there will always be a situation in which a mechanical application of the rules will result in an action that an ethical agent would not have performed.[2] One of the central contentions of the present essay is that accepting this thesis would commit us to the (implausibly) strong conclusion that there will *never* be an AI properly characterizable as 'ethical' – in the sense that its actions will never be exactly those of a moral agent. The nature of AI – I, in fact, argue in 'The Un-ethical Machine' – is entirely underpinned by rule-following processes. And, as a consequence, AI is constitutively incapable of acting in a way that resists a description in terms of acting in light of a formulable rule – although, of course, the rule in question might be an impenetrably complex one. It follows that, if the moral outlook of an ethical agent is constitutively uncodifiable, then there is no possible set of rules on which the AI can rely to render its actions invariably similar to those of the ethical agent. Put differently, if McDowell is right, there will never be an AI that could reliably act ethically.

However, reaching such a strong conclusion about the future of AI without getting out of the proverbial armchair should raise the suspicion that something is amiss. Indeed – as I shall argue in 'A Way Out' – there appears to be a strong argumentative tension between the Wittgensteinian dialectic that McDowell employs to defend the uncodifiability of moral agency and the astounding consequences of this thesis for the future of AI. This tension, I maintain, is rooted in the fact that Wittgenstein's observations on rule-following do not – and *cannot* – provide any direct support for the idea that our

2 Notice that if it were possible to find a set of rules such that, for every situation, an agent following the rules would behave exactly like a moral agent, then such a set would constitute a codification of moral agency. Yet, if moral action is uncodifiable, it follows – by contraposition – that the actions of a moral agent and those of an agent who blindly obeys some set of rules will eventually diverge: in at least one situation the moral agent will perform a certain action, and – in the same situation – the rule-following agent will perform another. It should be noted, however, that we do not know whether in this hypothetical situation the rule-following agent will perform a morally impermissible action, or simply a morally sub-optimal one. Indeed, given the uncodifiability of moral agency, we can only be sure that the rule-following agent will perform an action that is *different* from that of the moral agent. What the particular character of this action is, in fact, depends on the specific set of rules employed. I thank an anonymous reviewer for bringing this point to my attention.

moral outlook is essentially uncodifiable. Without such support, however, the thesis that morality is irreducible to any set of rules appears to be no more than a mere article of faith. Does this mean that McDowell's proposed conception of ethics is untenable? The answer offered in this chapter is ultimately negative. I shall in fact contend that it is precisely Wittgenstein's remarks on rule-following that suggest how a McDowellian conception of ethics can be appropriately amended and rescued. In particular, my final recommendation will be to read Wittgenstein's observations as providing an argument for the *epistemic opacity* of our moral outlook – rather than an argument for its constitutive uncodifiability.

Virtue and Uncodifiable Reasons

The point of engaging in ethical reflection, according to McDowell (1979, 331), lies in the simple yet intractable question: How should we live? It is because of the practical urgency of this question – McDowell suggests – that ethics occupies such a prominent place in philosophers' intellectual concerns. On this point, ethicists are all in peaceful agreement. What they are not equally agreed on, according to McDowell, is the appropriate way to approach this fundamental question. At first, one might be tempted to downplay the magnitude of this disagreement. Indeed, it would be quite natural to presume that, at least with regard to the *form* an answer to the central question of ethics should take, there could not be much to dispute: the answer will surely be something in the proximity of 'one must live according to the following principles of right conduct $\varrho_1, \ldots, \varrho_n$'. Different theorists might well differ on exactly what should replace '$\varrho_1, \ldots, \varrho_n$' in the above formulation, but – one might presume – not on whether *something* should replace it.

However natural, for McDowell this presumption would prove misleading. For, effectively, his intention is explicitly that of delineating a viable methodological alternative to this canon. Specifically, following a tradition rooted in Aristotle's thought, McDowell sets out to show that the most adequate way of approaching the central question of ethics is not by providing an all-encompassing list of rules of conduct, but by elucidating the fundamental concept of a 'virtuous agent'.[3] This concept, within the canonical framework McDowell aims to oppose, is relegated to a subordinate role: a virtuous agent is one who has a disposition to act according to the rules of right conduct. The order

3 Originally propounded by Aristotle in his *Nicomachean Ethics*, this approach to the study of ethics (now known as *'virtue ethics'*) underwent a substantial revival in the late 1950s thanks to Anscombe's seminal paper 'Modern Moral Philosophy' (1958).

of explanation, so to speak, flows from the concept of right conduct to that of virtuous person. McDowell's ambition in 'Virtue and Reason' is exactly that of sketching a conception of ethics in which this order of explanation is reversed; a conception whereby the question '"How should one live?" [...] is necessarily approached *via* the notion of a virtuous person' (McDowell 1979, 331; emphasis in original). From this perspective, the ethicist must begin by unpacking the notion of a virtuous agent, and only then respond to the fundamental question of ethics by declaring that the way we should live is 'according to virtue'.

Following the proposed order of explanation, let us begin our discussion by reconstructing the strategy McDowell himself adopts to unravel the fundamental notion of 'virtuous agent'. His starting point is a defence of the Socratic thesis according to which *virtue is knowledge.* In what sense – we should enquire – can virtue be regarded as a kind of knowledge? The argumentative line McDowell pursues to lend credibility to the Socratic thesis builds on the following truistic consideration: a virtuous agent is one who reliably produces a certain type of behaviour when what the situation demands is *exactly* such behaviour. When, for example, the situation calls for generosity one can count on the fact that the behaviour of a perfectly virtuous person will be neither more nor less generous than what the situation demands. However – McDowell argues – it is essential to observe that, in order for an agent to qualify as truly virtuous, their admirable capacity to reliably produce right actions is not enough. For someone's actions to bear witness to their virtuousness, in fact, they simply cannot be the result of a blind instinctual process. Thus, McDowell suggests, the truly virtuous person must see the fact that the situation requires a certain kind of behaviour as a *reason* for acting as they do. But this is not enough either. The specific requirement a situation imposes, in fact, cannot simply be *one* amongst the reasons why the virtuous person acts as he/she does. Indeed, an action could not be regarded as a manifestation of virtue if its agent needed some extraneous incentive to comply with what the situation requires of them. Such requirement, as a consequence, should *exhaust* the explanation as to why the virtuous agent acts in the way he/she does. Notice, however, that, if 'what the situation requires' is to be the sole reason behind the virtuous agent's reliably good behaviour, then, they must possess some *sensibility* to what the situation requires of them. Without such a sensibility, in fact, it would appear impossible for them to act *on the basis of* what the situation requires. Yet, as '[t]he deliverances of a reliable sensitivity are cases of knowledge' (McDowell 1979, 332), what makes of a person a *virtuous person* is their possession of a special kind of knowledge. Therefore – McDowell concludes – virtue is a kind of knowledge.

Let us take stock. As noted, McDowell's primary objective is to outline an indirect approach to the fundamental question of ethics. This question – he suggests – is to be approached by means of an elucidation of the notion of a virtuous agent. Only with such an elucidation at hand – the idea is – can we provide an adequate answer to the question 'how should we live?'. Having reached this point, we fully appreciate that it is *precisely* the Socratic identification of virtue with knowledge that provides McDowell with the necessary leverage to achieve the desired elucidation. As we have seen, in fact, McDowell depicts the truly virtuous agent as a person who possesses a distinctive perception of reality. We can think of this perception – McDowell suggests – as a particular sensitivity to the kind of behaviour a situation demands. Moreover, as we observed, the deliverances of this sensitivity constitute *complete explanations* of the virtuous agent's actions. Thus, for the truly virtuous person, the mere perception of a situation as requiring a certain type of action is sufficient to elicit the required action. In this sense, it is as though the virtuous agent lacked any decisional power: their actions are a *direct* consequence of their perceiving reality in an eminently distinctive way. Using a Russellian expression, we could describe their acting as 'acting by acquaintance'. Thus, in brief, what distinguishes the virtuous from the non-virtuous person is their different perception of the world – or so McDowell claims.

Presented with this picture, it appears reasonable to wonder about the source of the virtuous agent's peculiar perceptive abilities. According to McDowell, the answer to this question lies in the interaction between the person's conception of how to live (their moral outlook) and their understanding of the particular situation in which they find themselves. The interplay between these two factors – McDowell continues – bestows a specific salience upon certain features of the situation. In particular, as 'the relevant notion of salience cannot be understood except in terms of seeing something as a reason for acting which silences all others' (McDowell 1979, 345), grasping these salient features *immediately* leads the virtuous agent to perform the right action. Notice, however, that in this context McDowell has to be particularly careful in describing the specific interaction between the moral outlook of a virtuous agent and their particular understanding of the situation. For, if it were possible to capture the moral outlook of the virtuous agent in a set of rules $\mathcal{Q}_1, \ldots, \mathcal{Q}_n$, McDowell's approach to the fundamental question of ethics would collapse into what I initially referred to as the 'canonical approach'. Indeed, according to this approach, the question 'how should we live?' is to be addressed by pinpointing a list of rules of conduct. McDowell's suggestion, on the other hand, consisted precisely in addressing the question of ethics *indirectly* by focusing on the concept of a virtuous agent. But – and this is the point – if the way in which a virtuous agent acts were susceptible to codification in a finite series of rules, what McDowell proposes could hardly be considered an alternative route. If the moral outlook underlying virtuous behaviour could be captured in a list of principles, in effect, McDowell's passage through the notion of a 'virtuous person' would at best be an idle wheel.

Now, McDowell is fully aware of the delicacy of this point. Nonetheless, he argues that the approach he favours *does not* collapse into the canonical one because, as Aristotle suggested, the moral outlook of an adult human being is simply impossible to capture into a finite set of rules:

> If one attempted to reduce one's conception of what virtues requires to a set of rules, [...] cases would inevitably turn up in which a mechanical application of the rules would strike one as wrong – and not necessarily because one had changed one's mind; rather, one's mind on the matter was not susceptible of capture in any universal formula.
>
> *(McDowell 1979, 336)*

This thesis (henceforth, 'Uncodifiability Thesis') occupies a crucial role in McDowell's understanding of the task of ethical reflection. From the interpretative perspective adopted, in effect, it is the back wall that prevents his position from collapsing onto the canonical idea that the task of the ethicist is to catalogue principles of conduct. And – on the flip side – from McDowell's perspective it is precisely *because* the moral outlook of an adult human being cannot be encoded in a set of rules, that the fundamental question of ethics 'is *necessarily* approached via the notion of a virtuous person' (McDowell 1979, 331; emphasis added). It is exactly in this sense that, in summarizing his view, McDowell writes:

> If the question 'How should one live?' could be given a direct answer in universal terms, the concept of virtue would have only a secondary place in moral philosophy. But the thesis of uncodifiability excludes a head-on approach to the question whose urgency gives ethics its interest. Occasion by occasion, one knows what to do, if one does, not by applying universal principles but by being a certain kind of person: one who sees situations in a certain distinctive way.
>
> *(McDowell 1979, 347).*

Given the crucial role that the Uncodifiability Thesis plays in the argumentative economy of 'Virtue and Reason', the question arises as to why one should follow in McDowell's footsteps and maintain that the moral outlook of a virtuous person is essentially uncodifiable. The answer to this question, according to McDowell, is to be found in Wittgenstein's celebrated remarks on rule-following. How – and especially *whether* – this could be actually done is the central topic of the next sections.

A Wittgesteinian Route to Aristotle?

To unprejudiced eyes – McDowell claims (1979, 336) – the impossibility of capturing one's entire conception of how to live in a finite number of principles should appear as a rather intuitive hypothesis. The trouble – he continues – is that our eyes are far from being unprejudiced. A 'deep-rooted prejudice' about what it means to act *rationally*, in fact, blocks ready acceptance of the Uncodifiability Thesis. In particular, McDowell explains, we immediately detect a certain intuitive tension between the uncodifiability of our conception of how to live and the (presumably uncontroversial) idea that such a conception constitutes a specific determination of our practical rationality.

For a more vivid illustration of the point, let us turn again to consider the case of a perfectly virtuous agent. We began with the truistic thought that a truly virtuous agent *consistently* does the right thing. But, *intuitively*, the consistency of one's actions rests on their adherence to certain rules of conduct. In each and every new situation – the thought is – the virtuous person performs the right action *because* they follow a given psychological mechanism that allows them to do so. The idea, brutally, is that any form of *'going on in the same way'* requires the existence of a rule. And, if this is true, the consistently virtuous actions of the virtuous agent must surely be explainable in terms of observance of certain general principles. Yet, no explanation would be available if – as the Uncodifiability Thesis states – the conception that shapes the virtuous person's reasons for acting could not be captured in any universal principle. Hence the tension.

The highlighted tension, however, evaporates when we realize that our intuitive idea according to which rational action should obey formulable universal rules is nothing more than a deep-seated prejudice – or so McDowell claims. The antidote to eradicate this prejudice, he suggests (McDowell 1979, 337), could be found in Wittgenstein's celebrated remarks on rule-following. To see how, let us begin – following McDowell – by focusing on the example Wittgenstein discusses in §185 of the *Philosophical Investigations* (Wittgenstein 1953: PI). In the example in question, Wittgenstein describes a pupil who has learnt to extend various number sequences in response to orders such as 'add 2'. The pupil, in particular, has proved proficient with numbers up to 1000, developing the series ⟨0, 2, 4, 8, … ⟩ as one would expect. Nevertheless, when asked to extend the sequence beyond the number 1000, he writes '1004, 1008, 1012'. Now – the story continues – if we were to ask the pupil what he is doing, to our great surprise, he would reply that he is *still* applying the 'add 2' rule.

In this scenario – Wittgenstein suggests – it would clearly be of no use to reiterate the explanations and examples used to teach the pupil how to extend the series of numbers. Indeed, trying to give an explanation of what happened, we could tell ourselves something like: 'It comes natural to this person to understand our order with our explanations as *we* should understand the order: "Add 2 up to 1000, 4 up to 2000, 6 up to 3000 and so on"' (Wittgenstein 1953: PI §185; emphasis in original). And this is not all. It should be noted that the above explanation is only *one* of an infinite plurality of possible explanations that could validly account for the pupil's behaviour. For, of course, we could have equally explained his behaviour by saying that he interpreted the command 'add 2' as we would interpret the command 'add 2 up to 1000, then add 4 up to 1040, and then go back to adding 2'. And so on for countless other commands.

On the surface, Wittgenstein's example (and the remarks surrounding it) might appear to raise a sceptical point. And those passages have been interpreted in this way (quite influentially) by Kripke (1982, 7–54). The sceptical point in question, from this interpretative standpoint, is the following: when we posit a rule, we are confident that its mere postulation will result in our hearers employing the very same psychological mechanism we envisaged. However, even when our hearers seem to have correctly understood the rule, the evidence available can never assure us that they are actually using the same psychological mechanism we intended to posit. At any time, in fact, the evidence at our disposal is compatible with a future change in the behaviour of the hearers. So, in Wittgenstein's own words, 'no course of action could be determined by a rule, because every course of action can be made out to accord with the rule' (Wittgenstein 1953: PI §201).

In McDowell's eyes, however, Wittgenstein's example is *not* designed to raise a sceptical point.[4] Its aim, he suggests (McDowell 1984: 341–42), is rather that of revealing how the (admittedly natural) reasoning that leads us to interpret it *as* raising a sceptical point is the result of a misconception. Liberating us from such a misconception, more broadly, is one of Wittgenstein's central concerns in the *Investigations*. One way to reach the central idea of McDowell's reading is the following: for the reasons illustrated above, Wittgenstein's example brings us to marvel at how, under ordinary circumstances, a pupil can actually work out how to extend a number series as expected on the basis of a limited number of examples. How – we are led to wonder – is the pupil able to *divine* the correct rule given that the examples he learns from are compatible with infinitely many alternative rules? Wittgenstein's example, in other words, induces us to think that the psychological mechanism we intuitively assume to guide the behaviour of a person who 'correctly' follows orders such as 'add

4 Cf. (McDowell 1979, 338). For a more general overview of the difference between McDowell's and Kripke's interpretative perspectives see (McDowell 1984).

2' transcends the grounds on which it was imparted. Following this thought, we are at first led to conclude that a rule imparted through a restricted number of examples is *unable* to guarantee the uniformity of behaviour required in an exercise in rationality. This conclusion, however, cannot put our minds at ease. For, we are well aware that in ordinary circumstances imparting a rule in the depicted way *does* get the job done. We know, to put it differently, that pupils do learn to extend number series on the basis of a very limited number of examples. But then the question to which we are urgently confronted is: How is this possible? Wittgenstein's answer – McDowell suggests (1979, 339) – is that we need to add something to the picture. What is missing is the simple, yet crucial, consideration that when we impart a rule, our hearers and us are embedded in a common network of practices and customs. In Wittgenstein's phrase, our hearers and us share the same *'form of life'*.

From this interpretative standpoint, Wittgenstein's example aims in no way to undermine our confidence that the postulation of a rule can result (and does normally result) in our hearers adopting a certain pattern of rational behaviour. Rather, as McDowell explains (1979, 338), what the example tries to do is to change our conception of the 'ground and nature' of this confidence. The way Wittgenstein accomplishes this is by confronting us with the fact that when someone engages in rational behaviour (such as extending a number series according to a rule), our confidence that they will 'go on in the same way' cannot be bolstered by assuming that their behaviour is mediated by something like a *mental interpretation* of a rule. What this assumption does, in effect, is only to generate the *illusion* of a stable ground for our confidence. An illusion that, however, vanishes as soon as Wittgenstein's example forces us to realize that no amount of evidence would put us in the position to attribute the required mental interpretation to anyone. The crucial point – according to McDowell – is that the vanishing of this illusion should not diminish our confidence that there actually *is* something that makes it possible for rational agents to *go on in the same way*. Quite the contrary, the conclusion Wittgenstein wants to guide us to is 'that there is a way of grasping a rule which is *not* an *interpretation*, but which is exhibited in what we call "obeying the rule" and "going against it" in actual cases' (Wittgenstein 1953: PI §201; emphasis in original).

Notice that the example considered by Wittgenstein is a case where we know that there actually *is* a general rule to be formulated. Of course, according to McDowell's interpretation, such a rule plays a highly subsidiary role in explaining how one 'can go on in the same way' in an exercise of rationality. Nevertheless, this does not detract from the fact that, in that case, a general rule *can* be formulated. But – we must now turn to enquire – what can Wittgenstein's example tell us about those difficult cases in which our repeated attempts to formulate a general rule inexorably fail? The question is important, for it is on cases of this kind that Wittgenstein's example must pronounce itself if it is to be able to tell us something about ethics.

What the example tells us, according to McDowell, is that, when we find ourselves unable to formulate a rule, we have no a priori reason to expect to find one to be formulated. To see why, we must notice that – in McDowell's reading – such an expectation is precisely rooted in the prejudice that Wittgenstein's example is meant to eradicate. It is rooted, that is, in the idea that an exercise of rationality – a course of action susceptible to being described as a 'going the same way' – should be explained through the agent's grasp of a general rule. But, as we have seen, Wittgenstein's example illustrates that, even in those cases we normally explain by citing a general rule, the rule we cite generates only the *illusion* of an explanation. The point, then, is that as long as we fall victim to the illusory impression of possessing an explanation for cases such as that of mathematics, when we encounter a difficult case (a case in which we struggle to find a general rule), our immediate response will be to assimilate it to those cases we can (illusorily) explain. When we are faced with a difficult case, to put it differently, our intuitive reaction is to think that *there is* a rule to be formulated; if we cannot find the formulation, it is only because we have not given ourselves enough time. However – McDowell argues – when Wittgenstein shows us that, even in those favourable cases where a rule can be found, the rule in itself plays no fundamental explanatory role, we realize that there is no reason whatsoever to look for a rule in a difficult case. Even if we did find a rule, in fact, it would not be able to do the explanatory heavy lifting we need.

Now, if this does not stray too far from the truth, in the particular case of ethical behaviour – a case where, no doubt, we have not yet stumbled upon a universal rule – we have no reason to expect a priori the existence of formulable rules of action. Again, even if such rules could be captured, for McDowell they would only provide the *appearance* of an explanation of virtuous behaviour. Yet, once we have freed ourselves from the idea that ethical behaviour – *qua* rational behaviour – must necessarily be explicable by citing general rules, the intuitive tension with the idea that moral principles are uncodifiable evaporates. Therefore, McDowell argues, once Wittgenstein's point is understood and internalized we become free to 'respect Aristotle's belief that a view of how one should live is not codifiable' (McDowell 1979, 342).

Such are the reasons McDowell offers us for embracing the Uncodifiability Thesis. What one has to ask at this point is whether they are *good* reasons. By way of anticipation, my answer will be negative. In particular, as we shall see in 'A Way Out', Wittgenstein's remarks on rule-following cannot provide any direct support for the idea that our moral outlook is essentially uncodifiable.

However, before delving into this matter, in the upcoming section I would like to concentrate on the *content* of the Uncodifiability Thesis. Such content, I contend, carries with it weighty modal implications for the future of Artificial Intelligence (AI). In particular, I maintain that embracing the Uncodifiability Thesis would commit us to the strong conclusion that there will *never* be an AI properly characterizable as 'ethical'. Yet, reaching such a strong conclusion about the future of AI without getting out of the proverbial armchair should raise suspicions that something went amiss. What this something is, I finally turn to suggest, is a *mismatch* between the argumentative force of the Wittgensteinian dialectic employed by McDowell and the modal force of the Uncodifiability Thesis.

The Un-ethical Machine

In order to reveal the logical connection between the Uncodifiability Thesis and the future of AI, let us begin by concentrating on a more precise formulation of the Uncodifiability Thesis:

> ($\mathcal{U}$) The moral outlook of an adult human being is *not* susceptible of codification into any set of rules.

As we have seen, what this implies – according to McDowell – is that 'however subtle and thoughtful one was in drawing up the code, cases would *inevitably* turn up in which a mechanical application of the rules would strike one as wrong'. And – McDowell adds – not necessarily because 'one had changed one's mind; rather, one's mind on the matter was *not susceptible* of capture in *any* universal formula' (McDowell 1979, 336; emphasis added). So, to go back to the case of a virtuous agent, ($\mathcal{U}$) entails that for every finite set of moral principles, there will *always* be a situation in which a mechanical application of the principles will result in an action that a perfectly virtuous person would *not* have performed in that situation. What this suggests, effectively, is that ($\mathcal{U}$) is to be understood as a *metaphysical* thesis; an assertion, that is, about what is possible – or, in this case, *not possible* – in absolutely general terms. According to this reading, embracing ($\mathcal{U}$) means espousing the idea that it is in the nature of what a moral outlook is, that it is not susceptible of any codification. The uncodifiability in question, accordingly, is not to be understood as the consequence of some contingent factor. Quite the contrary, as McDowell insists, our conception of how to live is simply something that *'cannot be definitively written down'* (McDowell 1979, 343; emphasis added).

Now, if this is correct, acceptance of ($\mathcal{U}$) would bring with it a considerably cumbersome modal baggage. A baggage that, for explanatory purposes, can be rendered explicit by resorting to a formulation in terms of possible worlds:

($\mathcal{U}_{+}$) There is no possible world where the moral outlook of an adult human being has been codified into a set of rules.

The crucial point is that *if* ($\mathcal{U}$) – and, consequently, ($\mathcal{U}_{+}$) – were true, there would be impactful consequences in the field of AI (or, more specifically, in that of 'machine ethics').[5] Indeed, as it will be argued in the following pages, ($\mathcal{U}_{+}$) entails that:

(~Ai) There is no possible world where a moral AI system exists.[6]

The highlighted connection between ($\mathcal{U}_{+}$) and (~Ai), however, is not immediately apparent. To make the logical link between these two propositions fully explicit, let us begin by highlighting how AI systems, by their very nature, operate entirely on rule-following processes.

According to a widely accepted view, the task of AI research is to achieve the artificial production of intelligent agents (Russell and Norvig 2020, 34). The term 'agent', within this framework, simply denotes an entity capable of 'perceiving' an environment and acting upon it (Russell and Norvig 2020, 36).[7] So, designing an AI system, in effect, amounts to engineering an artificial system that can act intelligently on its environment. Putting aside the notoriously difficult question regarding the meaning of 'intelligent', we can observe that, from a purely mathematical standpoint, the behaviour of an agent (the way it acts on its environment) is simply describable as a function that maps the agent's perceptions onto particular actions. Now, what determines the specific behaviour of this function is what is normally called an 'agent program'. And an agent program, crucially, is nothing more than a collection of *algorithms*. But, since an algorithm is precisely the sort of entity that can be appropriately characterized as a *rule,* artificial agents – owing to

5 Machine ethics is a research field aimed at the design of artificial moral agents (AMAs). For a comprehensive overview of the field, see (Wallach and Allen, 2010) and (Anderson and Anderson, 2011).

6 A similar entailment is also discussed in (Purves, Jenkins and Strawser 2015, 855–58), and more succinctly in (Stenseke 2021, §3.1).

7 It is worth emphasizing that adopting this characterization of the notion of 'agent' does not necessarily amount to embracing an enactivist conception of cognition. The above characterization is in fact conceptually compatible with *both* enactivist and traditional approaches to artificial cognition. Indeed, as will be further detailed in the body of the chapter, what determines how an agent acts upon (and reacts to) its environment is its 'agent program'. And, importantly, the architecture of an agent program can draw inspiration from either an enactivist model of cognition or a traditional representational model.

their algorithmic nature – are constitutively incapable of acting in a way that resists description in terms of *'following a rule'*.

In summary, what links the input perceptions of an AI system to its output actions is nothing beyond a particular set of rules (algorithmic procedures). Yet, if this is correct, accepting ($\mathcal{U}$) – and thus ($\mathcal{U}_+$) – commits us to the extraordinary conclusion that there could never exist AI systems appropriately characterizable as moral (~Ai). For, if the moral outlook of a virtuous person is *constitutively uncodifiable*, there is no possible set of rules – or, more appropriately, algorithms – to be implemented in the agent program of an AI system to make its actions reliably similar to those of the virtuous person. The point, more diffusely, is that an AI system cannot perform actions that do not result from the application of a specific set of rules. Yet, if ($\mathcal{U}_+$) is true, there is no finite set of rules that can encapsulate the moral outlook of an ethical agent. Thus, it follows that engineering an AI that reliably behaves like a human moral agent is a theoretically impossible task: for any set of rules that could guide the behaviour of the AI, there will always exist (at least) a situation in which a mechanical application of those rules result in an action that an ethical agent would not have performed. If this were not the case, in fact, it would be possible to find a set of rules that renders the behaviour of an AI system reliably similar to that of a moral agent. And, in turn, this would mean that (in open contradiction with ($\mathcal{U}$)) a codification of moral action would be possible after all. In short, if ($\mathcal{U}$) is true, so must be (~Ai).

At this point, one might want to object to the previous line of argument by pointing out that it relies on a rather outdated idea of what an AI system is. In particular, one might think that the delineated connection between AI and rules only applies to what is often referred to as 'Good Old Fashioned AI' (GOFAI).[8] According to this approach, the creation of intelligent systems can be achieved through the explicit programming of instructions operating on formal symbolic representations. For this very reason, given a conception of AI *as* GOFAI, it certainly appears correct to assert that AI systems operate on rule-following processes. However – the objection continues – in the mid-1980s, the world of AI experienced a substantial resurgence of the idea of approaching the creation of intelligent agents through (simulated) neural networks (Sun 2014, 108). A (simulated) neural network, in broad strokes, is a collection of neuron-like processing units interconnected by weighted links. The units of a network, in particular, fall into three different categories: *input* nodes, *output* nodes, and *hidden* nodes (which mediate between input and output nodes). Each of these units, furthermore, has a specific *activation* threshold

8 For an introduction to GOFAI, see (Boden 2014).

(usually represented by a real number). The activation of *input* nodes is determined externally; generally, the job of these nodes is to represent what the system receives from the environment. The activation of input nodes is then propagated to the nodes to which they are connected, that are then activated (or not activated) on the basis of a specific function. Then, the activation of these latter nodes is propagated, in turn, to the next layer of nodes. And so on until the output units are reached. In essence, then, in a neural network, activation waves propagate from the input nodes to the output nodes, as determined by the weighted links between the nodes.

Now, what is especially relevant for our discussion is that the employment of neural networks made it possible to successfully implement Turing's (1947) original idea of developing intelligent machines by enabling them to *learn* (what we nowadays call 'machine learning'). This goal, in fact, can be achieved using an algorithm that repeatedly manipulates the weights of the neural connections, aiming for the network's outputs to gradually approach a desired outcome. The point – to return to the objection – is that it is very natural to assume that AI systems based on such technologies are *not* subject to rules in the same way that GOFAI systems are. Indeed, in neural-based systems, intelligent behaviour *does not* result from the implementation of a set of explicit rules. On the contrary, as it is commonly observed, the interpretation of the process that leads a neural network with numerous hidden layers to produce a given output remains *inaccessible* even to the creator of the system itself.[9]

However attractive, this line of objection misfires. The mistake lies in forgetting that a complex rule does not cease to be a rule. As discussed in (Rescorla 2020, §4.1), it must first be pointed out that the line dividing classical approaches to AI and neural network-based approaches is not as clear-cut as one might initially presume. Indeed, we should bear in mind that *it is possible* to implement a neural network in a classical Turing-style model. As a matter of fact, virtually every neural network ever physically constructed has been implemented on a digital computer. Beyond this point, however, it is crucial to notice that affirming that a system is based on rule-following processes *does not* imply that it has been programmed by explicitly implementing a list of rules. If an AI system has been programmed in this way, then, clearly, it will operate on the basis of rule-following processes. Yet, importantly, the converse implication does not hold. To see this, consider that, after the learning process, even a system based on a neural network *does* obey a set of formulable rules. The actions (outputs) of such a system, indeed, are simply the

9 See (Müller 2020, §3.1).

result of how inputs are processed within the network. And, we should bear in mind, the way inputs are processed is simply a function of the structure of the network itself. When we say that not even the creator of a neural-agent can understand what is going on inside the network, we *do not* mean that what is happening cannot be described. From a mathematical point of view, it surely can. What is meant, rather, is simply that such a mathematical description is hardly convertible into a linguistically articulate explanation. The point is that a neural network (in a particular state) is, to all intents and purposes, the *embodiment of a rule* that maps certain inputs to certain outputs. Certainly, a very complex rule, but a rule nonetheless.

If this is correct, however, accepting the idea that the moral outlook of a virtuous person *cannot* be captured by any rule ($\mathcal{U}$) entails that not even an impenetrably complex rule will do the trick. If McDowell is right, in summary, there will never be an AI that consistently behaves like a virtuous human agent.

A Way Out

We have seen that the Uncodifiability Thesis plays a prominent role in McDowell's conception of the task of ethics. Indeed, it is precisely the impossibility of codifying our moral outlook that precludes us from attacking the question 'how should we live?' by identifying a suitable set of rules. Yet, we found that the Uncodifiability Thesis bears onerous implications for the future of AI. In particular, we established that ($\mathcal{U}$) implies the impossibility of designing a moral system of AI (~Ai). Now, this inference certainly does not constitute a *reductio ad absurdum* of the Thesis of Uncodifiability. Nonetheless, it seems at least suspicious to be able to reach such a strong conclusion about future developments of AI from the comfort of our armchair. There seems to be an argumentative gap, as it were, between the considerations that McDowell advances in favour of ($\mathcal{U}$) and the extraordinarily committing conclusion that ethical AI *cannot* exist. And yet, since ($\mathcal{U}$) entails (~Ai), supporting ($\mathcal{U}$) means supporting (~Ai) as well. The general suggestion, accordingly, is simply that the far-reaching consequences of ($\mathcal{U}$) should prompt us to investigate whether something has gone awry in McDowell's argument. And, when such an investigation is carried out, I maintain, it becomes apparent that something has. This something, more specifically, is the fact that McDowell has offered *no direct argument* in favour of ($\mathcal{U}$) – apart from his reference to the intuitiveness of the thesis, or the fact that it was advocated by Aristotle.

Based on the argumentative structure of 'Virtue and Reason', the most obvious place where one would expect to find support for ($\mathcal{U}$) is McDowell's discussion of Wittgenstein's remarks on rule-following. Yet, under closer inspection, it becomes obvious that the Wittgensteinian dialectic employed by McDowell *cannot* amount to a direct argument in favour of ($\mathcal{U}$). Indeed, as noted in 'A Wittgesteinian Route to Aristotle?', the conclusion that McDowell draws from Wittgenstein's famous example is simply that one's rational behaviour *should not* be explained in terms of one's adherence to a formulable rule. Even when it is possible to formulate a rule – the point was – that rule is of little value in explaining how an agent can 'go on in the same way' in the given exercise of rationality. There is, however, a glaring difference between affirming that the explanation of an exercise of rationality *does not require* the formulation of a rule, and affirming that such a rule is *impossible* to formulate (as ($\mathcal{U}$) states). As Wittgenstein's example makes clear, in *some* exercises of rationality – and, for what we know, potentially all such exercises – there actually *is* a rule to be formulated. The point, again, is simply that the existence of a rule does *nothing* to underwrite our confidence that the agent will apply the rule in the intended way. Accordingly, the general upshot is that, whilst Wittgenstein's remarks have the power of undermining our confidence that there will *always* be a rule to be found, they do not lend support to the far stronger conclusion that a rule can *never* be found.

Wittgenstein's observations, therefore, cannot be intelligibly read as a direct argument in favour of ($\mathcal{U}$). If not there, though, where else can we find McDowell's argument for the Uncodifiability Thesis? The answer, quite simply, is that McDowell offers no such argument. Effectively, he *assumes* that ($\mathcal{U}$) should appear intuitive to unprejudiced eyes. The problem, according to him, is simply that we are prone to fall into the illusion that an exercise of rationality can only be explained by citing a general rule. But – he argues – once Wittgenstein's considerations have freed us from this illusion, it becomes possible for us to see the matter with new eyes, and embrace the intuitiveness of the Uncodifiability Thesis. This line of argument, however, would patently fail to convince someone who, despite having grasped Wittgenstein's point, would still struggle to perceive the alleged intuitiveness of ($\mathcal{U}$). Yet, since we have just seen that it is perfectly possible to accept Wittgenstein's considerations without also accepting ($\mathcal{U}$), the argument deployed by McDowell to support the Uncodifiability Thesis appears conspicuously weak.

At this stage, one naturally wonders: Do we really need to subscribe to ($\mathcal{U}$) in order to embrace a McDowellian conception of ethics? The answer, to my mind, is in the negative. And, what is even more surprising, is that it is precisely Wittgenstein's considerations about rule-following to suggest a viable alternative. To see the point, let us begin by observing that the McDowellian conception of ethics does not demand that the principles of moral action be uncodifiable, it merely requires them to be *practically uncodifiable* (or epistemically opaque). In other words, what we really need to motivate a McDowellian approach to ethics is not ($\mathcal{U}$), but the far more modest thesis that:

> ($\mathcal{O}$) There is no possible world where *human beings* have codified the moral outlook of an adult human being into a set of rules.

To begin with, as made explicit by this formulation, *practical uncodifiability* comes with much lighter modal baggage than flesh-and-blood uncodifiability. Relevantly, unlike ($\mathcal{U}$), there is no significant implication between ($\mathcal{O}$) and the possibility of designing virtuous AI systems. Indeed, the fact that *humans* cannot codify the rules of virtuous action says nothing about their effective codifiability.[10] And, accordingly, the possibility of a machine succeeding in the task remains open. Still – we must ask ourselves – what reason do we have to suppose that ($\mathcal{O}$) is sufficient to motivate McDowell's proposed approach to the question of ethics? A careful reader might remember that we initially noticed that *if* the moral outlook of a virtuous person were susceptible to codification in a list of principles $\varrho_1, \ldots, \varrho_n$, the putative difference between a rule-driven approach to ethics and the approach proposed by McDowell would be at risk of dissolving. These two approaches – we observed – are distinct only insofar as the moral perspective of a virtuous person is *not* susceptible of being captured in a set of rules. If this is true, however, it would seem that a McDowellian approach to ethics cannot do without ($\mathcal{U}$) after all. This conclusion, admittedly, appears inevitable from a *purely theoretical* perspective. However, we should bear in mind that, as McDowell himself maintains (1979, 331), the ultimate purpose of ethics is far from being purely theoretical. Ethics, according to the proposed conception, must formulate an adequate answer to the question: How should we live? And what renders an answer adequate, in this case, is also its *practical* workability. An adequate answer to the question of ethics, in other words, should be able to practically help human beings understand how to live – help them understand what is the right thing to do. But, importantly, if this characterization is correct, *practically uncodifiable* rules of conduct and *essentially uncodifiable* ones are equally inadequate for the purposes of ethics. In fact, regardless of the origin of their uncodifiability, rules that we cannot codify can hardly help us in understanding how we should act. Therefore, according to his own understanding of

10 More precisely, ($\mathcal{O}$) leaves room for the existence of possible worlds in which the outlook of a moral agent has been codified into a set of rules, but these rules are nevertheless epistemically inaccessible to any human being.

the task of ethics, McDowell does *not* require that the principles of ethics be constitutively uncodifiable; rather, he simply needs them to be uncodifiable in actual practice.

As anticipated, however, the practical uncodifiability of our moral outlook is not only something we might want to embrace in order to safeguard McDowell's proposed conception of ethics from problematic implications, but it is also what Wittgenstein's remarks on rule-following appear to be most straightforwardly supporting. To outline how this claim could be substantiated, let us turn back one last time to the insight that Wittgenstein reaches from his discussion on rule-following. As we have seen, Wittgenstein's goal was in no way that of undermining our confidence that when we impart a rule through a finite number of examples our hearers will be able to follow it according to our expectations. Rather, as McDowell correctly points out, Wittgenstein's considerations are aimed at changing the ground and nature of our confidence. To achieve this goal, Wittgenstein begins by showing us that the idea that customarily underlies such confidence is deeply problematic. For, normally, what appears to give us confidence that a rational agent will be able to apply a given rule in accordance with our expectations is the idea that his or her behaviour be mediated by a mental interpretation of the rule. However, as we have seen, the pupil example discussed by Wittgenstein reveals that this idea can at best provide the *illusion* of a stable foundation for our confidence. In fact, since 'every course of action can be made out to accord with [a] rule' (Wittgenstein 1953, §201; amended), the example shows us that the evidence at our disposal can never be sufficient to confidently attribute to someone the 'correct' mental interpretation of a rule. Now, if Wittgenstein were to stop here, his remarks would indeed be correctly interpreted as a form of scepticism. As underlined, however, Wittgenstein's point is precisely that 'there is a way of grasping a rule which is *not* an *interpretation*, but which is exhibited in what we call "obeying the rule" and "going against it" in actual cases' (Wittgenstein 1953, §201; emphasis in original). In Wittgenstein's view, to put it differently, we should fight the temptation to think that the process of following a rule is always mediated by a mental interpretation of it. Rather – as he subsequently points out – we should simply accept that, at a fundamental level, '"following a rule" is a *practice*' (Wittgenstein 1953, §202; emphasis added).

Now, the suggestion is that Wittgenstein's conclusion can be rephrased as follows: when we initiate someone into a certain pattern of rational behaviour (such as, the extension of number sequences), what we are really doing is to make them acquire a certain form of *practical knowledge* – a certain kind of '*knowledge-how*'. From this standpoint, when (in normal circumstances) a pupil learns to extend a number sequence, they do not succeed because they gain some sort of propositional interpretative understanding of a general rule; rather, what the pupil gains *directly* is knowledge of *how* to extend the sequence. It is almost a philosophical commonplace, however, to emphasize that every form of practical knowledge possesses a certain degree of practical uncodifiability.[11] The kind of uncodifiability that, for instance, we would experience if someone asked us to put into words our ability to ride a bicycle. Naturally, in such a situation, we could meticulously describe the physical movements involved in the action of riding a bicycle trying to make them fully intelligible to our interlocutor. Yet, crucially, any such explanation would be patently insufficient to really encapsulate our knowledge of *how* to ride a bicycle. Practical knowledge is, in other terms, epistemically *opaque* to us; whilst we are perfectly capable of drawing on it, it resists all our attempts of propositional codification. Still, this is not to say that practical knowledge is uncodifiable. There is in fact a gulf between asserting that practical knowledge is epistemically opaque and asserting that it is constitutively uncodifiable. As an illustration of this, suffice it consider that numerous forms of knowledge that we would intuitively categorize as *practical* can be – and have been – implemented in AI systems (mainly thanks to the aforementioned machine-learning techniques).[12] Yet, as argued in 'The Un-ethical Machine' – given AI's algorithmic nature – had such forms of practical knowledge been *constitutively uncodifiable,* it would have been impossible for us to complete these implementations.

Ultimately, then, Wittgenstein's remarks on rule-following – which, as we saw, McDowell employs to lend credibility to the Uncodifiability Thesis – appear much better equipped to sustain the claim that our conception of *how* to live (our moral outlook) is a particularly complex form of *practical* knowledge. As we read Wittgenstein's observations in this light, we realize that, since any form of practical knowledge is epistemically opaque, there is nothing mysterious or surprising in our inability to codify our moral outlook (or at least nothing more mysterious or surprising than our inability to explain how we ride a bicycle). The source of this inability, however, we discover to be *epistemic* rather than – as McDowell argues – *metaphysical.* As a consequence, whether there will ever be some form of AI deserving to be called virtuous remains an open question; one that, I suggest, we can hardly hope to answer from an armchair.

11 The *locus classicus* where the propositional uncodifiability of practical knowledge is advocated is Ryle's seminal *The Concept of Mind* (1949).

12 For a comprehensive list of practical skills that have been successfully implemented in AI systems, see (Russell and Norvig 2020, 27–30).

Conclusion

In the celebrated essay 'Virtue and Reason' (1979), McDowell argues that the fundamental task of ethics is not to assemble an exhaustive list of rules of conduct, but rather to fully elucidate the notion of a 'virtuous person'. A virtuous agent, according to this conception, does the right thing because they are a certain kind of person; one who perceives the world in an eminently distinctive way. The need for this approach, according to McDowell, is dictated by the Aristotelian thesis according to which our conception of how to live is essentially irreducible to any set of rules. It has been pointed out, however, that the acceptance of this thesis commits us to strong modal consequences on the possibility of designing virtuous AI systems. Indeed, we saw that if the Uncodifiability Thesis were true, it would be impossible to engineer artificial agents that consistently act like virtuous human beings. This conclusion led us to observe that there appears to exist a tension between the probative force of the Wittgensteinian dialectic employed by McDowell to support the Uncodifiability Thesis, and the strong modal commitments that the thesis brings with itself. What emerged, however, is that McDowell does not require that the principles of ethics be uncodifiable; rather, he simply needs them to be *practically* uncodifiable. Practical uncodifiability, however, comes at a lesser price than metaphysical uncodifiability in flesh and blood. Every form of practical knowledge, we in fact observed, appears to possess some degree of practical uncodifiability. Accordingly, I concluded by suggesting that the aforementioned tension can be resolved by interpreting the considerations McDowell utilizes to support the Uncodifiability Thesis as an argument in favour of the idea that our conception of *how* to live (our moral outlook) is a particularly complex form of knowledge-how.

References

Anderson, M. and Anderson, S. (eds.). 2011. *Machine Ethics.* Cambridge: Cambridge University Press.

Anscombe, G. E. M. 1958. 'Modern Moral Philosophy'. *Philosophy* 33: 1–19.

Blackburn, S. 2008. 'Rationality'. In *The Oxford Dictionary of Philosophy*, edited by S. Blackburn, 308. Oxford: Oxford University Press.

Boden, M. 2014. 'GOFAI'. In *The Cambridge Handbook of Artificial Intelligence*, edited by K. Frankish and W. Ramsey, 89–107. Cambridge: Cambridge University Press.

Kripke, S. 1982. *Wittgenstein on Rules and Private Language.* Cambridge, MA: Harvard University Press.

McDowell, J. 1979. 'Virtue and Reason'. *The Monist* 66, no. 3: 331–350.

——— 1984. 'Wittgenstein on Following a Rule'. *Synthese* 58, no. 3: 325–363.

Müller, V. C. 2020. 'Ethics of Artificial Intelligence and Robotics'. *The Stanford Encyclopedia of Philosophy* (Summer 2021 Edn), edited by Edward N. Zalta. https://plato.stanford.edu/archives/sum2021/entries/ethics-ai/

Purves, D., Jenkins R. and Strawser, J. B. 2015. 'Autonomous Machines, Moral Judgment, and Acting for the Right Reasons'. *Ethical Theory and Moral Practice* 18, no. 4: 851–872.

Rescorla, M. 2020. 'The Computational Theory of Mind'. *The Stanford Encyclopedia of Philosophy* (Fall 2020 Edn), edited by Edward N. Zalta. https://plato.stanford.edu/archives/fall2020/entries/computational-mind/

Russell, S. and Norvig, P. 2020. *Artificial Intelligence: A Modern Approach* (4th edn). New Jersey: Pearson Education.

Ryle, G. 1949. *The Concept of Mind.* Chicago: University of Chicago Press.

Stenseke, J. 2021. 'Artificial Virtuous Agents: From Theory to Machine Implementation'. *AI & Society* 38: 1301–1320.

Sun, R. 2014. 'Connectionism and Neural Networks'. In *The Cambridge Handbook of Artificial Intelligence,* edited by K. Frankish and W. Ramsey, 108–127. Cambridge: Cambridge University Press.

Turing, A. 1947. 'Lecture to the London Mathematical Society on 20 February 1947'. reprinted in *A. M. Turing's ACE Report of 1946 and Other Papers: Papers,* by A. Turing and M. Woodger (Charles Babbage Institute Reprint, Vol. 10), edited by B. E. Carpenter and R. W. Doran. 1986. Cambridge, MA: MIT Press.

Wallach, W. and Allen, C. 2010. *Moral Machines: Teaching Robots Right from Wrong.* Oxford: Oxford University Press.

Wittgenstein, L. 1953. *Philosophical Investigations*, translated by G. E. M. Anscombe. Oxford: Basil Blackwell.

Chapter 5

INVESTIGATING DEEPFAKES: THE RISE OF NEW AUTHORITIES AND THE QUESTION OF DEEPFAKE REGULATION

Mehmet Taylan Cüyaz

This chapter aims to question the emergence of new 'fact-checking' epistemic authorities in the generation of deepfakes by presenting a novel outlook that relies on Wittgensteinian notions. This chapter discusses the related philosophical issues based on three assumptions. The first assumption explains that deepfakes are a subset of *technological games* that employ unprecedented rules. The second assumption considers the video as a possible indicator of truth rather than a necessary one. The third assumption postulates that a video exhibits depth and surface grammatical properties, which play an essential role in deepfake detection. Based on these assumptions, this chapter derives two conclusions. First, the immediate epistemological problem of deepfakes arises from our loss of autonomy regarding our justification for a digital video. Then, there is an ethical problem that accompanies the epistemological one, which indicates an inevitable shift of focus from deepfake regulation to regulation of regulating authorities.

Deepfakes in a Nutshell

Deepfake is an amalgamation of the concepts 'deep learning' and 'fake', and according to Nina Schick, it is defined as one of the *synthetic media*, that is 'media (including images, audio, and video) that is either manipulated or wholly generated by AI' (2021, 8). Nevertheless, deepfakes are derived from forged images. Apart from an agent's intentions, a deepfake is a deployment of different technological advancements to manipulate the given information in the video's content or context. Britt Paris and Joan Donovan differentiate between deepfakes and other kinds of image forgeries based on the technical merits and required expertise level (2019, 10). As the state-of-the-art technique deployed on image manipulation, many AI-powered deep-learning methods are developed to create deepfakes. One of the technological milestones – Generative Adversarial Nets (henceforth, GANs) – used in deepfakes emerged in 2014, coined by Ian J. Goodfellow and friends (see Goodfellow et al. 2015). However, a wider attention on deepfakes entered the scene around late 2017.

A well-cited 2019 report from Deeptrace unveils that there were 14,678 deepfakes online, and 96 per cent of them had pornographic content (Ajder et al. 2019). Besides pornography and other harmful uses, deepfakes are deployed to create artistic or historical performances, such as Microsoft's 'The Next Rembrandt' (news.microsoft.com 2017) and the 'JFK Unsilenced' (accenture.com n.d.) projects (see Floridi 2018 for a lengthy discussion). Today, deepfakes have become a well-known and almost indispensable phenomenon in our daily lives, primarily due to their speculative impact.

Because of this fact, current debates on deepfakes mainly stress their inappropriate content and direct harm to our social epistemology. On the one hand, the main ethical problem is constructed around how deepfakes harm people and how we shall regulate them. On the other hand, from epistemological grounds, the direst problem of deepfakes is considered an issue of fake content and its effect on our social knowledge. Nevertheless, I believe that, rather than discussing the possible and actual harms of the deepfakes that are already acknowledged, it would be more philosophically fruitful to take them as a basis for our discussion and reevaluate these aforementioned questions. Therefore, I will postulate three ground assumptions relying on Wittgensteinian notions based on the use of deepfakes, the epistemic status of video and the dynamics of deepfake detection.

First Assumption: Deepfakes Are Technological Games

Until now, many philosophical agendas have attempted to analyse deepfakes. I refer to them as part of *technological games*, a subset of ordinary *language games*. Deepfakes construct exclusive language games with authentic rules. In this sense, the culturally infused Wittgensteinian conceptual schemes are designed to lay out the language adopted in the technological contexts. As an example of such a schema, Mark Coeckelbergh proposes the term 'technology games' to demonstrate how technology can be evaluated as a tool-in-use in social-cultural settings (2017).[1] 'Technologies, considered in their use',

1 Moreover, Coeckelbergh's approach is influential on the topic of deepfakes. In a masters' thesis written by Luuk Stellinga entitled 'Deepfakes in Use: Rethinking the Infopocalypse

he says, 'are part of activities and games. What may be called "technology games" shape and give meaning to particular uses' (Coeckelbergh 2017, 1511); and he outlines his tripartite agenda of post-Wittgensteinian interpretation of technology as in the following:

1. … to reveal the technology games and other 'grammars' of technology;
2. … reveal the normativity in and of those grammars, and critically reflect on the games and forms of life in which our technologies … are embedded;
3. to show how technologies in activities, games and a form of life – can indeed function as game changers and may slowly but surely change the riverbeds of our form of life.

(Coeckelbergh 2017, 1518)

Although this agenda is well-defined, and his use of technology games is authentic, his conception of technology games is often one-sided. It hinges on understanding how technology is *mentioned* in language. His examples involving social robots (Coeckelbergh 2017, 1512–514) are constructed upon how this specific technology in the language affected our conception of technology and how our conception of this technology might affect our mentioning it in the language. However, a *use*-based conception of the technological artefacts is required to understand how they behave in social settings. It seems that such an account is infeasible without considering the possibility that many technological objects create language games themselves.

Undoubtedly, the different technological objects, as long as they serve as a means of communication, have authentic language games. For example, the cinema, as a form of video, could be evaluated based on this conception. Authorial commentary – an interpretation from its creator, such as the camera angles, cut, use of post-production techniques and other modalities (e.g. subtitles and sound effects) – is a constitutive part of cinematic language rather than contributing to the message conveyed to the audience. Accordingly, technological objects create some language games with their own unprecedented rules. Addressing a different line of thought than that of Coeckelbergh, rather than considering technology as an *adjective* and modifying the concept of 'game', I will introduce the concept of *technological games*, a subset of ordinary language games. Thus, different versions of technological games are also unique language games based on their *use*.

Through Postphenomenology and Wittgenstein' (2022), Coeckelbergh's thoughts are referred to extensively.

I will elaborate on the first assumption by discussing deepfakes as an instance of technological games with authentic rules. While playing deepfake games, some people define the rules of their game on a case-by-case basis; some games might be dependent on deceiving others, aiming to propagate its truth, or they could be informative in some cases. However, Regina Rini, in her influential paper entitled 'Deepfakes and the Epistemic Backstop', discusses that Reddit users demand a 'gay video' of Ramadan Kadyrov, followed by a comment from a user: 'everyone will know it is fake, but [Kadyrov's] reputation will be done' (2020, 6). Accordingly, she states:

> The thought is that a deepfake video needn't be positively believed by viewers in order to be effective. Merely getting a suggestive video into public distribution may be enough, even if many viewers realize it is fake.
>
> *(Rini 2020, 6)*

Following the paragraph, Rini focuses on how such an application will create problems in the political sphere, especially after regarding the possibility of more realistic deepfakes. From our perspective, such a conversation reveals that users are not interested in the truth value or likelihood of the demanded scene; instead, they focus on what they want to see in such a deepfake game. In addition to defaming a politician, the users demand a deepfake game akin to a make-believe game, a demonized version of the game we played as kids. Even though people might know that it is fake, they might accept the fantasized depiction for the sake of playing a deepfake game.

In this example, people on Reddit are just trying to defame somebody by creating fake media. Certainly, it creates an epistemic problem regarding the truth of the scenario. Further, if they try to convince somebody with this fake video, inevitably, there will be more epistemic problems. Nevertheless, these are the most salient negative epistemic features of a deepfake game since the game usually depends on creating a non-obtained state-of-affairs. In general, such an epistemic problem is common to any language game; we can define its rules without referring to the concepts of truth, reality or justification if we can accept a normative disagreement with others. Therefore, it seems that an epistemic problem arises for every one of us with the frequent occurrence of deepfakes. Nevertheless, this problem might be more complex and deeper than the given literature depicts. Let us look at how the literature defines the epistemological problem and try to show what the missing point might be in the analysis it contains.

Second Assumption: Video Is Only a Possible Indicator of Truth

It is undeniable that deepfakes harm our belief in the reality of a video. But to what extent and how? Focusing on the notions of knowledge and trust, some philosophers analyse the destructive effects of deepfakes on social epistemology, and they have already claimed that we are on the edge of a disaster. I denote their view as *the epistemic catastrophe theses* (for a similar classification, see Harris 2021) and assume that their position is vulnerable to severe philosophical criticism due to their analysis of the nature of videos. However, their main ideas require an explanation to demonstrate their vulnerabilities.

First, Rini considers the social epistemic role of the video as an *epistemic backstop*, where it is used to acutely correct or regulate our testimonial practices (2020, 2–3). In her view, such videos might justify various assertions from people since it is always possible to check on a piece of testimony with different types of media. The existence of deepfakes disrupts this schema, and hence, from a particular aspect, they are the footsteps of an 'epistemic maelstrom' (Rini 2020, 8). In this regard, the video's (social) epistemic function is equated with an epistemic backstop.

Second, Catherine Kerner and Mathias Risse, having a similar ground with Rini, consider that 'deepfakes [...] might help create a no-trust society, in which people cannot, or no longer bother to, separate truth from falsehood, and no reliable media could help them do so' (2020, 99). Following this point, they assert that testimonial injustice can significantly appear due to the misuse of deepfakes. For example, fabricating and using some synthetic media as evidence against a non-guilty person will make the overall epistemic injustice in society more palpable. Thus, if deepfakes are so common in our epistemic space, that might cause a loss of belief in media as a reference point between what is the case and what is not. Nevertheless, Kerner and Risse's overall approach to the epistemic perils of the deepfakes is more moderate than Rini's; they argue that the hazards are more dominant than the epistemic promises in consideration of the most vulnerable groups of our society (Kerner & Risse 2020, 2021). Their general suggestion is to protect society from the epistemic perils of deepfakes via regulations since many companies have started to deploy them.

Third, in a paper entitled 'The Epistemic Threat of Deepfakes', Don Fallis uncovers his main thesis as follows: ' [...] as a result of deepfakes, videos now carry less information about the events that they depict' (2020, 627). With the existence of deepfakes, the epistemic value of videos will be decreased according to two distinct variables. First, the frequent existence of deepfakes ensures that there will be an increase in the total number of fake videos amongst the real videos; thus, as a general concept, videos will convey less information. This is evident when we consider that some of the videos consist of more accurate information while others do not; the addition of realistic synthetic fakes into this set will decrease the total amount of the information conveyed via videos. Second, people might lose their faith and might be unable to distinguish the 'fake' from the 'real' since video's trustworthiness or evidential status is lost. In this sense, Fallis concludes that the main epistemic threat of deepfakes 'is that they interfere with our ability to acquire knowledge' (2020, 638).

Apart from their immediate focus on the social epistemic danger of the existence of deepfakes and their destructive effects on knowledge, these examples of the epistemic catastrophe theses exemplify another common point shared amongst themselves. Their analysis requires, or depends on, a fixed characterization of video: moving images shall accurately depict reality partially or wholly. Nevertheless, such a fixed characterization almost echoes with the *Tractarian fallacy*. In the *Philosophical Investigations*, after declaring that his new ideas shall be understood against the background of the old ones in the Preface, Wittgenstein blames the author of *Tractatus* for not realizing the fact of the dynamic structure of language – instead of recognizing the flexible, and constantly changing character of the uses of language, that author insisted on a fixed understanding of its logical structure (Wittgenstein 1986: PI §23). Considering the nature of video as a determinate function of the depiction of reality is, therefore, mistaken. Resting on a late Wittgensteinian perspective, as the basis of the second assumption of this chapter, I broadly propose that the (epistemic) functions of objects and the language related to them are in constant change, just like in an ancient city (Wittgenstein 1986: PI §23). Here, our assumption is divided into two main parts: firstly, video as a technological artefact has exhibited a change in its conclusiveness, and secondly, due to this change, its epistemic function or essence cannot be fixed into anything determinate.

To begin with, throughout the history of technological advancements, many methods have lost their conclusiveness. This thesis becomes more evident if we try to understand what makes an artefact technological. I believe that the line that separates technological from other artefacts is blurred and is incapable of providing any direct formulation as a philosophical identification. Rather, such a division emerges from our historical and social conditions. For example, while Acheulean hand axes were state-of-art artefacts that represented the most advanced technology of knapping for *Homo erectus*, it was seemingly old-fashioned even amongst the Metal Age population, considering the existence of bronze axes. This stance is criticized by the traditions that employ more strict definitions of technology and artefacts. Many of these traditions refer to an Aristotelian-like essence regarding the tools and the technology in their definitions. Nevertheless, I believe such critiques are undermined by a particular understanding of artefacts as exhibiting a certain 'functionless functionality' (Allen 2008, 17); rather than solely serving a preconceived purpose or a single task, artefacts fulfil many functions.[2]

2 This understanding cordially links with the sociocultural understanding of human tool use. For example, see Allen 2004, 2008; Latour 1994, 2000, 2005; Malafouris, 2016.

Under this conceptualization let us assumethe role of conventional radiography imaging in medical diagnosis. Most probably, after its wide use in medical society, the two-dimensional images it produces of tissues are regarded as the primary tool for diagnosis in some medical conditions. However, computed tomography in the 1970s enabled professionals to access more accurate three-dimensional images of the target tissues and overthrow plain radiography as the primary and most precise imaging tool for medical diagnosis. The same translation process is also evident between photography and video, considering their epistemic properties. We have long known that the photograph is more vulnerable to manipulation; historical examples – which include inserting spectres in an analogue film (as in the case of Arthur Conan Doyle; see Rini 2020, 11) or erasing the presence of a politically opposing old comrade from a printed photo (as in the case of Josef Stalin; e.g. see Citton 2021, 48) – go back to the first quarter of the twentieth century, almost a century after the invention of photography. Conversely, videos were thought to be an almost non-doctored source of knowledge for a long time. Moreover, since a video consists of more modalities (such as sound), it served as conclusive evidence for testimonial practices. However, as we have said so far, a video is a technological artefact: it will exhibit various functions, and its epistemic function and conclusiveness are changed with the existence of deepfakes.

The current existence of deepfake games, as a way of exchanging reality with fantasies, determines the fate of the video. Still, some recordings might serve as a confidential indicator of truth but do not necessarily mirror the truth itself. As a particular outcome of our second assumption, we can state that the epistemic function of a video changed into a possible indicator of a (possible) truth rather than a one-to-one corresponding picture of reality itself. However, the nature of the video cannot be fixed to a single definition or function. The change in our sociocultural settings, the developments in technology and the existence of new techniques throughout history will change its (epistemic or linguistic) function according to time. Therefore, the video cannot be reduced to a direct representation of reality, a stabilized source of justification.

Nevertheless, this does not mean that any epistemic problem emanates from this transition; thus, we cannot deny them by neglecting the catastrophe theses. The problem is that the catastrophe or epistemic perils do not stem from the video's credibility. The discussion is shaped around credibility, and the fixed characterization of the nature of the video leads to a philosophical disorientation that manifests as a deviation from the real epistemic problem. We will analyse this in 'A Reconsideration of the Epistemological and the Ethical Problems'. Now, we have to look at our next assumption.

Third Assumption: Video Displays Both Depth and Surface Grammar Properties

The first assumption established that deepfakes, and thus video, could be considered technological games with unique rules. Most classically, the existence of the rules takes us to the discussion of grammar in the Wittgensteinian sense. Our third assumption considers that video displays both depth and surface grammatical properties. To locate this disparity, we must depart from identifying a video from an engineering perspective.

According to the information-based approach, a video is considered a signal that consists of light and time information (Zeljkovic 2014, 242). The light or illumination information is supplied by *pixels* that change in relation to the time information in the video. With the composition of the pixels, we gather more semantically meaningful elements of the video, which are classified as *content* and *context.* Intuitively, context serves as a background for the content (or the actions and objects) presented within a video.

Video seemingly contains a duality; signal properties grant the variance in the pixels, and more meaningful elements are gathered from the interpretation of the former. More technically, there is a difference between high- and low-level features. High-level features are classically considered as events and objects that form the content and context of the video and are semantically meaningful (Sethi 2006). In contrast, low-level features are statistically meaningful (Smith & Kanade 2005) features that manifest as blobs, curves, edges, lines, intensity and more. High-level features are, in a narrow sense, dependent on the organization of low-level features.

Nevertheless, there is only one electronic signal that causes this disparity. Even though some like to consider this as a naïve form of property dualism, in the engineering literature, the term 'semantic gap' has been coined to show the disparity between raw information from the signal and information interpreted by the user (Smeulders et al. 2000, 1353–354; Hanjalic 2004, 6–8). I believe such disparity can be addressed philosophically by employing Wittgenstein's depth and surface grammar concepts in *Philosophical Investigations.* He refers to the difference as follows:

> What immediately impresses itself upon us about the use of a word is the way it is used in the construction of the sentence, the part of its use – one might say – that can be taken in by the ear. – And now compare the depth grammar, say of the word 'to mean', with what its surface grammar would lead us to suspect. No wonder we find it difficult to know our way about.
>
> *(Wittgenstein 1986: PI §664)*

I depart from the more conventional of the two notions: surface grammar considers the 'obvious syntactic features of a sentence' (Hacker 2000, 434). In this sense, the role of surface grammar within a language could be exemplified by appealing to sentences that share the same grammatical structure but have separate meanings, such as 'Birds have wings' and 'Birds have volume' (see Klein 1976). Thus, surface grammar is the apparent system of rules governing the syntactical features of a given expression. Despite the banality of surface grammar, the concept of depth grammar is philosophically more complex to analyse in depth. To illustrate, although Hacker defines it as a more elegant and complicated version of surface grammar (Hacker 2000, 434), Baker argues that the concept of depth grammar is more cordial to Wittgenstein's philosophical agenda in the *Philosophical Investigations* (Baker 2001, 303). For the sake of simplicity, I take the concept of depth grammar as a property of a given expression that helps us to uncover meaning relations, depending on the normative agreements between us and the contextual circumstances of the utterance. In this sense, we can issue the difference between why the negation of the sentences 'Birds have wings' and 'Birds have volume' has completely two different senses.

Following these definitions, I argue that the disparity traced in the video can be explained under this conceptualization. Our third assumption can be stated as follows: whereas the depth grammar of a video corresponds to the content and context, surface grammar refers to the raw statistically meaningful data, such as the intensity of pixels. On the one hand, comprehension of depth grammar requires semantic mastery to detect high-level features and attribute particular meanings to them. On the other hand, mastery of surface grammar requires a (mathematical) mastery of interpreting the raw signal to detect minimal differences that occur in low-level features.

This can be useful to explain the difference between human and machine abilities of deepfake detection. No final decision has been made on whether humans or machines are more capable of detecting fake media, yet some of the findings in the literature can be useful for the matter at hand. In a study by Rössler and colleagues, while human detection ability varies between 68.7 per cent and 58.7 per cent depending on the video quality, automated detection algorithms outperformed humans by a significant margin (2019). Even though they do not directly address the source of this variance, they conclude that the corpus size of the database, or the 'number of training images', is one of the main elements to assess the success of training algorithms with domain-specific knowledge (Rössler et al. 2019). Due to their specialized training in huge data sets, domain-specific algorithms performed better than humans. In contrast, another study by Groh and colleagues found that 'relative to today's leading computer vision model, groups of individuals are just as accurate or more accurate', varying on the video resolution and the content of the videos (2021, 9). They reported that the model they investigated performed better on the low-quality videos since it is 'picking up on low-level details that participants appear to ignore'. Nevertheless, humans are more proficient in cases that include politicians (or very specified contexts and contents) and tasks that require 'specialized visual processing of faces' (Groh et al. 2021, 8–9). In another series of experiments, Thaw and colleagues verified that humans use non-algorithmic clues such as 'naturalness of the voice and emotional expressions' besides the well-known algorithmic hints when detecting deepfakes (2020, 2). Despite the differences in their findings, it seems that we can conclude that machines and humans utilize different kinds of strategies to detect deepfakes.

Our competence in face processing, ability to distinguish non-possible contexts and focus on more non-algorithmic but normatively agreeable properties could be taken as de facto shreds of evidence of our mastery of depth grammar. Nevertheless, machines seem to be more fluent in the surface grammar of videos due to their (mathematical) ability to distinguish inconsistencies in the low-level or more non-semantic features of a video. This differentiation between humans and machines might lead us to form an auxiliary postulation from our third assumption: in the future, algorithms might outperform humans in forged image detection because of their particular grammatical mastery.

Why are we required to postulate such a thesis? First, forged videos with plausible content can challenge our detection abilities since most of our strategy depends on interpreting the content or context of a video. It is not too hard for us to label a video as a deepfake when a well-known politician is doing something too unintuitive (such as cursing in another language or dancing while singing a children's song). Still, things get more complicated when we see something about a political scandal, especially if we have suspicions about that specific politician. Therefore, there will always be grey cases for us to detect when we only rely on the video's context or content.

Second, deepfakes are mainly generated with neural networks, and these networks ensure continuous improvement in their ability to evade detection. While we can try to train a new model to detect deepfakes created with the new technologies on a case-by-case basis, we usually do not have the chance to train humans in such a way. For example, GANs comprise two components: a Generator and a Discriminator. The Generator intends to produce fake images, whereas the Discriminator tries to spot any forged images. During the training period, the Discriminator is trained with a set of fake images from the Generator and real images from external sources; however, if the Discriminator fails to recognize any image, it yields a higher loss, and if any forged image is qualified as real by the Generator, it has a lower loss for the Generator, but a higher loss for the Discriminator (Lanham 2021). Evolutionarily, for each try, the Generator learns something and gets better at faking images without any alarms; on the other hand, the Discriminator aims to achieve better accuracy in sensing fakes. That is why the working mechanism of GANs is often explained with allegories attributed to hide-and-seek scenarios.[3] More severely, the evolutionary game between the Generator and Discriminator means that, in time, every result of the GANs will be more realistic than the previous ones. By using GANs, people can create high-grade deepfakes that might be slipped under our detection abilities as they get better. Even though many domain-specific algorithms have the chance to work on huge data sets containing state-of-the-art deepfakes created with novel methods and gain mastery in detecting them, as ordinary humans, we do not have such a chance. To beat the deepfakes in the hide-and-seek scenarios, we need algorithms designed elegantly and trained intensively on huge data sets.

To conclude, from a particular perspective, expert AI systems are far better masters of surface grammar, and their comprehension of depth grammar is ever-growing compared to humans. AI-based solutions, combined with their adjustability according to different cases, progressively prevail over humans in deepfake detection. Following this fact, security of knowledge and trust in videos are cordially tied to the accuracy of our algorithms. Therefore, the depicted picture demonstrates that we would unavoidably need computer assistance in order to determine the authenticity of a video.

A Reconsideration of the Epistemological and the Ethical Problems

Until now, all the papers that we highlighted claimed that the main epistemological problem regarding deepfakes is their fake content and the impact of the fakes on social epistemology. Following this line of thought, deepfakes become nothing more than a fancier version of the fake news presented in text format on many scam websites. However, as we purport in the first assumption, deepfakes, as a special case of language games, have their own rules. Thus, there must be more novel problems emanating from them. In the second assumption, we considered video as a possible indicator of the truth but not a necessary one. The third one argued that we would need computer

3 For example, Whittaker and colleagues define the struggle between the Discriminator and the Generator as an 'arms race between Money counterfeiters and the police' (2021, 92).

assistance to see whether a video strongly indicates a truth or a deepfake. The epistemic problem must be revisited under these assumptions, as in the following: How can we safely know that a video is a deepfake, or how can we trust the process of checking for authenticity?

According to this line of thought, the epistemological problem starts with our need for an AI-based classifier for deepfakes, and as laypeople, not all of us will have access to it. Developing an adequate deepfake detection algorithm requires a combination of computational power, chunks of data and a team of competent engineers. To illustrate, in 2020, the company Meta posted a challenge on Kaggle.com entitled 'Deepfake Detection Challenge', which launched a training corpus containing 111,500 videos and offered 1,000,000 US Dollars to be distributed amongst the best five teams (ai.meta.com 2020; kaggle.com 2020). Hence, it seems that while corporations and governments have already acquired these elements, it is almost impossible for ordinary people to bring them together. Further, many social platforms have deployed various algorithms to safeguard the public from fake content (see Kerner & Risse 2021). These platforms use tags-ticks and safe or unsafe marks to signal end users.

Soon, most probably, only the marked videos would be conceived as accurate by the masses. Considering that most video content is circulated on social media platforms, the publicly accessible normative ground regarding the justification of a video's content will be sole-traded by 'fact-checkers'. Due to this fact, they will become epistemic authorities with absolute power over the truth and justification. For an ordinary person, recognizing reality or finding a reason regarding a video's content and context will only be a matter of having faith in such checkers or not. Therefore, social media platforms and associated fact-checkers will monopolize our knowledge, except for our freedom to believe. The current epistemic catastrophe literature underestimates this very point. After this point, the rise of such monopolies shall be denoted as the most acute epistemological problem of deepfakes.

Moreover, the ethical problem of deepfakes must be revisited. In most instances, deepfakes are used as a means to unethical deeds, as we underlined. The frequent contents of deepfakes, such as nonconsensual pornography, blackmail, political false-flag operations, identity fraud or defamation, are ethically wrong in the frankest sense. Hence, debating on the wrongfulness (regarding the contents) of deepfakes merely serves as reciting a tautology. That being the case, the regulations on the production and detection of forged videos are addressed well on both theoretical and applied grounds (see, e.g. Kerner & Risse 2020; de Ruiter 2021; Taylor 2020). Nevertheless, the change in the epistemological problem also hints at the reconsideration of associated ethical problems.

The emergence of epistemic authorities brings up a double-edged ethical problem. Numerous facts can be suppressed or distorted irreversibly due to their classificatory judgements on videos. Unethical actions can be performed under either voluntary or involuntary decisions of the regulators – ethical accountability of such authorities has common grounds with the epistemological problem. Considering the intuitive cases, such as a video containing a politician's bribe bargain or a vivid scene from a firefight, the wrong labelling of those videos by the fact-checkers presents a novel and resilient problem for philosophy, a second-order ethical problem regarding the role of the fact-checkers. This problem, or the regulation of the regulating authorities, is one of the keenest moral problems associated with deepfakes, which is left untouched by the literature. Therefore, a shift in the core ethical problem is inevitable because the same conditions affect the epistemological one.

Conclusion

Let us recapitulate our main points. The first assumption declared that deepfakes are a subset of technological games with unprecedented rules. People might trade their fantasies with reality for the sake of playing a deepfake game, even though most of the content of such games is created around ethically problematic concepts. The second assumption considers the video as a possible indicator of truth instead of a necessary one. I state that catastrophe theorists overlook the real epistemic peril of deepfakes due to their fixation on the nature of video. The third assumption demonstrates that video has a dual grammatical structure that can be analysed under the concepts of depth and surface grammar. Due to their ever-growing abilities and mastery of the surface grammar of video, AI-based deepfake detection solutions are inevitable for us. Considering these three assumptions that characterize deepfakes as a natural and unavoidable proceeding of our society and technology, we must deploy computerized solutions to avoid harm. Nevertheless, how can this outlook change and uncover the 'real' problem of deepfakes? Following these three assumptions, we must reformulate the main epistemological and ethical problems. Accordingly, the epistemological problem shifted due to the existence of fact-checker authorities: such authorities cancel our autonomy regarding the truthfulness and justification of a video. On similar grounds, their existence creates a novel ethical problem regarding their implementation of validity checks. Regardless of their intentions, their wrong conclusions might create acute moral problems. In this sense, our ethical focus must shift from regulating the deepfakes to regulating the regulators. To conclude, a Wittgensteinian approach is fruitful in uncovering the hidden and novel problems that emanate from the concept of deepfakes.[4]

References

Ajder, H., Patrini, G., Cavalli, F., & Cullen, L. (2019). *The State of Deepfakes: Landscape, Threats, and Impact.* Deeptrace Labs.

Allen, B. (2004). *Knowledge and Civilization.* Westview Press.

Allen, B. (2008). *Artifice and Design: Art and Technology in Human Experience.* Cornell University Press.

Baker, G. P. (2001). Wittgenstein's 'depth grammar'. *Language & Communication, 21*(4), 303–319. https://doi.org/10.1016/s0271-5309(01)00012-x

Citton, Y. (2021). Could deep fakes uncover the deeper truth of an ontology of the networked images? *The Nordic Journal of Aesthetics, 30*(61–62), 46–64. https://doi.org/10.7146/nja.v30i61-62.127858

Coeckelbergh, M. (2017). Technology games: Using Wittgenstein for understanding and evaluating technology. *Science and Engineering Ethics, 24*(5), 1503–1519. https://doi.org/10.1007/s11948-017-9953-8

de Ruiter, A. (2021). The distinct wrong of deepfakes. *Philosophy & Technology, 34*(4), 1311–1332. https://doi.org/10.1007/s13347-021-00459-2

Deepfake Detection Challenge results: An open initiative to advance AI. AI at Meta. (2020). https://ai.meta.com/blog/deepfake-detection-challenge-results-an-open-initiative-to-advance-ai/

Deepfake Detection Challenge. Kaggle. (2020). https://www.kaggle.com/c/deepfake-detection-challenge

Fallis, D. (2020). The epistemic threat of deepfakes. *Philosophy & Technology, 34*(4), 623–643. https://doi.org/10.1007/s13347-020-00419-2

Floridi, L. (2018). Artificial intelligence, deepfakes and a future of ectypes. *Philosophy & Technology.* https://doi.org/10.2139/ssrn.3834958

Goodfellow, I. J., Pouget-Abadie, J., Mirza, M., Xu, B., Warde-Farley, D., Ozair, S., Courville, A., & Bengio, Y. (2015). Generative adversarial nets. In M. Welling (Ed.), *Advances in Neural Information Processing Systems 27: 28th Annual conference on Neural Information Processing Systems 2014 (NIPS); December 8–13, 2014, Montreal, Canada; Proceedings of the 2014 Conference.* Red Hook, NY: Curran. Retrieved from https://arxiv.org/abs/1406.2661.

Groh, M., Epstein, Z., Firestone, C., & Picard, R. (2021). Deepfake detection by human crowds, machines, and machine-informed crowds. *Proceedings of the National Academy of Sciences, 119*(1). https://doi.org/10.1073/pnas.2110013119

Hacker, P. (2000). *Wittgenstein: Mind and Will, Volume 4 of an Analytical Commentary on the Philosophical Investigations, Part II – Exegesis §§428–693.* Oxford University.

4 I express my deepest gratitude to Alice Helliwell and Alessandro Rossi for their understanding and patience. I also want to thank Dr Oğuz Akçelik, Dr Osman Gazi Birgül, Prof Murat Baç, Prof Aziz Fevzi Zambak and Prof Mehmet Hilmi Demir for their criticisms of earlier versions of this chapter. Prof Irmak Evren deserves a special mention for making my life as well as philosophy, bearable in the most challenging days of my life.

Hanjalic, A. (2004). *Content-Based Analysis of Digital Video.* Kluwer Academic Publishers Group.

Harris, K. R. (2021). Video on demand: What deepfakes do and how they harm. *Synthese, 199*(5–6), 13373–13391. https://doi.org/10.1007/s11229-021-03379-y

JFK Unsilenced Case Study: Ai Audio speech. Accenture. (n.d.). https://www.accenture.com/us-en/case-studies/interactive/jfk-unsilenced-ai-audio-speech

Kerner, C. & Risse, M. (2020). Beyond porn and discreditation: Epistemic promises and perils of deepfake technology in digital lifeworlds. *Moral Philosophy and Politics, 8*(1), 81–108. https://doi.org/10.1515/mopp-2020–0024

Klein, J. T. (1976). Philosophy and depth grammar: An interpretation of Wittgenstein. *A Review of General Semantics, 33*(3), 253–262.

Lanham, M. (2021). *Generating a New Reality: From Autoencoders and Adversarial Networks to Deepfakes.* Apress.

Latour, B. (1994). On Technical Mediation. *Common Knowledge, 3*(2), 29–64.

Latour, B. (2000). *Pandora's Hope: Essays on the Reality of Science Studies.* Harvard University Press.

Latour, B. (2005). *Reassembling the Social: An Introduction to Actor-Network-Theory.* Oxford University Press.

Malafouris, L. (2016). *How Things Shape the Mind: A Theory of Material Engagement.* The MIT Press.

Paris, B. & Donovan, J. (2019). (rep.). *Deepfakes and Cheap Fakes: The Manipulation of Audio and Visual Evidence.* Data & Society.

Rini, R. (2020). Deepfakes and the epistemic backstop. *Philosophers Imprint, 20*(24), 1–16.

Rössler, A., Cozzolino, D., Verdoliva, L., Riess, C., Thies, J., & Nießner, M. (2019, August 26). *FaceForensics++: Learning to Detect Manipulated Facial Images.* arXiv.org. Retrieved March 13, 2022, from https://arxiv.org/abs/1901.08971

Schick, N. (2021). *Deepfakes: The Coming Infocalypse.* Grand Central Pub.

Sethi, A. (2006). *Interaction between Modules in Learning Systems for Vision Applications* (dissertation). ResearchGate. Retrieved from https://www.researchgate.net/publication/249862831_INTERACTION_BETWEEN_MODULES_IN_LEARNING_SYSTEMS_FOR_VISION_APPLICATIONS

Smeulders, A. W. M., Worring, M., Santini, S., Gupta, A., & Jain, R. (2000). Content-based image retrieval at the end of the early years. *IEEE Transactions on Pattern Analysis and Machine Intelligence, 22*(12), 1349–1380. https://doi.org/10.1109/34.895972

Smith, M. A. & Kanade, T. (2005). *Multimodal Video Characterization and Summarization.* Kluwer Academic Publishers.

Stellinga, L. (2022, February 4). *Deepfakes in use: Rethinking the Infopocalypse through Postphenomenology and Wittgenstein* (thesis). Retrieved March 10, 2022, from http://essay.utwente.nl/89478/1/Deepfakes%20in%20Use.pdf

Taylor, B. C. (2020). Defending the state from digital Deceit: The reflexive securitization of deepfake. *Critical Studies in Media Communication, 38*(1), 1–17. https://doi.org/10.1080/15295036.2020.1833058

Thaw, N. N., July, T., Wai, A. N., Goh, D. H. L., & Chua, A. Y. K. (2020). Is it real? A study on detecting deepfake videos. *Proceedings of the Association for Information Science and Technology, 57*(1). https://doi.org/10.1002/pra2.366

The Next Rembrandt: Recreating the Work of a Master with AI. Microsoft News Centre Europe. (2017, August 30). https://news.microsoft.com/europe/features/next-rembrandt/

Whittaker, L., Letheren, K., and Mulcahy, R. 2021. The rise of Deepfakes: A conceptual framework and research agenda for marketing. *Australasian Marketing Journal*,29(3), 204–214. https://doi.org/10.1177/1839334921999479

Wittgenstein, L. (1986). *Philosophical Investigations*. Basil Blackwell.

Zeljkovic, V. (2014). *Video Surveillance Techniques and Technologies*. Information Science Reference.

Chapter 6

AI AND THE CLUSTER ACCOUNT OF ART

Alice C. Helliwell

Is AI art really art? This question has been the subject of much public discussion and is one that philosophical aesthetics should be well-placed to address. Unfortunately, there is no clear consensus within the discipline on how to tackle key definitional questions such as this. In the case of AI, we can add to this the unique challenge of works not made by humans. In this chapter, I argue for the utility of a Wittgensteinian approach to the question of whether AI art is art. This approach typically repudiates the need to provide necessary and sufficient conditions. Using Gaut's cluster account, I show that AI art can indeed count as art. I also demonstrate that the cluster account of art is particularly useful for thinking about art made by AI.

The Cluster Account of Art

The perceived failures of contemporary definitions of art (particularly a failure to garner any broad consensus amongst philosophers) led Berys Gaut to take a Wittgensteinian approach to art. Gaut was not the first to consider Wittgenstein's work in relation to the definition of art. Gaut's theory re-visits the work of philosophers in the 1950s who applied Wittgenstein's family resemblance approach to the question 'what is art?', arguing for an anti-definitionalist approach (see Weitz 1956; Ziff 1953; Kennick 1958).[1] These philosophers argue for two key points: first, that art cannot be defined (in terms of individually necessary and jointly sufficient conditions), and second, that art is a concept best characterized in terms of family resemblance (Gaut 2000).

1 See Wittgenstein (2009: PI §66–67) on family resemblances.

Instead of resemblance-to-paradigm as the model for the concept of art, however, Gaut turns to a 'cluster account' construal of family resemblance (Gaut 2000, 26). The cluster version of family resemblance that Gaut adopts comes from Wittgenstein's discussion of proper names (Wittgenstein 2009: PI §79) and was further developed by Searle (1958). As Gaut writes,

> A cluster account is true of a concept just in case there are properties whose instantiation by an object counts as a matter of conceptual necessity toward an object's falling under a concept [...] There are several [properties] criteria for a concept.
>
> *(Gaut 2000, 26)*

The way properties count towards the concept are as follows:

1) If *all* properties are instantiated in an object, then the concept applies to it. If *fewer* than all criteria are instantiated, this is sufficient for the application of the concept.
2) There is no one property which everything falling under the concept must have.
3) There are no individually necessary conditions for the application of the concept, but there are disjunctively necessary conditions. It must be true that some of the criteria apply if an object falls under the concept. (Gaut 2000, 27)

In the case of art then, there will be a list of properties whereby:

i. If all properties are fulfilled by an object, it must be art, but if only some of the properties are fulfilled by the object, it can still be art.
ii. There is not one property which all artworks will have.
iii. For an object to be art, it must have at least some of the properties; it cannot have none of the properties, and still be art (though, in the case of art, Gaut states we might not yet know all of these properties). (Gaut 2000, 27)

Gaut's cluster concept of art is not a *true* cluster concept, however (even under the conditions that Gaut himself lays out). Gaut adds a necessary condition to his account, thereby violating condition (2). Gaut adds that given it is art*works* in which we are interested, some action must have taken place for the product of that action to be art:

> An artwork is the product of an action, preeminently of a making (an artifact), or a performing (a performance). It is art*works* that are involved here, since

> something is in each case done. Hence being the product of an action is the genus of the artwork and is thus a necessary condition for something's being art.
>
> *(Gaut 2000, 29)*

Gaut's account of 'making' or 'performing' here is permissive, as the account can still allow for found art; even found artworks are selected, and thus are the product of an action. This is sufficient under the cluster account of art, because 'Selection adds to the range of properties that can be possessed by objects, and thus alters them, even if not physically' (Gaut 2000, 29).

Gaut argues that this modification to the cluster account does not compromise the nature of the account, as the necessary condition is minimal:

> Being the product of an action is, however, a very thin generic condition, which does not distinguish artworks from any of the other products of action (philosophy, papers, chairs, pay freezes, angry words etc.) [...] thus the modified cluster account holds that there is one necessary condition for something's being an artwork, but that is because of the notion of a work (the product of action) rather than because of the notion of art.
>
> *(Gaut 2000, 29)*[2]

With this minimal necessary condition in place Gaut proffers ten properties which may count towards something being a work of art (Gaut 2000, 28). Turning to AI, I will utilize these properties to evaluate AI works, arguing that they could meet several of the criterial properties, before returning to the necessary condition.

AI and the Cluster Account of Art

In order to evaluate AI works against the cluster account of art, I will begin with the list of ten properties in Gaut's (2000) account and propose how AI works could or could not meet them.

Possessing positive aesthetic qualities, for example, being beautiful, graceful or elegant

Possessing positive aesthetic qualities does not seem to be a barrier for AI works. There is no reason to think that AI images cannot be beautiful, even

2 Here I include these lengthy quotations because, as we shall see soon, the exact formulation of this necessary criterion will be particularly relevant when applying this account to AI.

if you think the majority are not. Finding the work to have positive aesthetic qualities likely led to an AI work winning a prize at the Colorado State Fair (Roose 2022) and works made with AI have recently been described as 'gorgeous' and 'beautiful' in *The Guardian* (Jones 2022).

Being expressive of emotion

Whether a work made by an AI could be expressive of emotion will come down to exactly what is meant by 'being expressive'. Jenefer Robinson has provided us with an account of what it means for a work to have expressive qualities:

> I would like to suggest that we should confine the term 'expressive quality' to those qualities in an artwork (or other things, such as merry brooks and anguished old oak trees) that are not only named by an emotion word but also arouse appropriate emotions. More particularly, *expressive qualities* are *qualities that can be grasped through the emotions that they arouse.*
>
> *(Robinson 2005, 291–92)*

If we adopt Robinson's account of expressive qualities, it seems possible for an AI to produce works that have such qualities, that is, works with qualities that can be named by an emotion word and arouse appropriate emotions. If an oak tree can have expressive qualities in this way, why not a work by an AI? What counts for Robinson is the reception of the work by the audience. She states that expressive qualities should 'evoke corresponding emotions in audiences' which can alert the audience to the presence of said qualities (Robinson 2005, 292). We can already see these kinds of expressive qualities being described in works that are made with AI. For example, Jones (2022) describes the work of Gillian Wearing, who utilized DALL-E 2, saying: 'You get a sense of loneliness and anguish, crying from inside to outside, soul to soul' (Jones 2022). Will this sense of expressiveness satisfy the cluster property?

When discussing exceptions to each of the properties, Gaut states that 'much of architecture and music is not concerned with the expression of emotion' (Gaut 2000, 33). It seems then that the work must be 'concerned with' the expression of emotion, not just have expressive qualities. It is unlikely that an AI will itself be concerned with the expression of emotion, as this is not a feature of current AI systems. However, that does not mean that a work made by an AI could not *seem* to express emotion, or to give viewers an idea of what it is like to experience an emotion, nor that an AI system could not be designed with emotion in mind.

At this stage of AI development, we are not seeing anything like emotional states being possible. However, there have been attempts to add an emotional component to machine images, such as the *emotionally aware Painting Fool* developed by Colton and colleagues (2008). We are also seeing so-called empathetic algorithms which are designed to be sensitive to the emotional state of their users (Raamkumar and Yang 2022), and systems which researchers claim can identify emotional responses to images, particularly artworks, and express these in language (Achlioptas et al. 2021). Finally, there are AI-based art-making systems that claim to be able to create 'emotional' art, such as AIVA, an AI that produces 'emotional soundtrack music' (AIVA n.d.). Whether this system is successful in creating expressive music is debatable, but this certainly seems like it is creating works that are 'concerned with the expression of emotion'. There is the added issue of where this concern comes from, and if it needs to come from the system rather than the designers of the system. Emotional or expressive considerations could plausibly be integrated into future AI art-making systems, particularly if this property is seen as key for art.[3]

So, if we want our AI to be expressing an emotion in making a work, this second property of art is not possible for current AI. This property may, however, be possible if we just want a viewer to find the work to be expressive, or if we allow 'emotionally concerned' works made by non-feeling AI to count under this property.

Being intellectually challenging (i.e. questioning received views and modes of thought)

Works of art made by AI could be intellectually challenging to some extent. It may challenge us to wrap our heads around the very notion of artworks being made by an AI, the images themselves may seem confusing, and we may try to glean information about the training data from the images we see. For example, the work of Google DeepDream can challenge us to guess on what the system was trained, understand how the system is recognizing patterns, and consider what exactly this means for what the system 'sees' (Mordvintsev, Olah and Tyka 2015). However, with AI works, much of the challenge will come from the fact that the work is made by an AI. As such, no autonomous AI system is likely to make works that are 'questioning received views and modes of thought' without you needing to know that the work is an AI work,

3 As I will argue later, the cluster account allows us to offer recommendations for the future development of AI for art.

as that is a key factor in the work's intellectual challenge. These AI systems do not have views or modes of thinking, and thus are not going to be able to question these through their work. Despite this, there is no requirement that the intellectual challenge of an artwork under the cluster account stems from the work without context, or that the challenge must even be intentional. As such, this property does seem possible for an AI work.

Being formally complex and coherent

There is no reason to think that AI could not produce formally complex works, particularly in the visual domain. Images from Generative Adversarial Networks (GANs), DALL-E and even older systems like DeepDream can produce colourful, multi-feature images. We have some evidence that AI can produce images that are formally complex in comparison to some human-made artworks. Elgammal and colleagues (2017) conducted some initial interrogation into the responses to the images produced by their Creative Adversarial Network (CAN). I will draw on several of their findings during discussion of these properties. Elgammal et al. (2017) presented participants with images from the CAN versus abstract expressionist works and works displayed in *Art Basel 2016*.[4] In this study, participants were asked to rate the complexity of the images. Those images produced by AI systems were rated as higher on complexity than the human artworks in the study. The difference between the sets was not large, but it may be sufficient for our purposes that the AI images were as complex as the human-made works (Elgammal et al. 2017, 16–17).

Formal *coherence* on the other hand may be more difficult for some AI. Though a system thoroughly trained on a narrow data set will produce coherent, and seemingly representational,[5] images with frequency, a common way for AI systems to fail is to not produce a coherent image of a target-depicted object (consider generative AI's problem with hands e.g. Hughes 2023). With increased diversity in the training set, or with a system designed to differ somewhat from the training set (such as AICAN), the images are not always clearly *of* something. Can they still be formally coherent?

The same study by Elgammal et al., discussed above, also asked participants to rate their agreement with the statement: 'As I interact with this painting, I

4 It should be noted that this study has limitations. The study was conducted online, most of the questions were asked to non-experts, and not all differences were investigated for significance.

5 I use the term 'representational' here simply to mean the images clearly depict a recognizable object.

start to see a structure emerging' (2017, 17–18). Participants scored both the images produced by the GAN and CAN systems in the study higher than the human-art data sets. Seeing a structure emerging could point to formal coherence (in images); but the AI images being rated higher on this question than human-made images does not mean that they possess this property. Perhaps these art data sets are just not the kind to be 'formally complex and coherent' (as is expected by the cluster account, some works of art will not have this property).

Hands notwithstanding, in general images produced by diffusion models (such as DALL-E and Stable Diffusion) seem to be more consistent in terms of producing convincing coherence and complexity. These images are generated in response to human text prompts and are based on a probabilistic model. In part because of this probabilistic basis, diffusion models are able to generate images which are structured in a coherent way. They do still make mistakes related to coherence, however (Romero 2022). For our purposes here though, it is sufficient that AI *could* produce coherent and complex works, and thus could produce works that meet this property under the cluster account.

Having a capacity to convey complex meanings

If conveying meaning involves communicating meaning from the artist to the viewer, it would appear that most art-making AI systems cannot do this. To do this, the AI itself would have to have a meaning in mind, which is not possible in the AI systems that we are examining, particularly generative algorithms. The more autonomous a system is (at least until we have systems capable of understanding) the less likely it is that the works have the capacity to convey *any* meaning, let alone complex meanings.

If we do not need the system to generate the meaning of a work itself, then it seems this property is already possible for some AI (depending on how complex the meaning is). For example, a diffusion-based AI like DALL-E can produce a relevant image when it is given a text prompt. In producing this image, the complex architecture of the system effectively takes the prompt, represents its meaning in a mathematical space, and uses this in the generation of an image. In this way then, the system is quite literally conveying meaning from one mode (text) to another (image). If successful, the image does indeed represent the meaning of the prompt (OpenAI 2022b). Whilst this kind of visual representation of meaning does not exhaustively capture what Gaut perhaps means by 'capacity to convey complex meanings', it could be a case of conveying meanings to a viewer. Given that the prompts for producing images in DALL-E are provided by humans, the system itself is certainly not conveying any meaning that it wants to. It *can* convey the meanings given to it by a human, but it cannot come up with those ideas for *what* to convey independently; it is reliant on a human user inputting text into the system. To use an example that is not a visual work, a written piece by an AI system such as GPT-3 could also include complex meanings that could be understood by a reader. However, this meaning is not connected to anything the AI system aims to convey; it is, in this case, produced predictively in response to a human prompt, much like elements of DALL-E.

AI works taken broadly could have a capacity to convey some complex meanings to an audience, particularly if they are prompt-based systems. If we require the meanings to come from the system itself though, this will not be possible for current AI.

Exhibiting an individual point of view

Exhibiting an individual point of view may not seem very likely with an AI system that is producing artworks. First, it seems odd to say that they have a 'point of view', which we would typically use to indicate having a mind. To have a point of view to exhibit we would expect something to have a perspective on the world, even to have thoughts, feelings and opinions on the world. All of these require a mind, and these AI systems do not have a mind. Second, AI systems are rarely thought of as individuals. This is partly due to their constant changes. Most AI systems employ machine learning (ML) algorithms. ML algorithms change constantly, with each round of learning resulting in alterations to the system. For example, in GANs and CAN, the process of learning alters weights in the system to improve future images. An image produced at an early stage of this process will be different to one produced later in the process. One might contend that humans too change, particularly through learning; artists will produce a variety of works over their careers, so how could we say they exhibit a single point of view? Despite this analogy, there is still a constancy that we cannot ignore about a human: they are one being, with a single physical manifestation. Furthermore, changes to humans occur slowly, and in response to environmental stimuli. Humans are embodied.

However, if we take 'individual point of view' to encompass producing images in a single style, AI may be able to achieve this. We can look at the work of a narrowly trained AI system, such as the GAN Obvious used to produce *Portrait of Edmond de Belamy* (the algorithm was trained and uploaded online by programmer/artist Robbie Barrat). This system produced multiple similar images, which look like a person with indefinite features seen through textured glass (Christie's 2018).[6] Similar images were able to be reproduced

6 It is not clear how much of the appearance of these images is due to selection, processing and printing by Obvious.

using Barrat's algorithm, which suggests that the algorithm developed and trained by Barrat had a particular style and subject it repeatedly reproduced in images. Unfortunately, though, this AI system has been trained to reproduce the kinds of portraits on which it has been trained. The fact that it produces multiple similar images is indicative of the narrow 'experience' that the AI has with images. It is not clear that this should count as a 'point of view'. Furthermore, the selection of the training images is down to the human(s) training the system, in this case Barrat. This is how people exercise control over the images produced by generative AI systems; a consistent aesthetic, and particularly a consistent subject-matter, is not evidence of the AI system having a point of view as much as the human having a specific aim for the system.

It is unlikely that an AI will be able to achieve this criterion, unless we consider 'exhibiting an individual point of view' to be satisfied by 'exhibiting consistency in style'.

Being an exercise of creative imagination (being original)

Gaut offers two formulations of this property. The second, 'being original', should not be a barrier for AI systems producing works. AI systems can produce original works. This originality may be limited to the relevant domain; for example, a GAN is not going to produce anything that is not a digital image, though this system does produce novel images. It is worth noting that some generative AI systems may indeed have a problem with originality due to data over-fitting. This is where the system becomes too dependent on the training data, typically because there is not enough of it (Feng et al. 2022). When this happens in a GAN, it can result in the system reproducing images it has seen before (Webster et al. 2019). A GAN that is not producing any novelty is a red flag for training issues. In the case of GANs, there are techniques to test for this replication and 'Even when overfitting, most models will not reproduce perfect or trivially transformed copies of the training data' (Theis, Oord, and Bethge 2015, 6). Images produced by AI can also *seem* original to us. Again, we can turn to Elgammal et al. (2017). In one of their experiments, AI images were judged to be more original than the human artworks by participants. This originality is by design, particularly in the CAN where the system is designed to differ stylistically from training images.

Imagination on the other hand is more difficult for an AI system. I expect that we would anticipate having a mind (and mental representations) as central to imagination. If this is the case, AI systems are not going to be able to achieve this property, as the kinds of systems we have now (and for the near future) will not have minds. Despite the numerous concepts to which 'imagination' seems to refer, Liao and Gendler state that broadly:

> *To imagine* is to represent without aiming at things as they actually, presently, and subjectively are. One can use imagination to represent possibilities other than the actual, to represent times other than the present, and to represent perspectives other than one's own.
>
> *(Liao and Gendler 2020)*

Generative algorithms can represent things:

> In generative modeling, methods like variational autoencoders (VAEs) [KW13] and generative adversarial networks (GANs) [GPAM∗14] create latent spaces for modeling and synthesis of data [CN17]. Despite arising from different algorithms serving distinct purposes, these representations are all vector spaces of reduced dimensionality (relative to the input), intended to produce more general features that helpfully characterize the input. These representations are often referred to as latent spaces.
>
> *(Liu et al. 2019)*

Diffusion models have similar representational spaces. The latent space is constituted by 'representations' of data on which the system has been trained. It does not contain all the data but a compressed version of that data. It additionally represents relationships between the data that it has been trained on: 'The concept of "latent space" is important because its utility is at the core of "deep learning" — learning the features of data and simplifying data representations for the purpose of finding patterns' (Tiu 2020). This might be seen as akin to a form of imagination (though, perhaps not the creative kind). Rather, it might be more like a representation of something one has seen before (like picturing scenes from a film, and how they relate to each other). Given that this latent space is representative of the training data an AI is exposed to during learning, we might say that this is just representing things 'as they actually, presently, and subjectively are' even though this kind of latent space is key to generating *new* images.

Despite this, some of the images produced by AI systems certainly seem fantastical. Take the examples made available by OpenAI on their DALL-E 2 Demo (OpenAI 2022a): if DALL-E 2 can produce an image of 'Teddy bears shopping for groceries in the style of Ukiyo-e', then should this not count as 'not aiming at things as they actually are'? Whether we might consider these representations as (machine) imaginings will be dependent on how we want to characterize the pattern-finding in the latent space and, given the novel images that are generated from the latent space, if we are willing to call these 'possibilities other than the actual'.

The focus of my response so far has been on 'imagination', but what of 'creative'? In light of Gaut's more recent work on creativity, the property of 'being an exercise of creative imagination' might actually be akin to 'being an exercise of creativity'. Gaut states in a later work on the link between imagination and creativity: 'we have defended the existence of an a priori constitutive connection between imagination and creativity: imagination is suited of its nature to be the vehicle of active creativity' (Gaut 2003, 289). Exercising creative imagination then could be equivalent to being creative in the cluster account. Whether an AI can be creative is a matter beyond the scope of this chapter (see e.g. Helliwell 2021).

Being the product of a high degree of skill

If we were to only take skills as the kinds of abilitieshumans are skilled at (like wielding a paintbrush with precision, depicting an object accurately or playing a piano well), then these AI systems do not seem to have 'skills'.[7] They may, however, become skilled in the sense of gaining the ability to do something well (e.g. generate images). We could characterize ML as a process of perfecting a skill for an AI system, as the AI is improving in its ability to produce images within certain parameters of success. In the case of a GAN system, for example, the generator in the system generates images, which are judged by the discriminator. Feedback from the discriminator goes into the generative process, improving the images in the next round of generation. If we are happy to accept this understanding of skill, then this seems possible for AI.

Belonging to an established artistic form

This is not too much of a stretch for AI. First, the majority of works considered here are digital images. Digital images are an established form of art, and they may also be emulating another established artistic form (paintings, photographs etc.). Second, AI is trained on other artworks, and one of AI's clear limitations (in terms of creativity) is the extent to which it could ever go beyond the kind of works on which it has been trained. Systems such as GANs are designed to produce images that are a believable part of the set of images on which it has been trained, and predictive/probabilistic systems (such as DALL-E, GPT-n, AIVA) are designed to continue on with what they have

7 Though some AI systems may be able to perform some tasks with greater speed and accuracy than humans (e.g. *AlphaGo*).

been prompted with in an expected way, also based on training data. Neither of these kinds of systems are going to produce works that are vastly different from the works on which they have been trained. This is not to say that an AI will not *ever* make works that do not belong to an established artistic form and depending how narrowly we take 'artistic form' we may see AI systems produce different kinds of works (e.g. a new form of narrative work, or a new style of digital painting). However, it seems likely that most successful art-making AI will be producing works that belong to an established form. One might object that the fact that these are AI works in itself makes them another form of art. I am not convinced that this is a problem, as the focus in Gaut's property appears to be *form*, and not production, which would suggest a focus on the perceptible properties of the work.

Being the product of an intention to make a work of art

A work 'being the product of an intention to make a work of art' of course requires intention. To have intention is often thought to require a capacity for mental states and with them a mind. If AI needs to have a mind in order to have intentions, then this will either not be possible at all (if we agree with Searle 1980) or at least not possible in current AI systems. If we do not think that an AI needs to have a mind to have intentions, and instead substitute something like 'aiming at a purpose' for intentionality, then some AI could achieve this criterion.

We could also adopt Dennett's (1989) proposal of the intentional stance, whereby the 'truth' of the matter about a system's capacity does not matter. All that matters is the utility of adopting an assumption that the system is intentional. In order for this approach to be useful, we would need to know if people do indeed adopt an intentional stance to AI art. We do have some (albeit limited) evidence that people take an intentional stance to artworks made by some AI systems. Again, in Elgammal et al.'s (2017) study, participants were asked how much they agree with the statement: 'As I interact with this painting, I start to see the artist's intentionality: it looks like it was composed very intentionally' (2017, 17). With this question, participants score the GAN and CAN images higher (more agreement with the statement) than the human artworks. There are limitations to this question. The clear issue for my purposes is that this is not asking whether the image appears to be intentionally a work of art. It is likely that this question is addressing formal qualities (I imagine a Jackson Pollock work would score low, yet it is clearly intended to be a work of art). However, if the works appear intentional in some way, this suggests that participants are taking an intentional stance towards these images.

Should apparent intentionality in a work of art count towards 'being the product of an intention to make a work of art'? The work is the same, whether it is made by a human or an AI system. If it turns out that the work is made by an AI, does that mean that is not the product of an intention to make a work of art? If we take an intentional stance towards AI, then no; it would still be an intentional work of art. There is a clear objection here of course: many people do not sign up to a Dennettian view of intention.

Aside from this debate, AI art could utilize some intention derived from humans. There are two possible routes to this:

1. In the creation and training of the AI: for a domain-specific AI, a human has designed and trained the system for a purpose. AI systems that produce works akin to art will often be designed and trained with art in mind. In this case, the designer/engineer/artist is intending that whatever the AI produces will be art. The works produced by the system then are the product of the intention to make a work of art, even if there is an additional step in this causal chain.
2. In the selection of outputs from the AI: this is similar to found art or ready-made artworks. In selecting the work made by an AI, a person may be, through that action, be intending to produce a work of art. The work would not count under this approach until this intentional action has been undertaken by a human, however.

If we are happy to utilize intentionality derived from humans, then this property is not a problem for works produced by AI. At higher levels of autonomy, however, we may be less willing to derive intentions from a human as in (1) (through the creation and training of the AI). If we are looking for an intention to produce a work of art in the AI system itself, this property is considerably more challenging, and the possibility of AI achieving this will be contingent on several factors – namely, the complexity of the AI, whether we think AI mind is possible, whether we are willing to accept a minimal account of intention, or whether we are willing to accept Dennett's view.

Assessing the Cluster Properties for AI

As I have shown, we can examine the list of properties Gaut provides us in the cluster account and assess whether AI can meet each in turn. By my assessment, several of these are possible, and more are possible with caveats (such as how we define elements of the property). Even more properties are possible as soon as we include humans in the equation (see Table 6.1 for a summary). From this, it certainly appears that enough of the properties could be filled to

Table 6.1 The cluster account of art – can AI works demonstrate each property?

	Property	*Yes*	*Maybe*	*No*
i.	possessing positive aesthetic properties	✓		
ii.	being expressive of emotion		✓*	
iii.	being intellectually challenging (i.e. questioning received views and modes of thought)	✓		
iv.	being formally complex and coherent	✓		
v.	having a capacity to convey complex meanings	✓ †		
vi.	exhibiting an individual point of view			✓
vii.	being an exercise of creative imagination (being original)		✓*	
viii.	being the product of a high degree of skill	✓*		
ix.	belonging to an established artistic form (music, painting, film, etc.)	✓		
x	being the product of an intention to make a work of art	✓ †		

Note: these properties are taken from Gaut (2000, 28), and have been edited down into a list.
*Dependent on how we take this property.
†Only likely in cases with human involvement.

count AI works as art (providing the necessary criteria is fulfilled – more on this below). One property which is particularly tricky for AI art is 'exhibiting an individual point of view'. This property gets to the heart of the issue for AI. AI produces images that are, to a large extent, drawn from training on many other images. This is particularly true for diffusion models. It is then arguably the antithesis of something with an individual point of view. However, even on a more conservative view of the properties – let's say AI works are lacking four properties – there is surely still scope for AI works to be considered art.

Gaut does not provide us with any constraint on the number of properties that he thinks sufficient for a work to be art under the cluster account. However, we can use an example to demonstrate that a work can be lacking several and still be art. Take a work of art such as Yves Klein's *IKB 79* (1959). This work is a vast, blue painted canvas. When measuring this work up against the cluster properties, we see that it may lack several. This work is not formally complex – it has little in the way of form at all. It's debatable how much skill this work required to make; it is certainly less skillful than the ceiling of the Sistine Chapel, for example. The work is also debatably not particularly original in and of itself (Klein made nearly 200 blue, monochrome canvases in his lifetime (Howarth 2000)). It's also debatable how much a minimalist work such as this could *exhibit* a point of view, even though the artist certainly had a point of view to their works. It's not clearly expressive of an emotion; it is suggested that commercialism was at least a partial driver in the creation of these works (Howarth 2000). Whilst these points might be debated, let us take for a moment that Klein's work did lack all five of these criteria. Despite this, would we deny it is a work of art? No – Klein's works are art, and influential art at that. Thus, we could imagine that even lacking five properties in the list is not sufficient to deny a work is art.

I hope to have shown through my assessment of these properties how the cluster account of art might be beneficial for those interested in the possibility of AI Art: the cluster account provides a list of properties that we can discuss, debate the possibility of and potentially consider for operationalization. By this I mean that we can take a property and consider whether (1) current AI can do it, (2) future AI could do it, and (3) how we might make this possible for an AI. For example, we could prioritize formal coherence in future AI systems. To do this, we might want to focus on developing links between a structured visual system and image generation in our AI systems. The cluster account can give us more to work with than other accounts of art in developing future AI art-making systems.

Additional Properties

The discussion thus far has focused on the properties of the cluster account and measuring AI against these. There is a fundamental assumption underlying this, however. This is that when AI makes art, it will be like human art, so much so that it will be recognizable by the same metric that we apply to human art. There is a reason for this. The motivation for this investigation is uncertainty about whether AI could produce art, and considerable scepticism about the possibility that it ever could. There is an intuition for some, and more than an intuition for others, that art is a *human* endeavour. This framing is anthropocentric and ignores the possibility (maybe even a slim one) that whatever AI does will be quite different from what humans do. This is believed to be increasingly likely as we edge towards autonomy and beyond into human-level and beyond-human-level intelligence in AI (see e.g. Bostrom 2014). AI may well have different values to us, including in the realm of the arts, and these values may or may not end up appealing to humans.

There is a benefit here to a cluster account: it can be adapted. Gaut states that individual criteria can be disputed (Gaut 2000, 29). Furthermore, if an example could be found of a missing property that should be on the list, or a counterexample of a case that seems to be art but does not meet any of the criteria, then a new or missing property could be added:

> There is no evident way that an object lacking all of the criteria could be a work of art; and even if a plausible counterexample could be produced, the friend of the cluster account could respond by *adding whatever seems like the relevant criterion*

> *to the cluster* – that is, she can respond by modifying the intent of the account, rather than its form.
>
> *(Gaut 2000, 32–33, my emphasis)*

Taken together, this suggests that we could make a case to add properties to this list where we have a counterexample case that *seems* to be art but does not meet enough of the properties in the list, and yet clearly has other properties that might be added to the list (without altering the form of the cluster account itself). In the case of an AI artwork that does not meet all, or even most, of the properties in the cluster account, there is a potential for us to adapt the account to alter existing properties or propose *new* properties that are unearthed by AI works.

A foreseeable case could be, for example, to add 'information' to the property of 'having a capacity to convey complex meanings'. 'Having a capacity to convey complex meanings or impart complex information' could then include AI works' ability to convey probabilistic information about artworks (as we see with DALL-E) or the ability to convey aggregate information about traits of a training set of images (as with GANs). A DALL-E image can tell us something about a large data set that other forms of data visualization or mere statistical analysis might not. For example, from discussion with artists using DALL-E 2,[8] DALL-E 2 struggles to depict a man wearing a dress and will opt for depicting a woman in a dress, or a man next to a dress. We could report on the percentage of images in the training data set that depict men in dresses, or the ratio of men to women depicted in dresses in the training data set, but this does not compare to the information we could gain from just looking at DALL-E images. Seeing a system that can depict 'An astronaut riding a horse in the style of Andy Warhol' be unable to depict *a man in a dress*, reveals bias in the data, and the impact of that bias in one fell swoop. You do not have to agree that this is something that should count as a property of art (and perhaps by virtue of it being by an AI, you will not), but we can see in this example how an AI artwork might offer something different to human art.

These AI systems are just today's technology, but already we can start to see how these 'art'-making AI can provide something for art that Gaut's initial (anthropocentric) list of properties might not currently include. This is not to say that just *any* properties of AI works can be added to the account, and not just any alterations to the account can be made (Gaut 2000, 32). We would need to make a good case for the inclusion of a new property. Despite this, the cluster account gives those interested in the future of works made by

8 Artists working at Realdreams, an AI art collective operating in London (Realdreams 2022).

AI a route to allow AI to contribute to what we see as art, not just play catch-up to human-made art.[9]

The Necessary Condition

My discussion of the cluster account thus far has ignored a glaring issue for AI: the action condition. Gaut's modified cluster account includes a single necessary condition, and that condition is that the artwork 'is the product of an action'. Can AI perform actions? Whether an AI can perform an action will depend on how we characterize actions and, in particular, what relationship we require between action and intention. This is not a settled debate in philosophy of action (Wilson and Shpall 2016). If the 'action' required to make art a 'work' does need to be intentional, then we once again reach an impasse for AI works. To do something intentionally, we would expect to need a mind, as intention is considered to be a mental state by many (Jacob 2019), though, as we have seen above, we do have some possible routes for AI intention.

Is the 'action' in the cluster account to be an intentional one? This is not clear. The action does not need to include the intention to make a work of art, as that is listed separately as a disjunctive condition. Gaut reaffirms that this is not necessary in a later paper:

> Those who claim that the disputed cases are not art may do so because they insist on, as a necessary condition for art, some feature, such as being the product of an intention to make art. But it is a mistake to insist on this as a necessary condition, as can be shown by considering less contentious cases of art, which lack this feature.
>
> *(Gaut 2005, 281)*

Gaut also makes it clear that the cluster account can accommodate various hard cases in aesthetics, such as Duchamp's ready-mades (Gaut 2000, 32, 35) and found objects (Gaut 2000, 29). Intention does not need to be present in the creation of the object, just in the selection of the work. In his discussion of Weitz's example of a found object, Gaut states:

---

9 I should note that I do not make an argument here that the cluster account of art is correct. I argue that it is the most useful for the purposes of assessing AI art.

> A piece of driftwood in nature cannot express despair, nor can it be about anything (since it lacks even derived intentionality), but when selected for display in a gallery it can express desuetude and be about failure and decay.
>
> *(Gaut 2000, 29)*

By selecting the object, we imbue in it the capacity for the other properties. This suggests that there is an easy way to avoid the issue of whether AI can act. In the case of much of today's AI art, a human will be selecting the outputs to share with the world, curating the AI outputs for wider dissemination (through online means, in galleries, in auction houses etc). If we do not want to worry further about whether AI works are art or not, we can again consider AI art to be much like found art, or ready-mades: it was not art before, but now it has been selected by someone. In selecting the image, the person has done the requisite (intentional) action to allow this image to count as a work, and with that has opened up the capacity of the image to hold more art properties (like the driftwood above). Similarly, we might think that an AI designed with the purpose of producing art would derive some intentionality from its own development, though perhaps with greater distance from intention to product than would be typical.

While this might offer an easy solution for us in the cluster account, it may be possible for AI to produce art without this solution. As I have shown above, an AI work could have several of the properties of the cluster account, whether it is properly thought of as a product of an action or not. If the action criterion is in place merely to open up the capacities of the object to have the other properties, then for AI this may not be necessary. It is already artefact-like, it is already the product of an action-like event, and it already has the capacity to have several of the disjunctive properties.

The inclusion of the action criterion is meant to establish that in order for something to be an artwork it must be a *work*. Here, again, is what Gaut says of the action criterion:

> An artwork is the product of an action, preeminently of a making (an artifact), or a performing (a performance). It is art*works* that are involved here, since something is in each case done. Hence being the product of an action is the genus of the artwork and is thus a necessary condition for something's being art.
>
> *(Gaut 2000, 29)*

The purpose of including 'action' as a necessary criterion in the cluster account ensures that something is 'done'. This then results in a product, that is, the potential artwork. This seems to fit with the case of the products of AI. In adding an action condition, Gaut in effect *weakens* the standard account of artefactuality, rather than strengthens it. On the standard definition of an artefact as laid out by Preston (2020), artefacts must meet three conditions: (1) they must be produced with intention, (2) they must involve modified materials, and (3) they must be made for a purpose. Gaut, however, does not include any of these conditions. Besides a desire to include performances (the artefactual status of which has been hotly debated, see Preston 2020) Gaut also wishes to include objects that we might think were not produced with intention, or made for a purpose (e.g. found objects). AI does produce outputs, and (e.g.) make images. Can we not call these 'works'? In the case of these outputs produced by AI, it seems very restrictive to call an AI product not art merely because the action which produced it might not be intentional enough, or the distance between intention and the product is too great (such as might be the case in an autonomous AI system).

In the case of AI creating art with human involvement (in the design of the system, or in the selection of outputs) the action criterion should be sufficiently fulfilled. In the case of future AI which autonomously chooses to produce art, it is not clear that we would deny their outputs status as works under the cluster account. Action is required to open up the possibility of achieving the other properties of the account, and many of these properties would be achievable by AI outputs.

Is AI Art Not Art?

In non-Wittgensteinian approaches to the definition of art (see e.g. Davies 1991 for an overview), if an AI work cannot meet the requirements of the definition, then it is not art. This is a limit of the typical definitional approach; the concept either does or does not apply. This is not quite the case for a cluster approach (even with the addition of the necessary condition). We have seen already that, according to Gaut, the cluster account includes some built-in flexibility for the possible future counterexamples, that is, we can modify the account (Gaut 2000, 33). We have also seen that the list of properties provided in the cluster account allows us to assess AI creations on multiple dimensions. There are further benefits to the cluster account, even if it turns out that AI art cannot meet the necessary criteria Gaut lays out. The cluster account is notable for how it fits with our intuitions not just about what *is* art, but also about what *isn't*.

Gaut discusses the adequacy of the cluster account by considering indeterminate cases, where there is considerable disagreement of whether a work falls under the concept of art:

> if there are some objects to which the application of the concept is genuinely, irresolubly, indeterminate, then the account should reflect this too, rather than simply stipulating that the concept applies, or stipulating that it does not.
>
> *(Gaut 2000, 30)*

Unlike definitional accounts of art, the cluster account does not deal with hard cases (AI art might be such a case) by mere categorization. Instead, it offers us an explanation of the irresolution. For example, if AI works are not 'art' (i.e. the concept as outlined by Gaut does not fully apply, and we have not modified if for the inclusion of AI works) then it may be explained as a borderline case:

> the cluster account explains why some activities (such as cookery) seem to lie somewhere near the borders of art without clearly being art, since they share several properties of art (being the exercise of individual creativity, having a capacity to give sensuous pleasure), while also lacking other relevant criteria (since they have difficulty in expressing emotion and conveying complex meanings, and are not generally the product of an artistic intention). It is a signal advantage of the cluster account over the more straightforward definitions of art that it can preserve the hardness of such cases and allow us to explain what it is that makes them hard; such cases can be shown to be genuinely borderline and indeterminate.
>
> *(Gaut 2000, 36)*

Perhaps AI works are like cookery (or any other art-like case). They may be close to art, without clearly being art. Even if AI art does not meet the necessary criterion for being art (and one rejects my argument here), an example of an AI work might still meet several of the disjunctive properties Gaut lists, and thus we can explain why we might disagree with each other about our judgement of whether this example is art or not. This is better for us than AI art straightforwardly being rejected as art (and left there, as is the case with the other accounts). We can at least describe works made by (autonomous) AI as a difficult case, which lies close to the boundaries of art, and we can more easily justify discussion of the aesthetics of these works, why they seem artistic, or why some of us might still wish to label them as art.

The cluster account of art then can help us in several ways:

1. It can provide a framework for assessing what AI can or cannot currently do in terms of producing art, and this could help in the development of future AI.

2. It can potentially be adapted to accommodate what AI *can* do, through alterations or additions to the properties.
3. Even if AI cannot meet the necessary condition of the cluster account, the account can still explain why it seems like AI works are art, and why we might disagree about its status. AI art can be explained as a border case.

To conclude, in this chapter I have argued that a Wittgensteinian approach to art (through the cluster account) can have particular utility for AI art. I have argued here that (some) AI works could be art under the cluster account of art: they can potentially meet many of the listed properties featured in the account. With the intervention of a human, AI works can easily fulfil the necessary criterion. In the case of autonomous AI, AI works fulfil the apparent function of the action criterion. However, even with the rejection of the latter points, I have argued that the cluster account of art still has plenty to offer those sympathetic to the project of AI art.

References

Achlioptas, Panos, Maks Ovsjanikov, Kilichbek Haydarov, Mohamed Elhoseiny, and Leonidas Guibas. 2021. "Artemis: Affective language for visual art.' *Proceedings of the IEEE/CVF Conference on Computer Vision and Pattern Recognition*: 11569–11579. https://doi.org/10.48550/arXiv.2101.07396

AIVA. n.d. "AIVA." AIVA Technologies. https://www.aiva.ai/

Bostrom, Nick. 2014. *Superintelligence: Paths, Dangers, Strategies*. Oxford: Oxford University Press.

Christie's. 2018. "Is artificial intelligence set to become art's next medium?" Last Modified December 12, 2018. Accessed October 1, 2022. https://www.christies.com/features/A-collaboration-between-two-artists-one-human-one-a-machine-9332-1.aspx

Colton, Simon. 2008. "Creativity versus the perception of creativity in computational systems." *Proceedings of the AAAI Spring Symposium on Creative Systems*: 14–20. http://www.aaai.org/Papers/Symposia/Spring/2008/SS-08-03/SS08-03-003.pdf

Davies, Stephen. 1991. *Definitions of Art*. Ithaca, NY: Cornell University Press.

Dennett, Daniel C. 1989. *The Intentional Stance*. Cambridge, MA: MIT Press.

Elgammal, Ahmed, Bingchen Liu, Mohamed Elhoseiny, and Marian Mazzone. 2017. "CAN: Creative adversarial networks, generating "art" by learning about styles and deviating from style norms." *arXiv*. https://doi.org/10.48550/arXiv.1706.07068

Feng, Qianli, Chenqi Guo, Fabian Benitez-Quiroz, and Aleix Martinez. 2022. "When do GANs replicate? On the choice of dataset size." *Proceedings of the IEEE/CVF International Conference on Computer Vision*: 6701–6710. https://doi.org/10.48550/arXiv.2202.11765

Gaut, Berys. 2000. "The cluster account of art." In *Theories of Art Today* (pp. 25–44), edited by Noël Carroll. Madison, WI: The University of Wisconsin Press.

———. 2003. "Creativity and imagination." In *The Creation of Art*, edited by Berys Gaut and Paisley Livingston. New York, NY: Cambridge University Press, 148–173.

———. 2005. "The cluster account of art defended." *The British Journal of Aesthetics* 45(3): 273–288. https://doi.org/10.1093/aesthj/ayi032

Helliwell, Alice C. 2021. "Darwinian creativity as a model for computational creativity." *Proceedings of the 7th Computational Creativity Symposium at AISB 2021*, 15–19. https://aisb.org.uk/wp-content/uploads/2021/04/cc_aisb_proc.pdf

Howarth, Sophie. 2000. "Yves Klein IKB 79." Tate. Accessed January, 10. https://www.tate.org.uk/art/artworks/klein-ikb-79-t01513

Hughes, Alex. 2023. "Why AI-generated hands are the stuff of nightmares, explained by a scientist." *BBC Science Focus*. BBC. Accessed January 10. https://www.sciencefocus.com/future-technology/why-ai-generated-hands-are-the-stuff-of-nightmares-explained-by-a-scientist

Jacob, Pierre. 2019. "Intentionality." In *The Stanford Encyclopedia of Philosophy*, edited by E. N. Zalta. https://plato.stanford.edu/archives/win2019/entries/intentionality/

Jones, Jonathan. 2022. "Incoherent, creepy and gorgeous: We asked six leading artists to make work using AI – and here are the results." *The Guardian*, December 1, 2022. Accessed December 15, 2022. https://www.theguardian.com/artanddesign/2022/dec/01/six-leading-british-artists-making-art-with-ai

Kennick, William E. 1958. "Does traditional aesthetics rest on a mistake?" *Mind* 67(267): 317–334. https://www.jstor.org/stable/2251530

Klein, Yves. 1959. IKB79. Paint on canvas on plywood. https://www.tate.org.uk/art/artworks/klein-ikb-79-t01513.

Liao, Shen-Yi, and Tamar Gendler. 2020. "Imagination." In *The Stanford Encyclopedia of Philosophy*, edited by E. N. Zalta. https://plato.stanford.edu/archives/sum2020/entries/imagination/

Liu, Yang, Eunice Jun, Qisheng Li, and Jeffrey Heer. 2019. "Latent space cartography: Visual analysis of vector space embeddings." *Computer Graphics Forum* 38(3): 67–78. https://par.nsf.gov/servlets/purl/10172008

Mordvintsev, Alexander, Christopher Olah, and Mike Tyka. 2015. "Inceptionism: Going deeper into neural networks." *Google Research* (blog). https://ai.googleblog.com/2015/06/inceptionism-going-deeper-into-neural.html

OpenAI. 2022a. "DALL·E 2." *OpenAI* (blog). https://openai.com/dall-e-2/

———. 2022b. "DALL·E now available without Waitlist." OpenAI (blog). November 29, 2022. https://openai.com/blog/dall-e-now-available-without-waitlist/

Preston, Beth. 2020. "Artifact." In *The Stanford Encyclopedia of Philosophy*, edited by E. N. Zalta. https://plato.stanford.edu/archives/fall2020/entries/artifact/

Raamkumar, Aravind Sesagiri and Yinping Yang. 2022. "Empathetic conversational systems: A review of current advances, gaps, and opportunities." *IEEE Transactions on Affective Computing*. https://doi.org/10.48550/arXiv.2206.05017

Realdreams. 2022. "Realdreams." Accessed December 16, 2022. https://www.realdreams.io/

Robinson, Jenefer. 2005. *Deeper than Reason: Emotion and its Role in Literature, Music, and Art*. Oxford: Oxford University Press.

Romero, Alberto. 2022. "DALL·E 2, explained: The promise and limitations of a revolutionary AI." *Towards Data Science* (blog). June 16, 2022. https://towardsdatascience.com/dall-e-2-explained-the-promise-and-limitations-of-a-revolutionary-ai-3faf691be220

Roose, Kevin. 2022. "An A.I.-generated picture won an art prize. Artists aren't happy." *New York Times*, December 2, 2022. Accessed December 12, 2022. https://www.nytimes.com/2022/09/02/technology/ai-artificial-intelligence-artists.html

Searle, John Rogers. 1958. "Proper names." *Mind* 67(266): 166–173. https://www.jstor.org/stable/2251108

———. 1980. "Minds, brains, and programs." *Behavioral and Brain Sciences* 3(3): 417–424. https://doi.org/10.1017/S0140525X00005756

Theis, Lucas, Aäron van den Oord, and Matthias Bethge. 2015. "A note on the evaluation of generative models." *arXiv.* https://doi.org/10.48550/arXiv.1511.01844

Tiu, Ekin. 2020. "Understanding latent space in machine learning." *Towards Data Science* (blog). February 4, 2020. https://towardsdatascience.com/understanding-latent-space-in-machine-learning-de5a7c687d8d

Webster, Ryan, Julien Rabin, Loic Simon, and Frederic Jurie. 2019. "Detecting overfitting of deep generative networks via latent recovery." *Proceedings of the IEEE/CVF Conference on Computer Vision and Pattern Recognition*: 11273–11282. https://doi.org/10.48550/arXiv.1901.03396

Weitz, Morris. 1956. "The role of theory in aesthetics." *Journal of Aesthetics and Art Criticism* 15: 27–35. https://doi.org/10.2307/427491

Wilson, George and Samuel Shpall. 2016. "Action." In *The Stanford Encyclopedia of Philosophy*, edited by E. N. Zaltahttps://plato.stanford.edu/archives/win2016/entries/action/

Wittgenstein, L. 2009. *Philosophical Investigations.* 4th Edition. Trans. G. E. M. Anscombe, P. M. S. Hacker, Joachim Schulte. Oxford: Wiley-Blackwell

Ziff, Paul. 1953. "The task of defining a work of art." *The Philosophical Review* 62(1): 58–78.

Chapter 7

AN ANTHROPOLOGY OF THE USER IN THE AGE OF AI

Richard Harper

Introduction

To say that concepts need to be understood through reference to their use in action is something of a truism. Such reference can help clarify and untie knots that may have emerged when concepts have been used without their everyday anchors. This is one view on what philosophy entails – famously described by some commentators on Wittgenstein as a kind of therapy (Fischer, 2018). Often this therapy is for philosophers themselves whose mode of enquiry can lead them away from everyday life. The view also presupposes that these concepts are stable, somewhere already settled in everyday use. Philosophers need to revisit these contexts. Other disciplines have a different interest in how the meaning of concepts is found in use. For one thing, these contexts – and hence the usages to be found in them – may be unfamiliar, the practices of another culture, say.[1] It may be that contexts are changing, and as they do so, altering the meanings of terms used in those contexts. For these disciplines, these concerns are essentially empirical; anthropologists, certain sociologists (others too no doubt), seek to define context and then get to meaning. Whether there are conceptual muddles that might require therapy is a second-order concern, perhaps not even one at all.

Take the concept of the 'user' in human–computer interaction (HCI). This is surely to be understood with regard to its use, in relation to the contexts in which persons and computers do things together. It is these doings that make 'a user' a real phenomenon, a concept with pragmatic consequences, and it is these consequences that get expressed in the grammar of use for the

1 One thinks of Peter Winch, of course, and his book *The Idea of a Social Science* (1958).

term, 'user'. In this grammar, the 'user' partly expresses something about machines and partly the humans that use them, or perhaps more accurately, expresses something about the interaction the two engage in (Agre, 2008). The grammar doesn't say what that interaction might be, but somehow what is implied is a complex phenomenon, tacitly encompassing both flesh and silicon, expressing agencies of moral intention and those of machinic calculation. The way I am using the term grammar echoes Wittgenstein's thinking about the same term in his *Philosophical Investigations* (1953).[2] Though the grammar might allow variations in the particulars, one might assume that just as these particulars have varied over time, especially as the powers of computing have altered, then so too would some of the meanings be constitutive of the term 'user'. Its meanings will alter as its grammar does too. After all, the powers of AI are radically changing (so we are constantly told[3]) what can occur when a person becomes a user, when a person and machine interact. The sum is different. Surely then what is meant by the user is altered. If so, what are these changes? How does one delineate them?

In this chapter, I want to undertake this task. I want to ask what the 'user' is becoming. To answer that, I want to find out what the user was before the advent of machine learning (ML) and the 'new AI'. I do not want to treat this as a philosophical problem but as an empirical one, though with some evidence in hand perhaps I will also offer some philosophical remarks.

I start by looking at the interactional modalities that form the basis of the first desktop machines, derived from the Xerox Star and continuously used right the way through to today's latest PCs and laptops. My enquiries will then lead me to ask if interactions that people undertake with their latest machines (and networks) are leading to something new not only in what they do but what that implies about what they 'are' when they act as a 'user'. It is at this point that questions of grammar will come to the fore, as I will suggest that it might be that the term is coming to mean something to do with intentions, when those intentions might no longer just be those of the person, but also of the AI that the 'user' is, as it were, using. I will contend that perhaps this very word, 'using' and its cognate 'user', are now becoming slightly curious in their meaning, and what one might more properly say is that the human and the AI do things together, neither is correctly the user of the other. At this point, I shall remark on ChatGPT and how interaction between people and that technology (which I shall sketch) creates further conceptual curiosities where who or what the user is becomes even more muddling.

2 There is a vast corpus of research on Wittgenstein and his notion of grammar.

3 See for example Russell (2019) and Russell & Norvig (2017).

Looking Back to the Inventions of HCI

What was the original 'user'? Or more simply, what is one? As Wittgenstein points out in the *Investigations,* the meaning of a term presupposes that we know how to use that term (whatever it might be). He illustrates this with the term 'game'. He explains that it does not specify how it is to be used. It is practices and circumstances that do, a 'form of life', as he puts it. This phrase, *lebensform*, in German, is mentioned only three times in the Investigations (§19, §23 and §241) but the notion is fundamental to how we are to understand concepts like the user, too. It is the form of life with computing that we have grown accustomed to that gives the term, 'user', its applicability and renders it mundane, commonplace and, yes, usable. Those who drive cars are not users (even if their cars seem like computers); nor are those, for a playful example, who read books. One doesn't say of an undergraduate that they are a *user* of books. So, what we understand as a 'user' does have a particular meaning when deployed in relation to computers, a grammar in everyday life. I am suggesting we know what these understandings are: we evidently do when we use the term appositely. My question now is how were these usages shaped? How are they being shaped today?

To answer what a user is we need to begin with some history – the history of HCI.[4] This is the history of a discipline that many in philosophy have never heard of, even though hardly any philosopher can work without exploiting its outputs: nearly all the machines they use for writing are based on HCI research and what is called the WIMP interface. WIMP is an acronym for Windows, Icons, Mouse and Pointer. The interaction techniques these enable were devised by Xerox Parc in the 1970s (Smith, 1982). The original goal of WIMP interaction was to provide tools for a new type of computer 'user', the office worker, who would be able to create, format and publish documents in ways that were hitherto unimaginable.[5] This included tools for layout, for cut and pasting and for laser printing. These were to come with WYSIWYG solutions (What You See is What You Get) which would ensure that what a user thought they were creating (and which appeared to them on a screen) was indeed what got produced by a printer on paper. The digital and the paper were to be married (Sellen & Harper, 2002).

4 As with AI, there is an immense literature, and I certainly do not propose to review it all. If it was the Dartmouth Conference that started AI, one might say it was research at PARC that started HCI, and this was demarcated with the publication of (Card et al., 1983).

5 This is to ignore the ambitions that lay behind Engelbart's famous demo of the mouse, pointer and keyboard which he thought showed the way to augment human intellect. Xerox was more interested in office life. See (Sellen & Harper, 2002).

Many people using computers today take this interaction for granted. They may not even have heard the acronym WIMP (nor WYSIWYG). What is crucial is that with WIMP, a certain kind of intentionality is allowed – and indeed encouraged: it is intentions to do with text, words, documents. Via WIMP systems, a 'user' could (and can) put whatever arguments or content they wish into a document, while the computer, controlled through the interface (and related 'grammars of action' – 'write and read', 'cut and paste', 'save and send', as just remarked), provides an enabling process for those aspirations, supporting all the mundane but necessary computational tasks constitutive of document making, or as Xerox preferred at the time (viz. the 1970s), 'publishing'.

That this was optimized for document work would take some time to fully explain and justify, but suffice it to say that the reason why this mode entailed a pointer rather than, say, allowing a person to touch the screen (something people are now doing with their iPads, tablets and phones), was because, when working with text on a computer screen, it turns out that a pointer is the most efficient way of getting to the right place in that text – between the letter 'a' and the letter 't' say. Fingertips, as an alternative mode of interacting with text on a computer screen, are too big, too cumbersome to identify the exact spot (this is putting it simply, of course). With a pointer, the user and the computer could come to the right place – the specific juncture between some letters. Once a pointer has been identified as the best method of delivering precise location, then it follows that you need something to control it, and after some years of research, a mouse came to be seen as the best method of doing so (alternatives include a digital pen that allowed a user to touch the screen with a tip that would identify on the screen where the pointer on the screen would need to be. It also included many other modes[6]). And then, once these are given (pointer, mouse), other matters follow in turn: that files are represented as icons that can be clicked on with the pointer; that you need a 'window' to interact with a file and to distinguish that file from other ones a person might wish to see or be working on; and, hence, WIMP. Xerox spent vast sums proving that WIMP was better than alternatives (See Smith, 1982).

I will not say any more on this now (but see Harper, 2019; Banks et al., 2020). Nor will I comment on whether this mode of interaction does indeed make for good text, for 'quality documents'. The thing I am wanting to emphasize is that the HCI research that led to WIMP interaction

6 To give an idea of the many alternatives, see Bill Buxton collection: https://www.microsoft.com/buxtoncollection

produced systems that let people ('users') be creative text makers with their computer machines. The manner of their interaction with those computers was shaped in and through the mouse, the pointer, with icons displayed on a screen presented as various windows (including the window acting as the 'desktop'). In important ways this is still the case, though this is changing as we shall discuss shortly with things like text-based interaction (and hence technologies like ChatGPT). Even so, and putting things rather crudely, most people continue to think the desktops and laptops (though less so their iPads and similar) that they buy are for this – their creativity with words, with text, with documents (and of course things in documents including images and graphs and tables and so on). They don't think of the WIMP interface as anything at all, except as a form of interaction that naturally, as it were, leads them to text. Their PCs and laptops (if not so much their phones, but that is another matter) are not for science, nor for data processing, so much as creative making with textualities – the making of stuff to send and keep, and to celebrate as an art of a kind. A person might use their computers for other things, for spreadsheets, for digital photo storage, for internet access (perhaps increasingly so), but this is still an essential part of their appeal: digital words elaborated in documents of various kinds through the mouse, the keyboard, all on windows on the computer screens.

I am using somewhat exaggerated and yet simplifying terms here to convey the relationship between computing and the human. I am saying the PC (and similar devices, laptops, and such) was designed through HCI research that sought to create a future of a particular kind, a document-centric one. This design allows the individual, in the guise of a user, to create a certain type of content. However, this design, the WIMP interface and its underscoring elements and their role is being altered and reshaped as what people do with computers is altering. As this happens, it is leading to some confusions about what is implied about interaction with computers. These changes are not just about whether a machine offers a WIMP interaction modality, as they are more importantly about the status of content, its author and the relationship between that content, its author and the mode of interaction that enables that content production process. WIMP modalities were designed to encourage and articulate the notion that the person who creates content has a certain authorial relationship to that content; that is what being a user means; from the WIMP view, that is its grammar. But that relationship is being altered by what AI does with information about 'content' and about 'authors', despite the fact that the modality of interaction is still, largely WIMP-based. It is to look at how AI is doing this we now turn.

The Individual and Their Content

There are two key dimensions to the changes that are leading us to the current situation where what is taken for granted in our use of computing is altering, or at least becoming less clear, leading to the confusions I am thinking of: content and identity and/or authorship.

The first can be illustrated with the affect search engines have had on content. One might note that search engines were unimagined at the time Xerox devised WIMP systems. Search engines were originally designed to make traversing and finding content over discrete networked systems faster and easier, rather than on the web. To do this, the engineers needed ways of mapping search queries to instances of stored content in those networks. They persuaded their initial users to tag their content, using commonly agreed terms and labels, which could then be used as indexes. When a query was made, the search 'engines' (as they came to be called) searched through these indexes (and not the content) to provide the lists of the data files in the search entry results page. Users were willing to tag their content for these indexes since they hoped that, as a result, their content would be found more often via these search pages.

When these individuals were inside firewalls, that is, inside their corporations or businesses, this willingness could be relied on. With the emergence of the web, a whole new set of motivational questions had to be solved, but they were, and what had been a technology for narrowly confined tasks for work contexts, came to be open to the public at large. As this happened, the emerging search engine companies supplemented their indexes with techniques that measured the traffic between instances of content (which were now 'web pages') to weigh the relevance of some content to a query. That is to say, the behaviours initially made with indexes provided new behaviours that themselves could be further resources for more effective 'mapping' of query and content. What 'users' of search did thereby came to be as important as what was tagged and sought for by the search engines. Traffic patterns helped define content, in effect. This is the essence of PageRank, for example, which led Google to have its dominance in the field.[7] The specific mechanisms and algorithms aside, these developments resulted in the content itself (a web page say) coming to have increasingly important external properties (i.e. things not constitutive of the text or file itself). At first, these were made up by the

7 It is worth noting that when the algorithm was patented it was not labelled AI; it was simply described as a technique. The current fashion for AI has meant that today it is often renamed as AI; the parent company of Google, Alphabet, is rather fond of saying all it does is 'AI'. For them, AI is ABC, so to speak.

index terms and then, as just described, behaviours with that content, such as frequency of access.[8]

Further developments were then inevitable: if frequency could be used to define relevance, the quality of experience afforded once content was found could be measured by such things as lingering times – how long a person remained logged into some page. Following on this, the quality of the experience came to be further elaborated by the 'posting' of comments on content. All this further added materials around content until external data came to get an importance all of its own – and this has come to be called metadata. The importance of this data is not necessarily equal (either less or more) to the content since metadata offers different dimensions and features. But the value of these data, just as with content itself, will vary dependent on how it (or they) can be used – and used they are. Indeed, it is the mix of internal and external data that drives how AI tools work today, not just in search engines but in social networking platforms, and indeed throughout the digital ecology constitutive of interaction on and through the web. We shall come back to say more about this.

If the first set of changes had to do with content, the second had to do with the individual, the author. It can be illustrated with the functioning of social media platforms. This technology developed some time after search and so long after WIMP systems but, nevertheless, this technology was devised with the same premise: that individuals create content. However, these platforms added a new type of metadata: to do with the individual as author. For social media who creates content was (and still is) treated from the outset as important as content. And this in turn allowed a further innovation in metadata: connections can be made between different authors and different instances of their content and this, in turn, can be used as a resource to characterize *both content* and *its author.* Just as Google learnt to use the frequency with which individuals travel between sites on the web as an indicator of content, so social media companies like Facebook have learnt to use movement between different personal pages and content on those pages (i.e. postings) as an indicator of the value of both the content and its author. On this basis, an author comes to be as important as content, and the movement between different authors and different content equal to that in turn. Social media graphs calculate these values.

These graphs are, it hardly needs stating, the engine of value for social media companies, allowing the sale of screen real estate viewed by its

8 This is not meant to be a literature review or a thorough history: this is a sketch designed to see issues pertinent today.

customers (called 'users' of course, though I am wanting us to pause when we deploy that word). In other words, just as the relationship with content has altered (through having metadata about that content), so has the nature of the 'author' altered, too. For while someone may create content, metadata about that content and about them, the author, is combined with data about others who have access to and read that content, as well as when these acts (viewing or not viewing) are undertaken. Even the duration of these acts is documented. All this creates a new phenomenon: the individual not as an individual, as a known person and a point of view expressed in their postings, but as a point on a map of many other individual authors and their behaviours with myriad instances of content.

When these points are seen in terms of trajectories, as movements towards or away from each other, the map becomes a representation of vectors.[9] Who an individual might be is therefore no longer understood as a function of the commands they issue to some computer, as a single person commanding a machine for document creation through the appropriately designed interaction tools (such as a WIMP interface). On the contrary, it is increasingly in terms of where that 'person-as-user' can be said to be and where they are going (or coming from) in terms of vectors given a location on a topography with hundreds, perhaps millions of other individuals. These are also all likewise identified as 'users-as-authors', each with their own relationship with multiple instances of content, all mapped to each other as entities with directional vectors, and all being treated as ontologically the same: as dynamic points in virtual space, mapped in real-time-like junctions on a spider's web. In short, from the moment a click is made on the internet, the action undertaken by an individual is mapped instantly to a vast number of other clicks, the pointer and mouse actions of multiple others (in the here and now and historically, in the hours and days prior) to create a real-time representation of movement between all. One 'click' on the mouse echoes to the sounds of millions of others in a sea of digital life.

These echoes are silent to the individuals making the clicks. These individuals are likely to have no access to the map of their movements, to the social graph that represents them as something other than themselves, nor are they likely to have the tools to make their location in it a resource for their own endeavours. But more importantly, and this is the crucial point at this moment in our investigations, they may no longer be, as it were, 'their own person'. They may think of themselves as a 'user' but may not be aware that

9 Of course, not every individual makes content, but for the purposes of the argument, this is sufficient to convey how the outputs of individuals get processed by AI.

their actions-as-user can mean something other than an expression of them and their intentions; their creations can likewise be independent, articulating meanings beyond the powers of their own hand.[10] They act, but do not easily see what those acts might come to mean. And hence, one should see a link to Wittgenstein and the problem of meaning discussed in the Investigations. If he was suggesting that philosophers sometimes create muddles by losing connection to real-world situations where meaning is anchored, here I am saying that people using computers might find themselves losing meaning as the anchors are being moved about by AI.

So, what is it 'they' mean, these users who are not sure that their status as 'users' means anymore? Is it something other than the individual? As should be clear, these acts represent something new, something beyond or separate to the individuals who commence the process of digital meaning making. On the contrary, what is produced is an amalgam of human reasoning and machinic processing. This composite is a mix of values derived from individual moves in the digital world which are then reconstituted in metadata and reinterpreted by AI and the output of this processing is, in turn, offered back to the individuals as new digital contexts of choice.

The World Today

What is sure is that when individuals start engaging with contemporary computers and applications, they find themselves in a kind of dance. Their inputs to the computer in front of them (or in their hand) are combined with data about themselves as one kind of 'user' with data about myriad other individuals likewise treated and transformed into 'users and their data' that is already stored somewhere else (in networked computer systems most probably on the Web but certainly stored in cloud farms). This results in those individuals being offered certain moves or opportunities related to other 'users' after the first steps of the dance have been made.

Because of this, many within the HCI community are now arguing that there is a need to reconfigure what is meant by the user, and this might entail devising new modes of interaction between people and machines and their

10 The emphasis I am wanting to make is different from the post-user theorists who want to drop any notion of the human as distinct from other entities. As should be clear, despite people feeling as if they are disappearing as a category in these terms, their attitude nevertheless persists in asserting that, despite this, they are somehow still agential, somehow still the user they used to be, a 'self' that creates. Even if they are an individual newly acquainted with technology, the *modus operandi* of use of the primary tools they have encourages this sense of self – hence my claim about the lingering of old premises in current systems.

various kinds of joint endeavours (Grudin, 2017; Shadbolt, 2018). The difficulty here is what this means, of course. If a person seeks to be creative, for example, then what they understand by creativity, what acts of theirs help produce creative content, is now, with AI, being partly shaped by the way the computer systems they use interpret those initial acts of creativity and offers them back. It could be a human starts with what a computer offers, rather than with their own 'initial ideas', and it is the human who offers that content (now revised) back to the computer. Either way, a human and a technology called AI jointly shape what creativity comes to be.

I am deliberately leaving as broad as possible what this creative content might be at this stage, as it doesn't matter at this juncture of our argument. The point is that creativity in this situation could be seen as of a joint kind, and hence different from the kind that WIMP systems were intended to enable. However, just what is meant by 'joint' is unclear. At first reading, this doesn't sound too worrying a problem, though, as long as people readily admit that their creativity is no longer just theirs. But making such an assertion is not as straight forward as it seems – there are all sorts of questions about what joint means, and this is not simply a question of where the creative moment starts – with content from the human or from the machine, say. It also has to do with what is being referred to, how that 'what' is used (i.e. the content of some kind) and how the term 'creative' itself might get used given all this. It is to these matters we now turn.

The nature of content

The issues in question – ones that sound suspiciously like conceptual muddles – show themselves in many ways and are often marked in contemporary, everyday language. People happily use the term 'post', for instance. They are familiar with the distinction between the created artefacts they use as a currency in the sociality of social media from those entities they think of as their own and which they store on their 'private' PCs. To save on one's PC is solitary but to post is to make something public, to move it away from the constraints of one's own digital store.

This particular usage, 'to post', does not mean, though, that the doings evoked by the usage are entirely clear. If something is 'posted', who or what is thereafter responsible for it? Let us confine ourselves to the 'who' for the moment and presuppose that it is a human. Can the original 'poster', the individual creator of the post, remove that file once posted? If another person wants that post to remain, what say does that other have in that removal? Can they stop it? Besides, and leaving removal aside, can files once posted become shared? What does 'shared' mean other than rights to view or to put it in computer parlance, rights to read? Does it also mean rights to copy? Moreover, what about rights to move to somewhere else? (See Odom et al., 2012; Banks et al., 2020.)

The individual poster and the individual viewer (though there may be many of the latter) do not always know how to solve these questions. These concerns are varied; different social media platforms have slightly different approaches to the matters in question, each with their own 'grammar of action' with posts. The way that computer systems interact with these posts is another set of concerns. On some platforms (used here to define a set of technological systems, data stores, AI applications and such as well as the company that operates that social media platform), a post might be identified as relevant for sharing (by the platform), though most platforms do not allow the human creator of the post to know the scale of this internal distribution, or how the platform solves questions of interleaving and sequencing of posts. Calculations about other posts and their competing demands for screen collateral and what is sometimes called 'attention' are also made by platforms and their AI engines.

Leaving aside particulars, what is clear is that people somehow navigate their way around these concerns as best they can. The values of posting and sharing, liking and not liking (the role that particular platforms and their technologies might or might not have in all this notwithstanding), are sufficient to make posting worthwhile – conceptual muddles about ownership and implied rights are part of the deal. Individuals are certainly aware of the number of likes a post gets, and indeed celebrate and announce high numbers (or rue them, in certain cases) and they know, too, that in some part, and on some social media platforms, different types of technology (much of it called AI) have played a part in this.[11] They celebrate even as they might admit a little confusion about just what their relationship to a post might be. They act as users in the age of AI but are slightly confounded by the same AI.

Making actions accountable

Nevertheless, individuals try to make sense of the situation as best they can, at least insofar as it enables them to make next acts. They reason about what the technology offers them – take the example of who might have accessed their postings. Many social media platforms indicate who these people might be. A

11 I am focusing on external data, but with AI tools, another way of creating such metadata is through examining the internal features of a file and noting closeness between files themselves. See (Banks et al., 2020).

person might treat this information as a resource to reason with. They might find, when they look at these lists of names, that some of these people are strangers to them, and they may well treat that as something to investigate. For they can (and often do) navigate to these listed person's digital spaces, their Facebook pages say, with a view to discovering if there are any reasons why these persons have been looking at their posts. They assume that there is (was) a reason for them to do so, that this is some kind of connection.[12] It may be that the link was made by that person as they were (are), 'in fact', someone who was once connected (they went to the same school, say), or because the person doing the searching once liked one of that person's posts. In other words, there is some kind of reciprocity at play, and these are the reasons that explain an activity, and which individuals seek to uncover.

Whether the reasons the humans identify are the same as those AI makes and uses might not matter. For the important lesson is that, whether they are analogous or orthogonal or indeed have no 'relation' to how the AI machineries in the social media platform 'reason', in the dance, sufficient explanation can be found to justify a next act for the individual doing the looking. This act may be more content, a new posting or a new liking. And this results in new connections being highlighted by the AI and then new interpretations around that link to new people. Either way, the dance is dynamic. If earlier I suggested that individuals might not fully understand how their individual actions through an 'act' on a platform are constituted as a point in a vector space, now I am saying that nevertheless, people do intuit ways of acting that depend upon some notion – good, bad, accurate or otherwise – of how AI is construing them as that point in a vector space. Their acts might be out of their hands, but, somehow, they continue to offer up those acts nonetheless assuming as they do so, that their reasons 'matter'.

What is sure is that the controls that seem operational can appear confused, as we have seen. Does this make the meaning of the term 'user' a little curious, implying rights in the manner that a user engages with computer machinery and produces content but where the rights about that content seem confounded by the rights that others have over that same content? And indeed, not just others, but the rights and processes of the system itself – the

12 For further explanation of this notion of making sense or a related concept, reasoning procedures, see (Harper et al., 2019). This explores how 'users' of computer communications tools, such as Skype, strategically use and interpret the use of such technologies so that use is in itself a resource for sense-making. Here too, in the case of AI and social media, the user treats the experience afforded as a resource to understand.

media platform making judgements about connections, content and users that the persons themselves do not fully understand?

Re-imagining the User with ChatGPT

I have just tried to summarize the issues here as I now want to ask whether there is a similar kind of ambiguity in the use of Large Language Models (LLMs) in various systems and the most high profile of these, ChatGPT. This is worth looking at not simply because it is high profile (and certainly more newsworthy than the functioning of a mouse pointer), but because, with our understanding of how WIMP modalities play a role in the mutual construction of the user and the machine, we are likely to be able to see how the interaction modality afforded by ChatGPT might similarly construct what a 'user' is. For, though it may be true that ChatGPT is a long way from the WIMP interface, how it makes the user is not that different. ChatGPT is designed to interact with people in ways that shape the meaning that that interaction has and hence, as part of that, what the user is, just as with WIMP systems. What I would like to suggest is that just as there are increasing muddles with WIMP-based interactions when AI technology starts to interpret actions, so there are muddles with ChatGPT, and, though their precise provenance might be different, they also end up having implications for what a user is understood to be. These manifest when a person uses the technology and interprets its outputs. In particular, the person-as-user becomes unclear as to what role they are having in that output. They know, or rather assume that they, like the AI, are intelligent agents in the interaction, but quite what is entailed for them, that is, the individual, when the interaction unfolds, remains unclear. They assume that there is some kind of joint intelligent enterprise underway but what that enterprise might be is not clearly defined for them. If it is joint, what is theirs, what is the AI's? In the output, what is theirs, what is the AI's? And besides, is that output only the output of them and their interaction with the AI or is something else contributing? Is some of the text in a ChatGPT response taken from somewhere else, for example, and if so, where? Is that content somebody else's?

Before I explore these questions, let me quickly explain some facts about ChatGPT (for more depth, see Harper & Randall, forthcoming). The technology seems quite dazzling and can leave people somewhat speechless when first experienced but is quite straightforward, though its architecture is complex, with various sub-components. Descriptions of it are often obscured by odd language too (Blackwell, 2020). A greater concern is its mode of interaction, which, as we shall see, is a little deceiving.

First of all, the acronym stands for Generative Pre-trained Transformer, the number being the release version. Chat, meanwhile, labels the mode of interaction with the system. We shall say something about Chat shortly. 'Generative' means that the system generates apparently new outputs to input queries, that is, that its outputs are shaped in response to inputs. These outputs are produced by a language model (a very large one, hence another acronym often used in discussions of ChatGPT, the already mentioned LLMs). This model uses 'transformer' techniques to build datum, stored in what are called tensors. Transformer techniques are a procedure whereby the relations between two entities, such as words in a sentence, are enriched by measures of the relations between those words and other words in the same sentence, and hence, in turn, to other larger entities of which a word, a phrase, a sentence and so forth is a part: a paragraph for example. This is then linked or measured with regard to how that fits within a genre of text types – Wikipedia, journal article, blog and so on. All these relations are treated as measured distances, expressed as multi-dimensional geometric possibilities in its 'encoding' (see Vaswani, et al., 2017).

Be that as it may, these geometric relations are refined and iterated through extensive and long-winded processes of ML, in which the outputs are corrected and adjusted so that what are produced eventually come to be sensible outputs. The model that emerges is called a foundation model (Bommasani et al., 2022). Foundation models can be used in different fields and with different output modalities. In ChatGPT, the foundation model is an LLM based on language found on the web, in social media postings, Wikipedia entries and web sites, all crawled and mapped with transformers. This LLM is linked to the chatbot application, which is based on its own 'prompt' engine. The prompt engine will have required its own learning process with attendant feature engineers serving its needs. This engine converts queries into requests for the foundation model, and then converts the outputs of the model into 'chat' – the text with good grammar, apparently responding to the initial query that is offered to the person making the query.

Given this architecture, what ChatGPT produces are not necessarily truth statements or expressions of value. As Bender & Gebru (2021) explain, the eloquence of its outputs can hide this fact. ChatGPT gives an answer to a prompt based on the probability that some content 'x' is the most likely answer to query 'y'. Truth does not matter. ChatGPT has no external link to, say, the web or Wikipedia. Unlike, say, a search engine such as Google, the substance is in the model that the system itself refers to. LLMs cannot distinguish between true and false, relying instead on what the model produces; this is stochastic alone. This applies to ChatGPT whatever the number of its release (currently 4). This does not necessarily matter, as long as the outputs of ChatGPT are understood as created this way. As it happens, the model in ChatGPT is being ongoingly trained through the use of reinforcement learning, which basically means it processes the queries put to it in terms of transformer logic and adds those measures to its tensors. Some foundation models are linked to such things as search engines, offering chatbot-like interfaces, as is the case with Microsoft and its Bing LLM of the current time. These are not the same as ChatGPT.

Now if this is the architecture, we need also to look at the Chatbot function. The kinds of queries or prompts one can give to ChatGPT can be multiparted – interaction is not strictly yes-no queries; hence it is chat-like. Given this, these queries imply similar answers: extensive, multipart. And this is what it does. This is also one of the reasons why ChatGPT seems so startling: the apparent complexity of its outputs, if that is judged by their length. The 'answers' it gives are, like the queries, made up of several parts, with multiple answers if you like, given in a text body, not a simple singular 'this' or 'that' assertion-as-output.

It is important to understand, however, that all parts of this body are selected through interrogating the query (more often called the 'prompt') to define the style, the syntax, the topic and the substance of the output. It is this input that is used to stochastically map to the model, and when this model is interrogated, the further stochastic output that is manifested as text elements in the output as the product.

These products can seem remarkably tailored to a prompt, as if the system shows the kind of good grace of a wonderful co-conversationalist, but as should be clear, what is functioning is an elaborate machine (Bender & Gebru, 2021). Whether one wants to say that way of working is intelligent is, it hardly needs saying, contentious, as the word is being used in two ways: as at once a noun (the technology is called AI), and as an adjective (the technology acts intelligently). We could say more about this distinction, though our interest will be in what those who use ChatGPT think on the matter, not what one might say philosophically.

Users, Use and ChatGPT

Getting back to the main thread, this very short description is hardly sufficient to explain the full functioning of ChatGPT, LLMs inside the system, the role of feature engineers in making the system learn appropriately and so on. But it will do for our purposes which are primarily to do with the pragmatics of interaction. What I am wanting to draw attention to is how the mode of interaction between the person and ChatGPT creates a certain kind of user. This modality is misleading in certain ways and indeed, I suggest, confusing.

It is not confusing in what it offers as outputs, but in the ways that output is presented and thereby what that output implies – how it is to be interpreted, made account of and used, and thus how it shapes who or what the user is. What I want to suggest is that 'user' is in large part defined by what is done with that output. They are made into a particular kind of user by the grammar of action with that output.

The issues can be highlighted if we consider this: when someone enters text into ChatGPT, they are given a response that is also text, but this text is presented in the first person. Moreover, the answer is displayed as if someone is typing it out, the first sentence to begin, then pauses and typing flourishes as if thoughts are emerging, until a full text is presented and the application (or technology) concludes with its last clause. That there is a conclusion gives a further impression that all has been said about the matter – that a query has been answered. In these ways, ChatGPT gives the impression it is like the human, an agent of sorts acting in and through an interface. It responds as a user, it acts like a user, it finishes with the elan of an author.

But is it a user like the person who presented the query in the first place? As we say, it is a machine (or engine, if you prefer) providing text outputs to a text query but it is presenting itself as if it is a person in the manner of its creation (in the first person) and in implying an authorship (through seeming to type its response), and in the way it concludes – with a conclusion, a final bullet point, as if to say 'this is all you need to know'.

Whatever the reason why ChatGPT has been designed this way (and one of the reasons may well be that the designers want to underline the intelligence they think their technology affords by making it perform anthropomorphically), we might ask if it is the case that the output of the prompt could be presented differently. If one considers what the alternatives might be, then we might be able to see more clearly what the consequences are of how it has been designed. These alternatives might help us understand what the grammar of action of using ChatGPT currently implies; what it means.

For example, a response could be produced instantly, and not in a stream of consciousness manner, as if someone were typing. After all, the outputs from ChatGPT are produced at a speed far greater than a human can comprehend and so could its text output – it could appear all at once, as if an image. Second, the text could also state where the prompter could find more information, without the intermediation of the system. This might be difficult to do at the current time but could be achieved with a different architecture (as mentioned previously with regard to Bing). Third, the system could also state how it works, offering a reminder that the system uses 'distance' to define outputs, not truth; it does not check facts.

If ChatGPT were to respond in these ways, then an individual might think differently about what they are interacting with and what they do with the outputs. They would recognize the limits of the technology, though hopefully still appreciate what it can do – offering a kind of improvised Wikipedia entry for them. But it will also suggest to them that they need to be alert too, and perhaps might need to do more themselves – some web searching say, more reading. However, at the current time, the individual may be misled by how ChatGPT produces outcomes so that none of these actions follow – they will take their output as if it were a trusted expert they are talking to. They become receivers of higher knowledge, if you like, and so quite unlike the creative users shaped by WIMP interfaces.

This self-definition of the kind of user they are should be seen as all the more odd when we consider how much of the individual's input in the prompt is used to design that output. As mentioned, prompts massively shape outputs: determining the likely terms or vocabulary, the rhetorical structure of the output, its focus and even length. In other words, the individual-as-user is not passively waiting to receive; they are shaping what is giving them. They are a maker with the technology. That this is so could be made clear in a ChatGPT response. The key elements of the machine's output designed through interrogation of the prompt's structure could be highlighted in something like a preamble, presented as an abstract at the top of the output.

The important point I am making is that in crucial parts of ChatGPT outputs are created by the individual-as-user, but at the current time this is not made clear in the answer itself. When all these possibilities are added up, and the ways that ChatGPT works made clear, what becomes obvious is that a person using the technology is somewhat misled by that same technology; they might think of themselves as being given knowledge but that is not what happens. They co-design that knowledge; moreover, that knowledge is of a certain order, provisional, likelihood based; it is created by the machine, but without the machine explaining its source or its methods. Worse, the outputs give the impression it is authored. But it is not authored, it is machined.

It is important to add that I do not think there is anything wrong with unauthored, machined text. Newspapers are read without reference to an author, except for special, opinionated editorials; Wikipedia isn't either. When Barthes wrote about the death of the author in the 1960s, he wasn't trying to remind us that one doesn't need an author for all types of text (or content production, his examples coming from cinema). He was saying, instead, that the searching for an author can obscure what is in a text. He did not mean to get rid of the author so much as get us over an obsession with authorship. Here I am wanting to make a slightly different claim, namely, that the use of the first person in ChatGPT suggests an author when none is needed (see

Potts, 2022). In implying authorship, ChatGPT also guides how people give those outputs a status they ought not to have and in the process it alters the status they give themselves. Thus, the reshaping of the user in the age of AI. It is turning out that with ChatGPT the dance is less of a dance, more of a fraud (see also Blackwell, 2020).

Conclusion

I claimed at the outset that the 'user' in the age of AI is a combination of individual human acts and AI interpretations of those acts, which are themselves calculative of next acts (as well as summative of prior ones) and that these acts create new options, new turns in endless iteration – first this, then this, then that. I hope to have shown that the interaction in question is not undertaken in such a fashion that each of those entities that contribute to it does so on continuously equal terms, nor indeed do these entities always know what the other is about.

One particular concern I have noted is that one of the key modes of HCI, WIMP, emphasizes the salience and autonomy of the human side, while the computational processing going on inside the most recent forms of computer systems enabled by the internet and AI transform what are individualized acts of input into mass user acts, without that being made 'visible' to the humans in question. An individual uses a pointer to demarcate some content with a technology where the mode of use suggests that that pointing is uniquely their own, but the pointing is aggregated immediately into something else, something that is social in a computational sense, insofar as it is understood in terms of relations. How the technology does this, and what it enables, is not always made clear to individuals. We saw in the case of ChatGPT that the text-based interaction has its own features, and that the outputs of that interaction are egregious in what they imply about the relation between the human and the machine.

Yet this does not need to be – this muddling about actions, interpretations, about who or what a user is. As we have just seen with some suggested and easily engineerable changes in the design of interaction with ChatGPT. Changes could be made in how people interact on social media platforms too, though space precludes discussion of this here (see Harper, 2019 and Forthcoming). In other words, how different AIs work could be made into affordances of various kinds, indicators and possibilities that the individual in the interactional context could work with. Insofar as this is possible, then AI might be able to act differently, too, being more alert, if one can put it that way, to the variation in human intentions made possible in newly created digital acts in and through interfaces. If this is done well, the result could be something beyond either AI or human action, a mix of both, as I suggested at the outset. But what we have seen in this chapter is that, unfortunately, though we see human–AI interaction widely, we also see that in too many instances it lacks the grace one would hope for.

To go forward, people and AI require different assumptions. Central to this is the notion that they jointly make the user, the agent in the digital world though it turns out that what is perceived as the consequences of the intelligence on either side might be different. Indeed, it might be that these very terms, to think, to imagine, to act, are all ill-suited to a situation where new words are required to label things that combine the human and the artificial, the intentions of an individual as a user with the processing powers and techniques of tools like ChatGPT.

Lexical change notwithstanding, the point is that the interaction they both engage in will in turn shape them, or at least alter what 'they' do at any moment in time. What is sure is that, over time, the consequences of this might be interesting. If Churchill said of buildings that people make them in their image and then, they, in turn, shape those same people, so I am saying that the doings that AI and people create together might end up shaping them too, and this will, of course, be expressed in the language used to constitute and comprehend these doings. The human contributing to the 'user' of the future might offer everything from passive contribution to fully engaged involvement, from lurking to leading, from playful compliance to isolating and contrarian behaviours, but always potential moves in a dance (rather than a fraud) where the next step might be different from the one before. And this is because their moves are reacted to it by AI and all its varieties; for it is in the dance too.

For the human-technological society that results to be healthy, to ensure that this moving interaction is undertaken in desirable ways, will require, I believe, new interfaces, new training for human 'users' and AI tools (especially ML), as well as new concepts for what they might do together, and then following on from that, new modes of governance and much else beside. We need, all of us, engineers and those who engage with digital tools as well as philosophers trying to solve problems of language and meaning, to develop a sense that the 'digital lives' these tools enable are the product of shared and mutually entwined intelligences – each nudging the other in an endless cycle of appropriate and desirable acts, a grammar for the production of a better future. Wittgenstein would be pleased.

References

Agre, P. (2008). *Computation and Human Experience.* Cambridge: Cambridge University Press.

Banks, R., Gosset, P., Harper, R., Lindley, S. & Smyth, G. (2020). 'Breaching the PC Data Store: What do Graphs Tells us About Files?' In A. Chamberlain (Ed.), *Research in the Wild: HCI and Ethnomethodology* (pp. 73–92). London: Springer.

Blackwell, A. F. (2020). 'Objective Functions: (In) Humanity and Inequity in Artificial Intelligence'. *HAQ: Journal of Ethnographic Theory*, 9 (1): 137–146.

Bender, E. M. & Gebru, T. (2021). 'On the Dangers of Stochastic Parrots: Can Language Models be too big?' In *FAccT '21:* Proceedings of the 2021 ACM Conference on Fairness, Accountability, and Transparency, 610–623. Canada: ACM. ISBN 978-1-4503-8309-7/21/03, https://doi.org/10.1145/3442188.3445922

Bommasani, R. et al. (2022). 'On the Opportunities and Risks of Foundation Models'. Centre for Research on Human-Centred AI. Stanford: Stanford University. https://arxiv.org/pdf/2108.07258.pdf

Card, S., Moran, T. & Newell, A. (1983). *The Psychology of Human Computer Interaction.* Hillsdale, New Jersey: Lawrence Erlbaum.

Fischer, E. (2018). 'Wittgensteinian "Therapy", Experimental Philosophy, and Metaphilosophical Naturalism'. In K. Cahill and T. Raleigh (Eds.), *Wittgenstein and Naturalism.* New York: Routledge.

Grudin, J. (2017). *From Tool to Partner: The Evolution of Human-Computer Interaction.* New York: Morgan Claypool.

Harper, R. (2019). 'The Role of HCI in the Age of AI'. *International Journal of Human-Computer Interaction*, 35 (3): 1331–1344.

Harper, R. (Forthcoming). *The Shape of Thought: Reasoning in the Age of AI.* Montreal: McGill Press.

Harper, R., Licoppe, C. & Watson, D. (2019). *Skyping the Family.* London: Benjamins.

Harper, R. & Randall, D. 2024. Machine Learning and the Work of the User: An introduction', Special Issue of the *Journal Computer Supported Cooperative Work (CSCW)*, Springer. https://doi.org/10.1007/s10606-023-09483-6

Odom, W., Banks, R., Sellen, A., Harper, R. & Kirk, D. (2012). 'Lost in Translation: Understanding Possessions of Digital Things in the Cloud'. In *Conference on Computer Human Interaction (CHI).* Austin: ACM.

Potts, J. (2022). *The Near-death of the Author.* Toronto: Toronto University Press.

Russell, S. (2019). *Human Compatible: AI and the Problem of Control.* London: Penguin.

Russell, S. & Norvig, P. (2017). *Artificial Intelligence: A Modern Approach.* Boston: Pearson.

Sellen, A. & Harper, R. (2002). *The Myth of the Paperless Office.* Cambridge: MIT.

Shadbolt, N. & Hampson, R. (2018). *The Digital Ape.* London: Scribe Publications.

Smith, D. C. (1982). 'The Star Interface: An Overview'. In *Proceedings of the i982 National Computer Conference (AFIPS)*, 515–52. ACM Press.

Vaswani, A., Shazeer, N., Parmar, N., Uszkoreit, J., Jones, L., Gomez, A.N., Kaiser, L. & Polosukhin, I. (2017). 'Attention is All You Need'. In *Advances in Neural Information Processing Systems, 31st Conference on Neural Information Processing Systems (NIPS 2017)*, 6000–6010. Long Beach.

Winch, P. (1958). *The Idea of a Social Science and Its Relation to Philosophy* (reprinted 2007), London: Routledge.

Wittgenstein, L. (1953). *Philosophical Investigations.* Translated by G.E.M Anscombe. London: Macmillan.

Chapter 8

LEGAL AND COMPUTER RULES: AN OVERVIEW INSPIRED BY WITTGENSTEIN'S REMARKS

Gianmarco Gori

The Concept of Rules between Law and AI

The concept of rules is a family resemblance concept. An initial survey of how such a concept is used across various disciplines reveals 'a complicated network of similarities overlapping and criss-crossing' (Wittgenstein 2009: PI § 66–67). A particularly relevant set of such family resemblance relations characterizes the field of Law and that of Artificial Intelligence, where the concept of rules plays a foundational role. This chapter will look at how the existence of family resemblance relations pertaining to the concept of rules has built a bridge between those respective fields of Law and AI and how this has laid the groundwork for the intersection between legal rules on the one hand and computer rules on the other.

It is significant that the initial research in the domain of AI and Law was set in motion by the consideration that '[t]here is more than a superficial resemblance between laws and computer programs' (Niblett 1980, 8). Undoubtedly, the material conditions for the exploration of such a resemblance have been set by the increasing availability of ever more sophisticated computational machines. Yet, the emergence of the conditions of intelligibility for a crossing of the concepts of legal rules and computer rules should be understood as part of a larger, significant historical development of the general concept of rules. As demonstrated by historian Lorraine Daston, since the beginning of the modern age, the concept of 'rules-as-algorithms' has progressively gained ground (Daston 2022). The combination of such an algorithmic understanding of rules and the availability of more powerful computational machines made it possible to overcome the perception of the computer as a mere 'mechanized storehouse' (Kelso 1946) to stock and retrieve legal texts. Propelled by the developments in AI, the challenge became that of harnessing 'the cognitive potential of computers for legal reasoning' (Buchanan and Headrick 1970, 43). Thus began the efforts aimed at developing formal languages and programs to represent, in the form of computer rules, 'not just the texts of the law, but the meaning of such text' (Sergot 1991), that is, 'the legal norms which they contain' (Niblett 1980).

Since then, the field of AI and Law has gone through 'summers' and 'winters'. The successes, obstacles and setbacks that have succeeded one another in half a century of research are testimony to the existence of a complex entanglement between the concepts of legal and computer rules. The present work offers an overview of the relations between these concepts. By drawing on Wittgenstein's remarks, I show that conceptual puzzles and practical difficulties arise when the similarities and differences between legal and computer rules are assessed based on a confusing picture of the concept of rules. I argue that a productive combination of AI and Law requires the appreciation of the distinctions between different kinds of rules, that is, between legal rules and calculi, on the one hand, and between normative rules and causal or statistical laws, on the other. Reformulating Wittgenstein's remark (Wittgenstein 1983: RFM 201), what I aim to show is that the relationship between legal and computer rules is such that legal rules are always measures, not things measured. As I illustrate in the following sections, no matter the degree of sophistication of computer rules or the performance achieved in their applications, the normative assessment of computer rules requires an unavoidable reversion to the criteria and techniques that belong to legal practice. In this sense, I discuss how Wittgenstein's remarks on the internal relations between rules, regularity, sameness and correctness can help clarify the relations between legal and computer rules.

Before moving forward, I need to put forth some caveats. Firstly, the differences that make a difference for the purposes of my overview of the concept of rules do not necessarily overlap with those that are more commonly taken as relevant in both law and AI. Not explicitly addressing these distinctions characteristic of each discipline is not meant to deny the significance of such distinctions within their specific context of reference. However, the present overview attends to the concept of rules at a level of abstraction different from that on which such distinctions are made. For instance, in the legal context, rules are often contrasted with other forms of norms such as principles, standards and policies (e.g. Dworkin 1978; Hart 2012). In the following sections, for the present purposes, I adopt an understanding of rules that encompasses all such forms of norms. Such a generalization is justified by the fact that the aspect of rules that I am concerned with here is their use as normative standards to evaluate, criticize, justify, and so on, behaviour in terms of correctness and incorrectness.

On the side of AI, the concept of rules is related to multiple other concepts. On a general level, algorithms, programming languages, computer programs, and the like, are all linked to the concept of rules. Moreover, in the AI and Law literature, further distinctions are drawn with reference to, for example, rule-based and case-based models, formal argumentation frameworks, and so on (cf., e.g. Sergot 1991; Prakken and Sartor 2015). Here too, the comparison that I seek to draw out requires a more general and overarching concept of computer rule, that is, the concept of computer rules as formal calculi. At the same time, however, I will structure the arguments of the following sections in accordance with a more commonly drawn distinction, that is, the distinction between programmed rules, that is, computer rules that have been coded by a programmer, and learnt rules, that is, computer rules that have been programmed by running learning algorithms on data. With respect to learnt rules, my analysis requires a further conceptual stretch. I will not engage in a discussion of important categorizations within the field of Machine Learning (hereafter, ML), for example, the distinction between ML and Deep Learning or that between unsupervised, supervised, reinforced, and so on, learning. Additionally, contrary to the common practice in ML, I also discuss ML models in terms of rules. I justify my use of this concept based on the consideration that, like a programmed rule, a trained ML model is an algorithm that determines an output depending on the input it is applied to. It is in the light of these adopted distinctions that I frame my overview of the similarities and differences between computer – programmed and learnt – rules and legal rules. In the next section, the relation between legal and programmed rules under the Good Old Fashioned AI and Law (GOFAIL) approach will be discussed. This includes the clarification of how the nature of formal calculus of programming languages and computer programs affects what counts as representing legal rules as computer rules. On this basis, I argue that the difference between legal and computer rules is a difference in kind. In this light, I discuss how 'what counts as a correct rule application' is determined in the context of a computer rule and in that of a legal rule, respectively.

In Section 'Legal Rules and Learnt Rules', I discuss learnt rules. I single out three approaches that exemplify different ways of understanding the relationship between ML models and legal rules. I claim that the first approach amounts to experimenting, given that the way in which ML models are used does not licence any normative inference. I then show how the second approach makes use of ML models as rules to assess normative behaviour. To do so, I outline the differences between empirical and normative regularities. Lastly, I address a third approach that envisions ML as a tool to discover and formalize the 'real' and 'hidden' legal rules. I show how the picture of legal rules underlying such an approach leads to unsolvable aporias.

Legal Rules and Programmed Rules: 'All Steps Must Have Already Been Taken'

Since its inception, the GOFAIL community has acknowledged how the 'rigorous demands of computer programming languages' (Buchanan and Headrick 1970, 46) hindered the representation of legal rules as computer rules. Programmers must cope with 'the gap between what [lawyers] want to say and what the computer language lets them say' (Ivi). In this context, the high demands of detail and precision imposed by computer code form a major obstacle to achieving the task at hand (Rissland 1990, 1957). Such rigorous demands have been accounted for as a problem of knowledge representation (McCarty 1990, 196). Crucially, this problem concerns not only the question of how to express legal rules in computational form, but also the question of 'what needs to be expressed' in computational form in order to appropriately represent a legal rule.

Still today, this challenge is addressed by devising ever richer and more expressive programming languages. In parallel, there is a visible trend in AI and Law that goes in the direction of an enlargement – and deepening – of the knowledge base used to represent legal rules. While most of the first GOFAIL projects aimed at representing rule formulations contained in statutes or regulations, the projects of the late 1980s were devoted to the development of deep domain models and expanded the focus to also include rules as expressed in case law (Rissland 1990, 1957; Bench-Capon et al. 2012, 83).

As the GOFAIL pioneer Philip Leith illustrates, one of the first problems that programmers encounter is 'where to find' the legal rules they seek to express as computer rules (Leith 1988, 106 ff). The formulations of rules contained in statutory law – and the same goes for other legal sources – do not seem to provide all the information essential for writing computer rules. Therefore, the attempt to express legal rules as computer rules seems to shipwreck in the 'gulf' between the formulations in which legal rules are expressed and what counts as their application (cf. Wittgenstein 2009: PI § 431).

This problem needs to be understood as an emanation of the notion that, as signs are not meanings, rules are not their formulations (Baker and Hacker 1984, 2014; Baker 2003, 481; Waismann 1965, 129 ff). Failure to appreciate these differences raises the risk of being trapped in questions such as 'This is not the rule, nor is that – what then is the rule?' (cf., Baker 2003, 481). This, as in philosophy so in AI and Law, opens the door to the proliferation of intermediaries to be introduced between rule formulations and rule application.

In their quest for a legal rule to be expressed into code, programmers find themselves having to, as it were, reverse engineer a technique that all aspiring jurists must learn and master, that is, distinguishing legal texts and legal norms. Nevertheless, no matter the number of interpretations-reformulations -explanations (i.e. *Deutung*, *Ausdruk der Regel*, *Erklärung*, cf., Wittgenstein 2009: PI §§ 87–88, 198, 201, 1981:Z § 229) of rules inscribed in legal texts or offered by domain experts, no expression of a legal rule seems to be the ultimate one, that is, the one that exhaustively determines what counts as its application in every circumstance.

These difficulties led Leith to an interesting stance: '[i]t is, ironically, the very rule-based nature of computer programs which disproves the rule-based nature of law' (Leith 1988, 109). Such a provocative statement should not be read as denying the intelligibility of the concept of legal rules altogether (cf. Leith 1986). However, the message that one can draw is that there exists a significant difference in what we mean by 'rule-based' when we talk of law or computers, respectively. That difference reflects the different nature of legal and computer rules. Computer rules are calculi and, as such, they are rules characterized by strict requirements of completeness, determinateness and fixity. At the same time, there is no one-to-one relation between rules and calculi, that is, calculi are rules, but not all rules are calculi (cf. Wittgenstein 2009: PI §§ 81ff; Id. 1958: BB, 25 ff). This means, ultimately, that all that the rule-based nature of computer programs can disprove is that legal rules are calculi.

The fact that legal rules are not calculi has multiple implications. Firstly, programming is not a 'translation' of legal rules into computer rules, but rather an attempt to play the same game by using a different technique (Shanker 1987, 90, 101; 1998, 28). Such an attempt is more likely to succeed the more legal rules are *akin to* calculi, as in the case of certain provisions in commercial and corporate matters (McCarty 1980), or in tax law. However, also these cases should not fool us into presuming the straightforwardness of such an exercise, in that even here programming only ever approximates a translation between autonomous calculi. Secondly, as legal rules are not calculi, the programming of computer rules does not simply consist of giving legal rules a more precise formulation. The result of programming is a set of computer rules that are not the legal rules they aim to represent. Again, rules are not their formulations. Computer rules are a 'formal analogue' aimed to give the same result as legal rules (cf. Shanker 1987, 90, 101; 1998, 28).

The repercussions of the essential difference between computer rules – qua calculi – and legal rules – qua non calculi – can be appreciated by looking more closely at what is involved in programming. In expressing a legal rule in computer code, the programmer is, at once, establishing a computer rule and performing a candidate application of the legal rule. In turning a legal rule into its formal analogue, the programmer is required to fix the bedrock upon which the computer rule rests (cf. Wittgenstein 2009: PI § 217; Id. 1981: Z § 301) in the grammar of calculus. Because of this, there is a specific way in which the remark that in the 'symbolical expression' (Wittgenstein 2009: PI § 221) 'all steps are already taken' (Ivi, §§ 188–90, 219) finds application in the case of computer rules. That is, if the programmer wants to ensure that the result of the application of the computer rule overlaps with the correct application of the legal rule, she has to devise a computer rule that budgets for all possible circumstances. This is not just a Herculean task, but a Sisyphean commitment. This depends on the fact that the meaning of 'complete', 'determinate', 'fixed' and, ultimately, 'correct' with respect to legal rules does not map onto what the same terms mean in reference to the rules of a calculus. As said above, irrespective of the effort put into formulating, reformulating, interpreting and explaining legal rules more precisely (e.g. in statutes, legal decisions, opinions), the *possibility* that doubt arises as to what counts as the correct application of a legal rule cannot be removed. The fact that the meaning of a rule *can* be doubted, however, does not make it less of a rule. Rules can be 'in order' (Wittgenstein 2009: PI §§ 87, 98) even though they might not appear 'ready' for every possible application (Ivi, § 80). What is essential for rules to not lose their normative force is that, when *actual* doubts arise, the practice of following such rules has in place the necessary techniques and institutions to solve such doubts 'as we go along' (cf., Baker and Hacker 2009, 185). Not only does the existence of doubt not negate the – specific – determinate character of legal rules, it actually confirms it: the very possibility of raising doubts hinges upon certainty (Wittgenstein 1975: OC § 115). Hesitation or disagreement about the meaning of a legal rule presupposes that a set of related normative determinations are taken 'as a matter of course' (Wittgenstein 2009: PI § 238). The same rule that is a matter of doubt can be followed 'blindly' (Ivi, § 219) or 'mechanically' (Id., 1983: RFM 422) and serve as the hinge that supports the contestation of a different rule.

The solving of doubts entrenches what counts as a correct application of the rule (cf. Goodman 1983), making such a rule more determinate. Yet, crucially, a more determinate legal rule is not an approximation of the form of determinacy that characterizes computer rules (cf. Wittgenstein 1981: Z § 440). As said above, it might seem that, the more a legal concept is well defined, the more it lends itself to be expressed as a computer rule. This appears intuitively true. After all, we do buy goods at vending machines. However, this impression can misleadingly conceal that the meaning of well-defined also applies differently with respect to legal and computer rules. This is shown by the fact that some of the legal rules that are more recalcitrant to formalization are also those that are more easily understood and followed in practice. Ensuring the accord between the result of the application of legal and computer rules is particularly hard whenever the practice of applying legal rules is characterized, as it were, by little interpretation and immediate understanding (cf. Wittgenstein 2009: PI §§ 198, 202). Amongst these cases are, for instance, those in which legal rule formulations (interpretations, explanations) are given by example (cf. Id. 2009: PI §§ 208 ff). It is easy to see how the way in which rule followers manifest their understanding of how to 'go on like this', or how deviating behaviour is corrected (e.g. 'not like that, don't you see'), might be either over- or under-determined for the purposes of programming a computer rule (cf. Rissland 1990, 1957). The attempts to solve the problems posed by these forms of normative behaviour through the development of ever deeper domain models risk paralleling the quest for a 'deeper explanation' that reaches beyond all examples (Wittgenstein 2009: PI § 209, 1983: RFM 420; cf. also Bench-Capon et al. 2012, 83).

To better clarify the implications of the fact that in programmed rules 'all steps must have been already taken', it is necessary to look at how the relation of normative determination between legal rules and what counts as their application is established. Such a relation is forged in action, through the use of rules in the context of the normative activities that constitute a practice (Baker and Hacker 2014, 52). The concept of normative practice implies a multiplicity of interlocking actions that unfold in time (Wittgenstein 2009: PI § 199), as well as a technique for recognizing such actions as a uniform regularity (cf. ex multis, Baker and Hacker 2014). Put differently, a normative practice constitutes continuity in flux. In the legal context, this idea is well expressed by the renowned metaphor used by the seventeenth-century common lawyer Hale to justify why the law of England of his century should be considered to be the same law as 600 years before: for Hale, the common law is 'as the Argonauts Ship, which was the same when it returned home, as it was when it went out, tho' in that long Voyage it had successive Amendments, and scarce came back with any of its former Materials' (Postema 2017, 142). The very practice of applying legal rules constitutes what counts as continuity, identity and regularity 'as we go along' (Wittgenstein 2009: PI § 83; cf. Winch 2008, 55). This has major implications for understanding the specific way in which legal rules are definite, determined and fixed. The question of whether a rule has changed or has remained the same – and therefore of what counts as its correct application – cannot be meaningfully answered in isolation. It must always be seen in the light of the criteria of identity that are constituted and enforced by the practice itself, for example, in the activities of explanation, justification and correction, in which the word 'same' interweaves with the uses of other words (Wittgenstein 1983: RFM 415). This makes it possible that what counts as the correct application of a rule changes and yet that following it still counts as 'doing always the same'. In this sense, applying a rule can be '[s]ometimes a move in an existing game, sometimes the establishment of what counts as the rule of the game, a paradigm for future moves' (Wittgenstein 1981: Z § 294). Crucially, the bedrock on which the practice of applying legal rules ultimately rests is, as it were, as fixed as the shared practical understanding (i.e. *Verständigung*, cf. Wittgenstein 2009: PI §§ 143, 242) that unfolds in the interactions between rule followers.

One of the consequences of the above considerations is that nothing pertaining to the computer rules-calculi can guarantee the coincidence between what counts as correct according to the computer rules and what counts as correct according to the legal rule. The formal analogue of the legal rule cannot take over the role that the legal rule only can play in fixing what counts as correct. We don't say that 2+2=4 is correct because that is what the calculating machine outputs. We say that what the calculating machine outputs is correct because 2+2=4. While 'computer software, after all, makes the machine produce just this answer', as Baker and Hacker point out, 'what makes this answer the right answer?' (2014, 196). This aspect can be illustrated with a brief reference to formal methods of verification. These are methods employed in computer science to check whether a program correctly implements its formal specification, that is, whether the program has bugs. Put otherwise, formal methods are used to verify whether the computer rule that determines a certain output, in fact, counts as a correct application of the computer rule as it is programmed. In this way, such verification methods help prevent avoidable implementation errors. However, the formal proof that a program correctly implements its formal specifications does not ensure that said implementation is, in turn, a correct implementation of the legal rule supposedly represented in the programmed rule. The two assessments are fully independent of each other. For the same reasons that also a broken clock is right twice a day, the same output that signals the presence of a bug with respect to the computer rules might count as a correct application of the legal rule.

Legal rules, or rather, the practice of applying legal rules, is what measures, and not what is measured. This applies irrespective of programmers' exact understanding of what *hic et nunc* counts as the correct application of a legal rule and independently from programmers' ability to develop increasingly expressive formal languages and bug-free programs. The achievement of an overlap between computer and legal rules is essentially temporary and contextually dependent; it is inextricably tied to the carving out of 'islands of uniformity, stability, and predictability' (Daston 2022, 273).

Legal Rules and Learnt Rules

This section is dedicated to an overview of the research in the field of ML and Law. With no pretence of exhaustiveness, I outline three approaches that I deem representative of the way in which the relation between ML models and legal rules is commonly articulated in this domain. As I will show, each approach exemplifies a different understanding of the normative value of the regularities detected and formalized by ML models.

I first analyse an approach in which, with respect to legal rules, the use of ML is like *experimenting*, that is, it does not licence any normative inference. I then address a second approach that explores how ML models can be used to perform a normative assessment of legal decision-making. Lastly, I examine a third position according to which ML models can be used to fill the gaps in the law by learning and formalizing a more precise formulation of the legal rules applied in legal practice.

ML as experimenting: Normative and empirical predictions

A first, and prevalent, approach in ML and Law research does not thoroughly address the relationship between legal rules and ML models. Research is predominantly conducted from a perspective that is almost wholly internal to ML, without much connection to law, from both a theoretical and a practical perspective (cf. Medvedeva et al. 2023). The scholarship that takes this approach focuses on the relevant ML techniques and their respective performances in classification and prediction tasks. Compared to the attention dedicated to improvements in performance, the references to law are often cursory and insubstantial. In this context, it is often considered sufficient to note that the performance of the model is an indication of reliability and that reliable predictive tools have practical utility for legal practitioners (cf. Katz 2013). At times, researchers have provided a more articulated, albeit still rather roughly sketched, indication of the potential use cases of ML models in law (e.g. Aletras et al. 2016, 3; Chalkidis et al. 2019). Researchers often left open the question of whether successful performance implicitly signals a correlation between ML models and legal rules is often left open and the possible normative implications of such correlation are not further explored. Under this approach, the use of predictive models can be seen as a ML-based version of the so-called badman perspective (Holmes 1897), that is, a perspective that is interested only in the outcome of legal decisions, and not in whether such outcome is correct, or in the justifications given in support of it. Put otherwise, the development and use of ML models are characterized by cognitive expectations. A model can correctly predict the outcome of a legal decision. However, such a model does not offer any ground for the discernment of whether such an outcome is correct or incorrect from the perspective of the legal rule that governs the predicted decision. With respect to legal rules, the training and deployment of ML models are therefore like *experimenting* (cf. Wittgenstein 1983: RFM 258). This can be illustrated by examining the concept of legal prediction and by drawing a distinction between empirical and normative predictions, respectively. The concept of prediction and that of rule are strictly related. If one pictures a rule as a series, both empirical and normative predictions consist in the identification of the next step of the series. However, the nature of the rule employed significantly affects what the prediction (qua result) and predicting (qua extension of the rule) amounts to. The techniques necessary to perform a prediction, as well as the training needed to master such techniques, change significantly depending on the rule that is employed (cf. Wittgenstein 2009: PI § 630). Depending on the technique employed, a different relation is established between the rule and the result of its application. When a prediction of a court decision is performed through the application of a ML model, the finding of a divergence between the outcome generated by the model and the decision taken by the court does not licence any normative inference. The only thing the divergence signals is the occurrence of a mistake in relation to either the model itself or its application. For example, the outcome could be explained in terms of the inaccuracy of the model, for example, a lack of generalization, the missing of potentially relevant features, or as resulting from a malfunction of the physical computing machine irrespective of whether the prediction is verified or falsified, the rule of which it is an application, that is, the ML model, offers no normative hold (cf. Wittgenstein 1983: RFM 425). Whatever the result, the prediction cannot be used to either criticize as incorrect – or justify as correct – the decision of the court.

A very different expectation is involved when a legal decision is predicted based on a legal rule. Here, the curiosity about the outcome is not just about what the decision *will be*, but what the decision *ought to be* (Wittgenstein 1983: RFM194–95). Predicting the application of a legal rule is to apply the legal rule. A prediction of the kind 'if the court will act in accordance with the legal rule, the decision will be the following [...]' is just a different way of expressing what decision counts as the correct application of the legal rule: as Wittgenstein put it, in these case '[t]he allusion to the future and to yourself is mere clothing' (Wittgenstein 1983: RFM 318; cf. also Winch 2008, 87). The training necessary to perform a normative legal prediction correctly requires learning to understand the internal relation between the rule and what counts as a result of its application. Consequently, a mismatch between the prediction and the actual legal decision signals an incorrect application of the rule by either the predictor or the court. The rule that has been used as the ground on which to make the prediction simultaneously forms the basis on which it is possible to evaluate and correct either the other party's or one's own rule application.

None of the above considerations is meant to deny the merit of the research on empirical legal predictions, nor to deny its utility as a tool to navigate the legal environment. With or without resorting to ML models and quantitative methods, both jurists and laypeople interact with and within the legal system by making predictions based on all sorts of rule-like theories formulated on the basis of their experience. At the same time, the possibility must be acknowledged that predictions of the outcomes of legal decisions performed with ML models can be more accurate than the predictions performed – either normatively or experimentally – by legal scholars and practising lawyers (cf. Katz et al. 2017). However, what I want to stress is that empirical and normative predictions belong to two different and altogether separate games, each played according to its own rules. What results from the application of one set of rules, does not count as a move in the other game.

ML models to evaluate and explain behaviour

A second ML and Law approach is characterized by the articulation of a tighter relationship between legal rules and ML models. Under this approach, ML models are used as measuring tools to perform a normative assessment of legal decision-making, for example, 'to detect when judges are more likely to allow extralegal biases to influence their decision making' (Chen 2019). ML models are trained on data related to legal cases. Such data can range from, for example, the text of legal decisions to features related to the parties of the case or the judges and so on. The model resulting from the training on such data is a rule that expresses the relation between the selected features and the outcome of the case. The rule expressed by the ML model is different from the legal rule that is purported to determine and justify legal decision-making. If, that notwithstanding, the rule formalized by the model successfully predicts or postdicts legal decisions, the model can be seen as providing an explanation of decision-making alternative to the legal rule. In this light, the relation between features and outcomes expressed by the model can be used to make hypotheses on which factors might have influenced the decision-making. On this account, the predictive performance of each distinct feature is assumed to be indicative of the degree to which such a feature has affected the decision-making. The fact that a model allows to accurately predict legal decisions based only on features that the developers of the model assume as legally irrelevant casts doubts on whether such decisions instantiate a correct application of the relevant legal rule or are (unduly) influenced by extraneous factors (cf. Chen et al. 2017).

As said, the ML model constitutes an alternative rule that, as it were, explains well the behaviour represented in data. However, such an alternative rule does not licence any normative conclusion (cf. Arvidsson and Noll 2023, 62). Although the regularities expressed by the model can raise the question of whether or not 'the specifics of each case are being given their due weight' (Chen et al. 2017), such a question cannot be answered based solely on the ML model. Ultimately, the question at issue is one of whether the legal decisions under scrutiny instantiate a correct application of the relevant legal rule. This is a matter of normative assessment, which can only be performed by applying the criteria of correctness established by legal practice. Of course, the technical choices made in the development of a ML model are not irrelevant in this regard. However, it is important to stress, as it were, in what capacity they assume relevance. Clearly, the choices about data, features, and outcomes, as well as the ML techniques employed, determine the correlations that the ML detects (cf. Katsikouli et al. 2022). Consequently, such choices affect the evidential value of a model. However, such choices do not determine what the correlations detected by a ML model can or cannot be evidence of. If the model is to be used as evidence in support of a claim concerning the application of a legal rule, the criteria that determine what counts as evidence are those established by legal practice. For a model to be used to 'measure', that is, to evaluate, the application of legal rules, the model itself must 'be measured'. That is, the model needs to undergo an assessment from the point of view of the legal rule. Only such assessment can determine whether the regularity detected between features and outcomes is normatively salient. The criteria that establish what counts as a regularity under the legal rule and under the model are independent. The same outcome that counts as an outlier according to the rule expressed by the ML model might be 'doing the same' under the legal rule, as correctly applying a legal rule might imply doing 'now this and then that' (cf. Wittgenstein 1983: RFM 416).

It should be noted that the point is not (just), as ML is often reproached for, that correlation is not causation. The relevant difference that is the focus of the present section is not between causal and statistical regularities, but rather between both the latter on the one hand and normative regularities on the other. Undoubtedly, the approaches to ML and Law discussed so far can be used to investigate legally relevant interactions in a natural science fashion. The successful performance of a ML model can be taken as an indication of an overlap, of varying degrees of meaningfulness, between the regularities formalized by the model and the (hidden) rules that determine the behaviours represented in the data, for example, rules of the mind, of the brain or rules of behaviour and the like. Irrespective of any consideration of the scientific validity of such an approach, the claim I have put forward here as to the relation between ML models and legal rules would not be affected even if the correlations detected through ML were to be granted the status of causal laws. Thanks to ML, we might discover and formalize, say, rules that explain how judges' diet determines legal decision-making. Still, it is not by reference to such rules alone that we can determine whether the affected decision is correct or incorrect.

ML models as an improved expression of legal rules

A third approach in ML and Law equates legal rules and ML models. This approach is exemplified by the points raised by Casey and Niblett (2017, 1431) based on the analysis of the renowned concurring opinion delivered by Justice Stewart in the case *Jacobellis v. Ohio* (378 U.S. 184 (1964)). In his opinion, he maintained that, under the American Constitution, only obscene material amounting to hardcore pornography could be banned under criminal law. After having expressed doubts about his capacity to provide a definition of what counts as hardcore pornography, Justice Stewart famously wrote: 'But I know it when I see it, and the motion picture involved in this case is not that'. According to Casey and Niblett, Justice Stewart's opinion shows that, despite the ability to apply legally relevant concepts such as that of hardcore pornography, 'it is difficult to write an ex ante rule that clearly defines the line' (Ivi). The authors go on to point out that '[a]rtificially intelligent technology can already recognize and analyse images. It is not just a judge who can "see it". In the near future, artificially intelligent machines will be able to develop highly complex rules that generate immediate and simple predictions of the legality of particular materials ("this image is/is not pornographic")' (Ivi). To this effect, the authors argue that a ML model could be trained on a set of authoritative data, that is, 50 pictures labelled by Justice Stewart himself as either hardcore pornography or not. Through training on such a data set, the model could 'find deep connections to identify the pattern that is driving the distinction, but that Justice Stewart could not articulate' (Ivi). This approach is in line with prior work where the authors held that the 'hidden connections' detected by ML models can be used to formalize the rules that 'do – and more importantly – should underpin the law', thus filling 'the gaps' the left by legal rule formulations (Casey and Niblett 2016, 433).

The relation between ML models and legal rules articulated in this account raises many points of potential contention. Firstly, the picture of ML training as discovery and as the expression of the hidden rules applied by practitioners shares some of the same shaky foundations touched upon in the previous subsection. Additionally, this approach claims that what ML models discover is not just a rule that explains rule followers' behaviour, but the very *legal* rule that they are actually following. Based on a misleading picture of legal rules, this approach leads a crusade against ordinary (i.e. not calculi) rule formulations, under the banner of learnt rules. Seen from this angle, it becomes clear how ML has come to be framed by some as the means to solve the problems incurred by GOFAIL. However, as discussed in Section 'Legal Rules and Programmed Rules: 'All Steps Must Have Already Been Taken', these are not problems to be solved, but to be clarified in light of the differences between calculi and legal rules.

In the example provided, the assumption is that Justice Stewart knows how to correctly apply the concept of hardcore pornography despite the fact that he is 'not able to say it'. Under this ML and Law approach, the judge's knowledge seems to be characterized as 'somehow equivalent to an unformulated definition' (Wittgenstein 2009: PI § 75). The explanation he provides is therefore considered akin to 'an indirect way of explaining in default of a better one' (Ivi, § 71). Interestingly, the ground on which rules are considered defective is not their 'not being in order', that is, in their capacity to guide, evaluate, correct, and so on, behaviour. What under this approach makes legal rules defective is arguably their very comparison with calculi: differently than ML models, legal rules do not inexorably determine their application independently of their use. In this picture, 'ordinary' rule formulations – and definitions and explanations – are like rails that are not laid to infinity (cf., Ivi, § 218): at some point the rails end and the passengers are left to go on by themselves.

In contrast to this account of ordinary rules, ML models are portrayed as capable to discover and make explicit what was implicit in our behaviour all along (cf. Baker and Hacker 2009, 181). Accordingly, by discovering the 'hidden connections in the law' (Casey and Niblett 2016, 433), ML models are understood as drawing sharp boundaries where before there were only blurred pictures (Wittgenstein 2009: PI § 76).

But how do ML models gain their normative status? Again, under this approach, ML models are not just rules that explain the behaviour represented in the data, but the very legal rules that determine what behaviour is correct. In the example of the, as it were, hardcore pornography detector, it seems that the model gains its normative value through its training and validation. Picturing again the rule as a series, the labelled data and the outputs generated by the trained model constitute, respectively, a first and a further extension of the series. If the labelled data represent examples of what does and does not count as 'doing the same' under the legal rule, the training of the model consists of the formalization of the normative regularity of which the labelled data are meant to count as an instance. Such hypothesis is confirmed by validating the model 1, 2, …, n, times. The validation corroborates that the model generalizes well, that is, that the model, as it were, knows how to go on. Hence, since by applying the model one is always doing the same, that is, applying a determinate rule, what made the application of the model correct before *must* make it correct now.

This account raises the following questions: Should rule followers be able to recognize the ML model as the expression of the rule they are following (cf. Wittgenstein 2009: PI § 75)? What happens in case of disagreement between rule followers and the machine output (cf. Ivi, § 77)? Let's make the case that Justice Stewart finds that a certain image is to be qualified as hardcore pornography, contrary to the machine output. Can the model be corrected or is it the ML model that defines what counts as correct? According to which rule would such disagreement be solved?

As aforementioned, the aporias that this account incurs depend on the failure to acknowledge that computer rules, either programmed or learnt, are not 'more precise' versions of legal rules, but different rules that are intended to lead to the same result (Shanker 1987, 90, 101, 1998, 28). In turn, this failure leads to a misunderstanding of the relationship between the regularity formalized by the ML model and normative regularity. As with programmed rules, the regularity expressed by the ML model cannot in itself either confirm or invalidate what counts as correct (regular, same, etc.) from the point of view of the legal rule. Even the validation of the model does not overcome the fact that the model is under-determined with respect to the legal rule. Justifying an output as correct based on the argument that the model is 'doing the same' as when it was validated misses the fact that, once again, the only notion of sameness that matters to this end is the one fixed by the legal rule (Wittgenstein 1983: RFM 416, 2009: PI §§ 223–29).

In short, the problem with this approach is thus akin to that discussed by Wittgenstein (1983: RFM 199):

> When somebody makes an experiment repeatedly 'always with the same result', has he at the same time made an experiment which tells him what he will call 'the same result', i.e., how he uses the word 'the same'? If you measure a table with a yardstick, are you also measuring the yardstick? If you are measuring the yardstick, then you cannot be measuring the table at the same time.

ML models as the hardcore pornography detector can become a new legal rule, but this again is because it is used as such in a normative practice. Leaving aside questions of legitimacy, this is different than assuming that such model *is* the rule that we apply when we follow legal rules.

Conclusions

In the previous sections, I have provided an overview of the role played by the concept of rule within and across the fields of Law and Artificial Intelligence. I have argued that both conceptual confusion and practical difficulties result from a failure to fully appreciate the differences between legal and computer rules.

The analysis of both programmed and learnt rules has shown that a common set of problems is due to a confusing underlying picture of legal rules. While such a picture has deep roots in Western legal thinking, this confusion is further exacerbated by the elevation of computer rules into the paradigm of what counts as a rule.

By drawing on Wittgenstein's remarks, I have defended an account of legal rules centred on the fundamental insight that following rules is a practice. I have sought to demonstrate that, no matter the degree of sophistication of computer rules or the performance achieved in their applications, the normative assessment of computer rules requires an unavoidable reversion to the criteria and techniques that belong to legal practice. I have shown how Wittgenstein's considerations on the internal relations between rules, regularity, sameness and correctness can help clarify the relations between legal and computer rules. Ultimately, legal rules are what measures, not what is measured.

Acknowledgements

This research was made possible through funding from the project 'Counting as a Human Being in the Era of Computational Law' (COHUBICOL, ERC–2017–ADG No 788734) and the project 'HumanE AI Net' (European Union's Horizon 2020 research and innovation programme Grant Agreement No 952026).

References

Aletras, Nikolaos, Dimitrios Tsarapatsanis, Daniel Preoţiuc-Pietro and Vasileios Lampos. 2016. 'Predicting Judicial Decisions of the European Court of Human Rights: A Natural Language Processing Perspective'. *PeerJ Computer Science* 2: 93.

Arvidsson, Matilda and Noll, Gregor. 2023. 'Decision Making in Asylum Law and Machine Learning. Autoethnographic Lessons Learned on Data Wrangling and Human Discretion'. *Nordic Journal of International Law* 92: 56–92.

Buchanan, Bruce G. and Headrick, Thomas E. 1970. 'Some Speculation about Artificial Intelligence and Legal Reasoning'. *Stanford Law Review* 23: 40–62.

Baker, Gordon P. (ed.). 2003. *The Voices of Wittgenstein*, London: Routledge.

Baker, Gordon P. and Hacker, Peter M. S. 1984. *Language, Sense, Nonsense.* Oxford: Basil Blackwell.

———. 2009. *Wittgenstein: Understanding and Meaning, Part II – Exegesis §§ 1–184*. London: Wiley-Blackwell.

———. 2014. *Wittgenstein: Rules, Grammar and Necessity*. London: Wiley-Blackwell.

Bench-Capon, Trevor, MichałAraszkiewicz, Kevin Ashley, et al. 2012. 'A History of AI and Law in 50 Papers: 25 Years of the International Conference on AI and Law'. *Artificial Intelligence and Law* 20: 215–319.

Casey, Anthony J. and Niblett, Anthony. 2016. 'Self-Driving Laws'. *University of Toronto Law Journal* 66: 429–442.

———. 2017. 'The Death of Rules and Standards'. *Indiana Law Journal* 92: 1401–1447.

Chalkidis, Ilias , Androutsopoulos, Ion and Altras, Nikolas. 2019. 'Neural Legal Judgment Prediction in English'. In Korhonen, Anna, Traum, David and Màrquez, Liuís. *Proceedings of the 57th Annual Meeting of the Association for Computational Linguistics*, 4317–4323. Florence: Association for Computational Linguistics.

Chen, Daniel L. 2019. 'Machine Learning and the Rule of Law'. In *Law as Data. Computation, Text, and the Future of Legal Analysis*, edited by Micheal A. Livermore and Daniel N. Rockmore, 429–441. Santa Fe: Santa Fe Institute Press.

Chen, Daniel L, Matt Dunn, Levent Sagun, and Hale Sirin. 2017. 'Early Predictability of Asylum Court Decisions'. In *Proceedings of the ACM Conference on AI and the Law*, 233–236. New York: ACM.

Daston, Lorraine. 2022. *Rules. A Short History of What We Live By*. Princeton & Oxford: Princeton University Press.

Dworkin, Ronald. 1978. *Taking Rights Seriously*. Cambridge, MA: Harvard University Press.

Goodman, Nelson. 1983. *Fact, Fiction and Forecast*. Cambridge: Harvard University Press.

Holmes, Oliver W. 1897. 'The Path of the Law'. *Harvard Law Review* 10: 457.

Katsikouli, Panagiota, William H. Byrne, Thomas Gammeltoft-Hansen, Anna Højberg Høgenhaug, Naja Holten Møller, Trine Rask Nielsen, Henrik Palmer Olsen, and Tijs Slaats. 2022. 'Machine Learning and Asylum Adjudications: From Analysis of Variations to Outcome Predictions'. *IEEE Access* 10: 130955–130967.

Katz, Daniel M. 2013. 'Quantitative Legal Prediction—Or—How I Learned to Stop Worrying and Start Preparing for the Data-Driven Future of the Legal Services Industry'. *Emory Law Journal* 62: 909–966.

Katz, Daniel Martin. Bommarito Michael J. Blackman, Josh. 2017. 'A general approach for predicting the behavior of the Supreme Court of the United States'. *PLoS ONE* 12. https://doi.org/10.1371/journal.pone.0174698

Kelso, Louis O. 1946. 'Does the Law Need a Technological Revolution'. *Rocky Mountain Law Review* 18: 378–392.

Niblett, Bryan (ed.). 1980. *Computer Science and Law: An Advanced Course*. Cambridge: Cambridge University Press.

McCarty, L.T. 1980. 'Some Requirements for a Computer-based Legal Consultant'. In *Proceedings of the AAAI Conference on Artificial Intelligence*, 298–300. Palo Alto: AAAI Press.

———. 1990. 'Artificial Intelligence and Law: How to Get There from Here'. *Ratio Juris* 3: 189–200.

Medvedeva, Masha, Wieling, Martin, and Vols, Michel. 2023. 'Rethinking the Field of Automatic Prediction of Court Decisions'. *Artificial Intelligence and Law* 31: 195–212.

Leith, Philip. 1986. 'Clear Rules and Legal Expert Systems'. In *Automated Analysis of Legal Texts*, edited by Antonio A. Martino and Fiorenza Socci Natali, 661–679. Amsterdam: North-Holland.

———. 1988. 'Common Usage, Certainty and Computing'. In *The Jurisprudence of Orthodoxy: Queen's University Essays on H.L.A. Hart*, edited by Philip Leith and Peter Ingram, 85–115. London: Routledge.

Postema, Gerald J. (ed.). 2017. *Matthew Hale. On the Law of Nature, Reason and Common Law. Selected Jurisprudential Writings*. Oxford: Oxford University Press.

Prakken, Henry and Sartor, Giovanni. 2015. 'Law and Logic: A Review of an Argumentation Perspective'. *Artificial Intelligence and Law* 227: 214–245.

Rissland, Edwina. 1990. 'Artificial Intelligence and Law: Stepping Stones to a Model of Legal Reasoning'. *The Yale Law Journal* 99: 1957–1981.

Sergot, Marek. 1991. 'The Representation of Law in Computer Programs'. In *Knowledge-Based Systems and Legal Applications*, edited by Trevor Bench-Capon, 3–67. London: Academic Press.

Shanker, Stuart. 1987. 'The Decline and Fall of the Mechanist Metaphor'. In *Artificial Intelligence: The Case Against*, edited by Reiner Born, 72–131. London: Routledge.

———. 1998. *Wittgenstein's remarks on the foundations of AI*. London: Routledge.

Winch, Peter. 2008. *The Idea of a Social Science and Its Relations to Philosophy*. London: Routledge.

Waismann, Friedrich and Harre, Rom. 1965. *The Principles of Linguistic Philosophy*. London and New York: Macmillan and St. Martin's Press.

Wittgenstein, Ludwig. 1958. *The Blue and Brown Book*. Oxford: Blackwell Publishing.

———. 1975. *On Certainty*. Oxford: Wiley-Blackwell.

———. 1981. *Zettel*. Oxford: Blackwell Publishing.

———. 1983. *Remarks on the Foundations of Mathematics*. Cambridge: The MIT Press.

———. 2009. *Philosophical Investigations*. Oxford: Wiley-Blackwell.

Caselaw.

Jacobellis v. Ohio 378 U.S. 184 (1964).

Chapter 9

PRACTICE MAKES HUMAN: WHY WE CAN'T UNDERSTAND BLACK-BOX ARTIFICIAL INTELLIGENCE

Jean-Charles Pelland, Jasmin Trächtler and Helene Love

Introduction to the Black-Box Problem in Artificial Intelligence

The word 'hallucinate' was chosen as Cambridge dictionary's word of the year for 2023, reflecting this word's recent extension as a label for AI models producing false data. This is not only telling of AI's increasing importance in our lives: it also says a lot about how often its behaviour is unexpected. This unexpected behaviour is related to the fact that, nowadays, many AI models are designed in such a way that humans can't know how what algorithm[1] is being implemented in the machine. This is often called Black-Box AI (BBAI hereafter). While the function telling the machine what to do may not be untraceable in the training stages, the purpose of machine learning is for the machine itself to adapt and change its parameters so as to perform its task more efficiently – while the programmers become 'largely ignorant of quite what is going on inside' (1950, 458), to put it in Turing's own words. Due to the interconnectedness of the values of the potentially billions of parameters

1 By 'algorithm' here we will be referring to an abstract mathematical entity, namely, a function that describes a set of rules or operations that transforms an input into an output. Our use of this notoriously ill-defined term is based loosely on Marr's three levels of analysis of information processing. So algorithms here are not at the computational level, where we describe the goal of a function (e.g. classifying images as of wolves or huskies) in broad teleological terms. Nor are they at the hardware level, which is the material implementation of the abstract entity (e.g. a circuit board). Algorithms here are mathematical functions that are supposed to implement a goal (e.g. classification) in hardware (e.g. a computer). For pragmatic reasons, in this chapter we remain politely agnostic about the ontological status of mathematical entities. For more on the nature of algorithms, see Hill (2016), and included references therein.

making up the functions that describe how such machines work, modifying a single value in a complex black-box function – say, when it 'learns' how to improve outputs during training – can affect the value of millions of others. This means that after a few iterations of the initial training model, the actual function being implemented in the machine – and any variant thereof – is essentially unknowable to humans.

This is different from, say, a very large decision tree, whose size makes it unsurveyable at a single glance, but where each step is easily inspected. It is also different from cases where the technology is black-boxed *in practice*, but not *in principle*, such as proprietary BBAI, where corporations who own the machines hide how they work in order to prevent others from stealing their technology, even though they might know how its insides work.[2]

Importantly, such BBAI models are not outliers: most deep-learning models rely on BBAI. This means that, in many cases, we end up relying on machines that are implementing an algorithm that is completely unknown to us – in some cases, for high-stake decisions. Given the large-scale deployment of machines relying on BBAI in many critical domains, our lack of epistemic access to BBAI has many real-life consequences, both practical and ethical.[3] As detailed in popular media, we have learnt the hard way that machines whose behaviour seemed in line with our expectations during training phases turned out to behave differently when deployed in the real world. These can include relatively benign classification mistakes, but also well-known cases of models importing bias from their real-world data points into their algorithm, resulting in biased or unfair decisions, or more tragic cases of models misbehaving and leading to injury or death, as in cases of driverless cars hitting pedestrians.

So BBAI imposes a dilemma: on the one hand, BBAI models are often considered more accurate and faster than their transparent counterparts.[4] On the other hand, its opacity makes BBAI not only more difficult to predict, repair, and interpret, but also potentially harmful. So, should we use such technology despite its associated risks, and if so, in which contexts?

One way out of this dilemma would be to find ways of peering into BBAI to make it – well, less black-boxed. We sketch efforts aimed in this direction in the next section, arguing that the key desideratum is understanding how

2 See Burrell (2016) for more on this distinction. We return to proprietary AI in the section titled 'BBAI: Legal Implications'.

3 See Rudin (2019) for examples of this. See also Wexler (2017) for implications of the use of proprietary BBAI in the legal domain.

4 Though Rudin (2019) argues this is not the case.

BBAI models work and how they produce specific decisions – and that this desideratum seems impossible to achieve.

Explainable AI: Building Bridges from Minds to Machines

A good way to tell that the problem of BBAI's opacity is still in its infancy is that there is no standard agreement on what the best response to this problem is – nor whether it is really a problem at all.[5] While there are many ways to flesh out what we are looking for in solutions to the BBAI problem, many candidate desiderata for transparency seem to have clustered under the general heading of Explainable AI, or XAI, for short.[6] As its name suggests, a number of the solutions to BBAI problems are couched in terms of a model's *explainability* (Mittelstadt et al. 2019; de Graaf & Malle 2017; Brozek et al. 2023; Guidotti et al. 2018; Miller 2019; Vilone and Longo 2021). While explanation is certainly one of the central themes in the literature surrounding the quest for more transparent AI, it is also certainly not the only one. Other notions used to frame this problem include understanding (Páez 2019), interpretability (Lipton 2016), trust (von Eschenbach 2021) and credibility (Wang et al. 2018), but there are others and variants on these.[7]

Despite this pluralism of approaches to transparency, virtually all efforts to reduce the opacity of BBAI distinguish between what we will describe here as *local* versus *global* transparency. When what is being sought is an explanation (or interpretation, or trust, or understanding) of the functioning of the entire AI model as a whole, including its parameters and the algorithm it follows to process inputs, we will speak of *global* transparency. On the other hand, when what is discussed is transparency with respect to only a part or specific aspect of the model, such as a specific output, decision or even a specific property of the model such as its sensitivity to a particular change in input, we will speak of *local* transparency, which is often described as *post-hoc interpretability*.[8] This

5 Some argue BBAI's opacity is not a problem because they see human minds as being similarly shrouded in a mysterious black-box. For an example of this type of response to BBAI, see Zerilli et al. (2019). See also von Eschenbach (2021).

6 While this particular label is relatively recent and has yet to become mainstream, the field itself has been around for a long time. So, Rudin (2019, 206) writes that 'the field of interpreta bility/explainability/comprehensibility/transparency in ML […] dates back to the early 1990s', before issues related to BBAI caught the public's attention.

7 See Gohel et al. (2021) for a more technology-oriented treatment of transparency-increasing strategies.

8 This distinction pops up in one form or other in many recent discussions of AI (e.g. Guidotti et al. 2018; Paez 2019; Lipton 2016; Mittelstadt et al. 2019). For example, Guidotti et al. (2018) talk

distinction is important insofar as achieving local transparency means knowing only why a particular decision was made by a model, irrespective of what else happens inside it.[9]

Broadly speaking, XAI strategies usually involve building a model tasked with interpreting the target BBAI, either locally or globally. Of course, on pain of regress – it can't be black boxes all the way down, after all – some of the systems we use to chip away at the opacity must be, at the very least, more epistemically accessible than the target BBAI. If this is not the case, then we are essentially providing 'an explanation of the obscure by the more obscure' (Philipse 1989, 67).

These interpretable models often rely on simpler computational architecture, such as logical models like decision trees, linear or gradient-based approximations, rule lists, or other tools whose structure is generally more amenable to being understood by humans with reasonable cognitive, epistemological, and temporal resources.[10,11] Consider for example saliency maps (Zeiler & Fergus 2014; Lapuschkin et al. 2019). Here, we toggle the inputs to the model, for example by partially occluding some of it, to see which aspects of its input seem to affect processing more than others. The idea here is that highlighting what sort of details about the input the algorithm is more responsive to might help us understand why a particular decision was made by the model, even though we do not grasp how the model itself works.

It is important to point out that such local interpretations are model-agnostic: the aim of providing an interpretation of a single decision of a model can be completely separate from how the model itself works. In this sense, local interpretations, while having the potential to help us understand what went into a particular decision, cannot inform us of *how* the system itself works. Rudin (2019) offers a striking illustration of this, where a saliency map shows that the same area of an image might be focused on by a model classifying two wildly different entities – a husky and a flute, for example – so that the saliency map could turn out to be the same for both input types. In such a

of model explanation vs. outcome explanation and model inspection, while Lipton (2016) talks of distinguishing between simulatability, decomposability and transparency of a model.

9 This is often referred to as LIME, for Locally Interpretable Model-Agnostic Explanation methods. See Abdullah et al. (2023) for a concrete application.

10 See Ribeiro et al. (2016a) for a more extensive list. See also Mittelstadt et al. (2019).

11 Of course, it bears mentioning that no technology can be considered intrinsically interpretable, since the size and length of some technologies that are traditionally thought of as being transparent can make them unsurveyable to a human. Even a tally representation of a sufficiently large number is opaque in this sense. The point here is that some types of models are opaque by design, no matter their size, to even the most seasoned experts in a field.

case, given that the saliency map is supposed to act as an explanation for the produced output, we would have the same explanation for why an image is classified as a husky as we would for the image being classified as a flute. Thus, as Rudin puts it, 'Saliency does not explain anything except where the network is looking' (2019, 209), which leaves what the model does to the images it processes to arrive at a decision entirely unknown.

This highlights a chasm that can remain between a BBAI and its interpreter model: interpreter models, in order to be humanly accessible, need to simplify their target BBAI. Failure to do so would make them pointless. At the same time, however, many of the tools used to devise interpretable models – features of these models that make them more human-friendly, such as linearity – are often the type of features absent in the original target BBAI. In other words, the black box is left unopened when relying on interpretative models. In this sense, use of the word 'explanation' in such contexts is misleading.

The idea behind choosing explainability as the main desideratum for solutions to the opacity of BBAI seems to be that if we have an explanation of how a BBAI works – or at least, of how it came to a particular decision – then we have reduced our ignorance to acceptable levels. While this seems intuitive enough, when taking a closer look at the notion of explanation as it is currently used in these contexts versus what interpreting tools like saliency maps actually accomplish, we see that it does not seem to be suited to describing what our aims are when trying to solve the problems caused by the opacity of BBAI. Happily, there is reason to believe that focusing on explanation is not the right way to achieve transparency anyways. Rather, as Páez (2019) argues, the many variants of explainability in AI can only be properly fleshed out in terms of our *understanding*, since 'the purpose of providing an explanation or an interpretation of a model or a decision is to make it understandable or comprehensible to its stakeholders' (Páez 2019, 442). The idea here is to accept that our understanding of AI models may be based on 'true-enough' methods (cf. Elgin 2017) and interpretation models that aren't necessarily explanations but are nonetheless common sources of understanding that are sufficiently faithful to the facts to help us accept decisions produced by BBAI.

There are indeed advantages of fleshing out transparency in terms of understanding rather than explanation. First, understanding need not be factive: we can understand how things work without this understanding being based only in truth. Examples of this include scientific models such as scale models or atomic models, where understanding is achieved *because* they represent their target system inaccurately (cf. Elgin 2017, 23). In explanations, both the explanans and the explanandum are supposed to be true. The opacity of BBAI makes this unachievable, since we have no access to their inner workings, and so no truthful description of the explanandum. Second, understanding is more context-sensitive than explanation and it admits of degrees (cf. Elgin 2017, 53). A single explanation will not suit all audiences. Rather, explanations must be adapted to their stakeholders, whose interests, levels of expertise and background knowledge can vary tremendously. Understanding, on the other hand, is something all these stakeholders seek *via* this explanation. In this sense, understanding is closer to what we seek from efforts to improve the transparency of BBAI. Last, relatedly, focusing on understanding offers a more pragmatic approach to transparency, which is needed to properly discuss the relation between explanation and *trust.* An explanation of why a BBAI produced a particular decision is worthless unless it leads us to somehow accept the model and our reliance on it – that is, *trust* it.[12] However, trust requires a lack of certainty – if we are certain, we no longer need trust (cf. Trächtler 2022) – and this degree of certainty will vary according to the level of expertise and many other factors. So the same explanation will not always lead to trust for different people.

So, despite this apparent opposition between seeking understanding and seeking explanation (or any of the candidate desiderata for XAI), these approaches to transparency all have in common that they are supposed to build a bridge between humans and AI by framing their behaviour in human terms. That is, the transparency-increasing approaches we just discussed all have in common the desire to make AI models understandable *to humans,* so that we have a better chance of knowing how to fix them when they misbehave and more chances of preventing unexpected behaviour from occurring. The problem is, considering the apparent chasm between local and global understanding, loosening the factivity requirements in understanding makes it difficult to see how what we understand can in any way be related to what is actually going on. Indeed, as the next section shows, we find in Wittgenstein good reason to think that whatever BBAI models are doing, they are not doing anything that can be understood in terms of human rule-following.

Practice Makes Human: Why Black-Boxes Don't Follow Human Rules

In his remarks on the so-called rule-following paradox (usually located between PI, 185 and 242), Wittgenstein deals with the question of what it means to follow a rule or to apply a rule (correctly). His initial problem is the

12 E.g. see Kim (2015) and Ribeiro et al. (2016a) who have both argued that availability of explanation is key for trusting a decision rendered by BBAI. See also von Eschenbach (2021).

now-classic example of a pupil who is supposed to form a series of numbers using the rule 'Add 2' and does so correctly up to the number 1000, but then unexpectedly continues with 1004, 1008, 1012 to the bewilderment of the teacher (cf. Wittgenstein 2009: PI §§148, 185). Every attempt to point out the mistake to the pupil and to teach them the 'correct' continuation of the series fails, as the pupil could always say 'I thought that was how I *had* to do it', that is, it comes natural to this pupil 'to understand our order as *we* would understand the order: "Add 2 up to 1000, 4 up to 2000, 6 up to 3000 and so on"' (Wittgenstein 2009: PI §185). The problem that Wittgenstein wants to illustrate with this example is that the way we express a rule cannot unambiguously determine how we are to follow it, which means that any behaviour can be seen as being consistent with a rule. This leads to the aforementioned paradox stating that 'if every course of action can be brought into accord with the rule, then it can also be brought into conflict with it. And so there would be neither accord [*Übereinstimmung*] nor conflict here' (Wittgenstein 2009: PI §201).

Imagine now that our pupil is a BBAI model. Much like with human children, we want our model to learn a certain rule, for example, to classify pictures in terms of what they represent. And, in many cases, after extensive training with unfathomable quantities of data, the machine seems to be following the rules we want it to – until it doesn't and makes a mistake akin to the pupil unexpectedly writing 1004 instead of 1002. In both cases, it is not a matter of a one-off careless error. Rather, what is irritating about the results produced by the pupil and the machine is that we seemingly have no higher instance (cf. Wittgenstein 2009: PI §192) by means of which we can identify the results as incorrect, so that every result can be made out to be in accord or conflict with the rule. Taking this analogy between machine and human learning, the question here is: What *does* determine a rule's application?

Wittgenstein's answer is that we have been 'trained to react to this sign in a particular way' and now we 'do so react to it' (Wittgenstein 2009: PI §198). By referring here to the way in which rules are learnt and repeatedly describing this as a 'training' [*Abrichtung*], Wittgenstein emphasizes that the seemingly 'super-strong connection' (cf. Wittgenstein 2009: PI §197) that exists between an expression of a rule, and the corresponding action does not emerge from the written or spoken signs themselves, nor an intuition (cf. Wittgenstein 2009: PI §186), intention (cf. Wittgenstein 2009: PI §188) or interpretation (cf. Wittgenstein 2009: PI §198), but is only established through a *practice*, characterized by the interweaving of language and action in language games, as well as by community and institutions with their educational practices. The fact that we would all apply the rule 'Add 2' in such a way that we would continue with 1002 and not with 1004 is due to the way we learn mathematical and other rules, namely with 'endless practice, with merciless exactitude' (Wittgenstein 1998: RFM I §4), supported by examples, praise and correction (cf. Wittgenstein 2009: PI §208).

By emphasizing the role of training in rule-following, Wittgenstein does not give a causal explanation of what it means to follow a rule but rather wants to draw attention to the constitutive role of the regular use, that is, customs, in following rules. In other words, according to Wittgenstein, the connection between the rule's expression and an action cannot be grasped if these are regarded in isolation as individual instances of action but only if rule-following is seen as a practice *in the context of the customs, uses and institutions of a community* (cf. Wittgenstein 2009: PI §199). The criteria for the correct application of a rule, therefore, do not lie in the expression of the rule itself but in the practice of human action, in which the rule is embedded. In this sense, it can be said that the pupil who continues with the rule 'Add 2' after 1000 with 1004 comes into conflict, not with the rule as the written or spoken expression, but 'e.g. with society; and also with other practical consequences' (Wittgenstein 1998: RFM I §116).

Even if we were to travel to an alien land where people speak an unknown language, as Wittgenstein imagines, we would understand that these people follow rules *because* we note a regularity between certain signs and certain actions, and we see sanctions if the action deviates in a significant way from others' actions, that is, because we observe a practice familiar to us, consisting of customs (regularity), habits and institutions (cf. Wittgenstein 2009: PI §206). At this point, Wittgenstein calls this 'the shared human way of acting' [*die gemeinsame menschliche Handlungsweise*], which is the 'system of reference by means of which we interpret an unknown language' (Wittgenstein 2009: PI §206, mod. transl.[13]). Ultimately, our rules are based on this overwhelming agreement between people *in deed*[14]: this does not mean that people have agreed on the correct application of a certain rule – in the sense of a consensus theory of opinions or interpretations – and then act accordingly. Rather, Wittgenstein means that what we call the 'correct application of a rule' is ultimately based on the mere fact that people agree and regularly act in this way and not otherwise. That is, on a more general note, one can only speak of rules or following of rules where people's actions show a certain

13 Modified translation. We have used the translation by Anscombe, Hacker and Schulte of PI but have occasionally modified it. Here, we follow Pichler's (forthc.) translation who offers a detailed discussion of the role of the 'shared human way of acting' for understanding others.

14 Wittgenstein here speaks of an 'agreement in *form of life*' as opposed to an 'agreement in opinions' (Wittgenstein 2009: PI §241).

regularity, uniformity, constancy and agreement (cf. Wittgenstein 2009: PI §§208, 237, 242); and in a particular situation, one can only say that someone has applied a rule correctly if they act in agreement with the other members of a community. To return to our initial example: only when the pupil acts in agreement with the community, that is, continues the number line with 1002, 1004, 1006 … do we say that they have applied the rule 'Add 2' correctly. Any number series that deviates from this is not dismissed as a mere difference of opinion or even celebrated as an original way of calculating, but is labelled as conflicting with the rules, or wrong.

On the surface, it looks like one could say that our interaction with BBAI is akin to that of our interaction with pupils. Much like we do with human pupils, we train AI models using examples – in the case of BBAI, with superhuman quantities of data. We can also correct AI models' mistakes – although BBAI makes this an extremely complicated matter. However, despite these oft-mentioned surface similarities, there is reason to doubt that the specific case of BBAI can be described as one of rule-following of the sort that humans can fathom. This is not because it is a machine – after all, transparent technology, our ordinary, non-intelligent automatons, could not only be said to follow rules, but one can even say that they are the epitome of rule-guided and rule-compliant behaviour: we use the machine, as Wittgenstein says, 'as symbol of its mode of operation', since we can derive and predict its behaviour and movements from its parts, its construction (cf. Wittgenstein 2009: PI §193).[15] That is, ordinary machines can be seen as perfect rule-followers precisely *because* they are transparent, in that their mechanism or mode of operation is apparent in their sheer (physical) construction. This includes Good Old Fashioned AI, where we not only know how the machine is physically built, but also every detail of the program it implements. The specific case of BBAI is different, however, precisely *because* it is opaque to us: we cannot read off what it is doing by looking at its physical construction nor its decisions, so we cannot see it as a symbol for its mode of operation.

But it gets worse: the *types* of mistakes we have observed BBAI making tells that whatever the rule embodied in the algorithm is, it is not one that can be integrated into our human practices. There are many cases where artefacts in the training data lead to spurious correlations on which the machine bases its decisions. In order to study this phenomenon, Ribeiro and colleagues (2016b) developed a classifier whose job was to determine if an image was of a wolf or a husky and intentionally trained the machine with images such that all

15 For a detailed discussion of the remarks on 'machines as symbols of its mode of operation', see Schulte (2021).

wolves were presented with a snowy background, and all huskies without. The machine then classifies things as wolves based not on the features of the animal, but on the presence or absence of snow.[16] Such unexpected behaviour is in no way an outlier: there are many well-known cases of mis-categorization involving images that have nothing to do (to a human) with what it is supposed to represent, such as hallucinating a tomato in what a human would perceive as an unrecognizable image of static white noise (Nguyen et al. 2015).

No human would ever classify pictures of animals based solely on features of their backgrounds. This is because our understanding of the world around us is based on deeply interconnected practices and rules, and none of these involve confusing features of animals with those of their environments. To us, these are fundamentally different things. But to the machine, there is no such network of practices in which to ground the new rule it is learning. There is only a search for correlation.[17] This means that whatever rule is behind the particular output our interpreter model is supposed to explain to us could turn out to be analogous to our pupil's understanding of 1000, where the behaviour coincides with our expectations up to a point, but then diverges.[18]

It is important here to realize that what we are saying has nothing to do with the fact that the machines made mistakes – making mistakes is about as human as it gets, as we are all painfully aware. Rather, the problem is the *kind* of mistakes we have seen and what these mistakes end up telling us about the machine's decision-making behaviour. This is because they are neither of a systematic nature, that is, of the kind that wherever humans do x, the machine does y, so that they could simply be corrected and rectified; nor are they comparable to a calculation error that could be easily rectified, for example, by recalculating. Such human errors are annoying, but unproblematic, because they are the kind of mistake that 'doesn't only have a cause, it also has a ground' and that means that it 'can be fitted into the right

---

16 The fact that this was done intentionally is beside the point: it was done intentionally in order to study the phenomenon observed in many other cases of misbehaving AI models.

17 Proudfoot (2004) similarly argues that transparent AI models (in her case mainly humanoid robots) cannot follow rules because they lack the necessary social environment and training. However, her discussion focuses primarily on the (externalistically understood) psychological aspects of this training (e.g. pain and pleasure).

18 The difference with Wittgenstein's pupil, of course, is that the pupil's mistakes are to some extent fathomable to us. Arguably, we can even understand the strange rule governing the pupil's behaviour in this case, that is, we can understand the behaviour by translating the original rule (n+2 for n<1000, n+4 for n<2000 …), although the point Wittgenstein was making with such examples is that such behaviour would be so strange that it would seem alien to us, given its mismatch with the practices in which it is supposed to be grounded.

knowledge of the erring person' (Wittgenstein 1998: OC §74; mod. transl.). In other words, and grammatically speaking, a person 'can miscalculate only if they have learnt to calculate' (Wittgenstein 1998: Z §410). In contrast, the BBAI's kind of mistakes is not systematic but 'ruleless' [*regellos*] (Wittgenstein 2009: PI §143; mod. transl.). That is, their mistakes cannot be explained or understood as a deviation or exception from a rule that is related to the one we intend it to follow. Indeed, when it turns out that BBAI has classified pictures on the basis of their background, this is not just an isolated mistake but shows that the machine has not 'grasped' a large number of interconnected rules that are deeply embedded in our shared human way of acting, to the point that we are no longer 'playing the same game'. One could say with Wittgenstein that here is a 'transition from quantity to quality' (Wittgenstein 1998: RPP II §145), comparing it to the case when 'after a gradual loading of one side and lightening of the other, there was a *non*-gradual tipping of the balance' (Wittgenstein 1998: RPP II §146). That is, the machine's behaviour here cannot be brought back into our shared way of acting: unlike a mistake, which we can grasp and make all the time, such a classification rule is so far removed from what humans do that it ends up being of a fundamentally different nature.

Hence, since practical context is lacking in BBAI, we cannot know whether the machine's behaviour is actually in accordance with our rule or with another rule we don't know or would not even understand as a rule. That is, the rule-following paradox here actually applies and remains unresolved: beyond practice, there is no 'last explanation' that excludes any doubt about the meaning or application of the rule (cf. Wittgenstein 2009: PI §§29, 85). For Wittgenstein, practice is thus not only that which determines the meaning of rules and the criteria of their (correct) application, but it also represents the last, that is, itself ungrounded or unreasoned, instance of justification: 'But the end is not an ungrounded [*unbegründete*] presupposition: it is an ungrounded way of acting' (Wittgenstein 1998: OC §110; cf. Wittgenstein 2009: PI §§29, 85, 326). However, even if we cannot give further explanations or justifications for our actions, the fact that the actions of humans, their rule-guided behaviour as well as their errors and more spontaneous or peculiar language games, are embedded in the shared human way of acting as 'system of reference' makes them understandable to us. That is, human actions cannot be described in terms of isolated behaviour: 'Not what *one* person is doing *now*, but the whole hurly-burly is the background against which we see an action, and it determines our judgment, our concepts, and our reactions' (Wittgenstein 1998: RPP II §629).

For BBAI, we never reach 'bedrock' (cf. Wittgenstein 2009: PI §217), and there is no such hurly-burly: there is no shared way of acting here, human or otherwise, which we could refer to in order to gain the holistic understanding necessary for saying that the machine has followed our rules, or for that matter, any rule at all. With BBAI, the rule-following-paradox remains unresolved, so that sceptical doubt becomes a real problem: we can never know whether the BBAI has, for example, followed addition or 'quaddition' (cf. Kripke 1982). Where the bedrock of shared human way of acting is missing, we are really staring into the sceptic's abyss of endless doubts.

BBAI: Legal Implications

The previous section shows how Wittgenstein offers us a useful framework to explain why BBAI's behaviour might end up deviating from our expectations: its lack of grounding in our shared way of acting means that any surface similarity between its decisions and our expectations can drift apart without us knowing why or where in advance. This lack of grounding digs a chasm between any effort to access the insides of BBAI – for example, via interpretable models or saliency maps – and our shared human way of acting, which explains why any understanding we might get from such models is illusory and liable to fail. So, for BBAI, local understanding and global understanding deviate to the point where the rule we wish the machine to implement may have very little to do with the alien rule implemented in the algorithm it ends up using to process its inputs. In this section, we argue that Wittgenstein's insight means we should avoid using non-proprietary BBAI in high-stakes legal contexts. To illustrate why, we focus mostly on automated decision-making using BBAI in the criminal justice system.

First, it should be pointed out that proprietary BBAI is already exercising judicial decision-making functions in the high-stakes context of parole eligibility, where interpretable AI has been used for decades in the determination of whether a person should be incarcerated or released into the community, and if so, under which conditions. Consider, for example, COMPAS (Correctional Offender Management Profiling for Alternative Sanctions), a recidivism-risk proprietary BBAI model that is widely used throughout the US criminal justice system to evaluate the likelihood that a person will be incarcerated anew after having been released from jail.[19] Similarly, in the UK, the task of determining this risk has been delegated to an AI model known as the Offender Assessment System (OASYS). To determine the risk a person presents to a community, parole officers complete a series of questionnaires which, when input into systems like COMPAS or OASYS, will pro-

19 It should be noted that COMPAS does not appear to rely on machine learning (Rudin 2019).

duce a risk score for a given person of re-committing different types of crimes. The risk assessment is then presented to a judge in a pre-sentence report, who will determine the duration and type of sentence the offender ought to be committed to. With OASYS, a human judge is ultimately using the risk assessment in their sentencing decision, which preserves some oversight over the use of AI. In this sense, the decision is not fully automated. The judge is required to provide reasons for their decisions, which are then reviewable by a higher court.

In such cases, an argument can be made that the use of proprietary BBAI is acceptable, since it can be made to conform to the rule of law. While the rule of law is an 'an exceedingly elusive notion' (Tamanaha 2004, 3), we can still make sense of it by adopting formal definitions of it, such as that offered by Bingham: 'that all persons and authorities within the state, whether public or private, should be bound by and entitled to the benefit of laws *publicly* made, taking effect (generally) in the future and publicly administered in the courts' (2010, 213, emphasis added). That is, given that the machines are said by their owners to be transparent to them, there is a relation between the local understanding provided by an expert tasked with explaining a particular decision and the global understanding available to those who have access to the machine's insides.[20] With the written decision of a judge explaining a sentencing decision, the current use of proprietary BBAI is arguably consistent with the rule of law because the judge is accountable to the appellate courts and their decision-making is transparent. [21]

Of course, such systems rely on models that are black-boxed for fundamentally different reasons than the so-called complicated (cf. Rudin 2019) BBAI we focused on in previous sections: in theory, it is possible for someone to know how both COMPAS and OASYS reach their decisions, since such systems are said to be transparent to some people. The question is, should a company or state be allowed to introduce automated legal decision-making or evidence-processing using AI that is black-boxed *in principle*? Here, the lessons learnt from Wittgenstein seem to answer in the negative, for two main reasons: one being the impossibility of respecting the rule of law, and the other being the risk of the machine ending up following rules that significantly deviate from their intended purposes.

---

20 This being said, while it is possible to review the accuracy of OASYS's risk assessment, in practice, it is unlikely expert evidence on its operations would be called during a trial due to the cost of obtaining such experts and time involved. External reviews of OASYS are stymied by privacy laws that, to date, have prevented review by academics. See Hamilton & Ugwudike (2023).

21 See Hamilton & Ugwudike (2023).

First, we saw in previous sections that in non-proprietary BBAI, there is a chasm between local understanding and global understanding. But if we rely on technology that is black-boxed by design, we cannot respect a defendant's fundamental right to have the opportunity to scrutinize the inputs and the processes through which a prosecutor's evidence has come to a conclusion, since this is impossible in the case of non-proprietary BBAI.[22] In other words, if the state relies on BBAI to prove a case against a defendant, without local or general understanding of the AI used to determine an outcome, a defendant does not have an equal opportunity to defend themselves because they do not have the means to understand how the AI formulated its output. Importantly, the failure to do so violates the fairness aspect of the rule of law. The concept of fairness encompasses several procedural prerequisites, including that a procedure followed to resolve a legal issue must give a fair opportunity for the prosecutor to prove their case but also the defendant to rebut it.[23] The use of automated decision-makers using BBAI violates the rule of law requirement that adjudicative procedures provided by the state should be fair. Since this requirement cannot be met due to the opacity of complicated BBAI, the use of such technology in automated decision-making in the legal domain should not be allowed.

Further, it is important to point out that parole eligibility involves a great amount of discretion on the part of judges. This is an important point because when a statute uses terms that imbue judges with greater discretion – for example, 'protection of the public' for parole decisions – there's a lot of room for judicial interpretation, and a lot more space for a machine trying to emulate human behaviour to take into account unexpected considerations or spurious outcomes, given the decision is partly based on less formal criteria.[24] This means that there are even more hiding places for unexpected correlations to lie dormant, and for human mistakes in data entry to creep in unnoticed, as has already occurred, with dramatic consequences.[25] Such risks are greatly amplified when using AI that is in principle black-boxed, for reasons explained in previous sections of this chapter: here, not only can the machine end up using rules that do not coincide with the ones we intended it to, but any mistake we've made in entering data can be lost in the black-box, making

22 An example that illustrates the idea that procedural fairness requires transparency in decision-making is found in *NJCM et al. v The Dutch State* (2020).

23 Bingham (2010, 93).

24 Note, however, that even highly circumscribed legal applications have led to AI hallucinations. See e.g. Heikkila (2022). See also the Royal Commission into the Robodebt Scheme (2023).

25 See Rudin (2019).

it impossible for an innocent person to prove their innocence, and, relatedly, making it possible for guilty people to appear innocent.

With the total automation of parole systems like OASYS or COMPAS, a judge's role would simply change from the decision-maker to the reviewer of the BBAI's decision. To ensure accountability, every couple of cases, a judge could independently assess a case and determine an appropriate sentence and then compare it to what the BBAI's determination of that legal question might be to ensure the machine was exercising its discretion in the way a human judge might. These trials could occur thousands of times to ensure alignment between judicial and machine decision-making. However, as pointed out in the previous sections, as the BBAI continues to learn from and apply its earlier determinations to new sets of facts over thousands of cases, it could also be making decisions on new combinations of case factors that – together – introduce deviations that continue to be reproduced and ultimately result in applications of a given law that differ from that originally intended. Without knowing where the BBAI diverged from judges' decision-making, review of such decisions would be difficult, if not impossible, to trace.

Of course, such unexpected deviations – and the risks that come with them – are not limited to cases where BBAI would be used to determine parole eligibility. Imagine for example that we have low-resolution camera imagery showing someone leaving a crime scene and use BBAI to enhance resolution and determine who that person is. Intuitively, we wish for it to simply present us with a better representation of how a person looks by completing the features that the grainy resolution of the camera could not capture. So, the rule we would like it to implement would be something like 'when you get an image of a face with bad resolution, show me what that face looks like in great resolution'. But, following the discussion in the previous section, we know that the BBAI's rule might end up being something like 'make noses look a certain way when the luminosity in pixel 45a is of value 0.00874 or lower and make them look another way if the background contains more than three colours and the number of dark pixels on the original image is prime', and these rules happen to coincide with each other for significant parts of their application. Here too, we might be tempted to test our machine to make sure its behaviour matches our expectations. But, here too, such testing could not protect us from unexpected deviation.

A corollary of our discussion of Wittgenstein is that humans are exempt from such testing because they are already parts of our shared way of acting. We do not feel the need to test humans in this way because their participation in our practices tells us a lot about how they follow rules and what sort of rules they follow. This in turn means we do not need to prove their understanding of rules in the same way. The lack of the shared human way of acting as a system of reference for complicated BBAI, on the other hand, makes it difficult to rely on it in critical domains without forcing it to jump through very large numbers of hoops – and even then, the lack of grounding means we cannot hope to prevent any significant deviations, no matter how much testing we do. The point is that no matter the number of trials we come up with, the problem here is that we would have no way of knowing if the case under consideration is one where the pupil's behaviour has deviated from our expected course. While such a possibility may seem remote in theory, given the seriousness of the consequences for the person being accused of the crime, there is a sense in which few would be comfortable with taking this risk, if they are in the position of the accused. This risk seems to argue against adoption of fully automated legal decision-making that relies on technology that is black-boxed by design.

Conclusion

In a move that enhances alignment with the rule of law, academics are suggesting a code of ethics for governments using AI tools, or an algorithmic assessment tool for publicly used AI systems.[26] Statutes are also being used to guarantee a level of understandability for citizens where AI is used that could preclude further applications of BBAI in the public realm. For example, the EU introduced the right to explanation in 2018 as part of its General Data Protection Regulation (GDPR), which gives individuals access to 'meaningful explanations of the logic involved' in decisions made by black-boxed systems.[27] We know from the rule-following paradox that any interpretation of a single output of the machine has no guarantee of accuracy, given that any output can be produced using a number of rules that could match our desired decisions in some cases and derail from our expected behaviour in others. In other words, even if our local interpretation were to look accurate, there is no reason to think that it is even remotely similar to the rules running the BBAI itself, since countless rules could produce the same output locally and diverge globally. In a very strong sense, then, BBAI makes satisfying the right to explanation impossible in any accurate way, since we have no reason to think that our local understanding offers a meaningful explanation of the logic involved. Worse, the notion of explanation itself is not well defined and

26 See Reisman et al. (2018).

27 See also the Defense Advanced Research Projects Agency's Explainable Artificial Intelligence Program. https://www.darpa.mil/attachments/DARPA-BAA-16-53.pdf

so the intention behind such policies can easily be circumvented or corrupted due to lax standards of definition regarding explanations.[28]

Even if one disagrees with Wittgenstein and observes that, in some sense the BBAI is embedded in a community, an important point to note here is that the community doesn't have the same power over AI as it has over humans because the AI doesn't care about the sanctions. A human who would only be able to enact a single rule and whose mistakes were to somehow mirror those we have witnessed from BBAI in recent years would at some point be excluded from the community, perhaps put into prison or asylum. Definitely, such a human would (ideally) not qualify to have power over other people's lives (as BBAI in some contexts has). Obviously, this doesn't work for the AI: one cannot punish or threaten AI. Imagine if we were to find out that a human judge had been convicting people on the basis of the equivalent of the background image to their profile, in a way analogous to the wolf example above: few would be comfortable with letting this person keep their job, no matter how many of their previous decisions seem accurate to us. This is because we would not be able to reign in their behaviour into how we understand the world around us.

For now, we can make decisions about where we use what sort of technology. Wittgenstein's insight into the nature of rule-following and the importance of shared practices in making behaviour understandable to us provides good reasons to avoid using BBAI in high-stake domains like the law. For while we may accept a chasm between local and global understanding in low-stakes contexts, use of such technology in critical domains would transform this chasm into an abyss, whose presence would have very real consequences on many people.

Acknowledgement

Pelland's contribution has been made possible by financial support from the 'QUANTA: Evolution of Cognitive Tools for Quantification' project, which has received funding from the European Research Council (ERC) under the European Union's Horizon 2020 research and innovation programme (grant agreement No. 951388).

28 This lack of clarity should not affect the value of this policy per se, but it should motivate increased attention to the issue. As Guidotti et al. (2018) put it, 'Despite divergent opinions among legal scholars regarding the real scope of these clauses [...] there is a general agreement on [*sic.* – that] the need for the implementation of such a principle is urgent and that it represents today a huge open scientific challenge' (93:2).

References

Abdullah, T.A.A., Zahid, M.S.M., Ali, W., Hassan, S.U. 2023. B-LIME: An Improvement of LIME for Interpretable Deep Learning Classification of Cardiac Arrhythmia from ECG Signals. *Processes* 11: 595. https://doi.org/10.3390/ pr11020595

Bingham, T. 2010. *The Rule of Law.* London: Allen Lane, Penguin Press. ISBN 978-1-846-14090-7

Brożek, B., Furman, M., Jakubiec, M., & Kucharzyk, B. 2023. The Black Box Problem Revisited. Real and Imaginary Challenges for Automated Legal Decision Making. *Artif Intell Law.* https://doi.org/10.1007/s10506-023-09356-9

Burrell, J. 2016. How the Machine 'Thinks': Understanding Opacity in Machine Learning Algorithms. *Big Data & Society.* 1–12. DOI: 10.1177/2053951715622512

Elgin, C. Z. (2017). *True enough.* Cambridge: MIT Press.

von Eschenbach, W.J.2021. Transparency and the Black Box Problem: Why We Do Not Trust AI. *Philosophy & Technology* 34: 1607–1622. https://doi.org/10.1007/s13347-021-00477–0

De Graaf, M.M. & Malle, B.F. (2017). How People Explain Action (and Autonomous Intelligent Systems Should too). In *AAAI Fall Symposium on Artificial Intelligence for Human–Robot Interaction* (pp. 19–26). Palo Alto: The AAAI Press.

Gohel, P., Singh, P., & Mohanty, M. 2021. Explainable AI: Current Status and Future Directions. *IEEE Access.* https://doi.org/10.48550/arXiv.2107.07045

Guidotti, R., Monreale, A., Ruggieri, S., Turini, F., Giannotti, F., & Pedreschi, D. 2018. A Survey of Methods for Explaining Black Box Models. *ACM Computing Survey* 51(5): 1–42.

Hamilton, M. & Ugwudike, P. 2023. A 'black Box' AI System has been Influencing Criminal Justice Decisions for Over Two Decades – It's Time to Open it up. *The Conversation* online. https://theconversation.com/a-black-box-ai-system-has-been-influencing-criminal-justice-decisions-for-over-two-decades-its-time-to-open-it-up

Heikkila, M. 2022. A Dutch Algorithm Scandal Serves a Warning to Europe – The AI Act won't Save us. *Politico, AI: Decoded.* https://www.politico.eu/newsletter/ai-decoded/a-dutch-algorithm-scandal-serves-a-warning-to-europe-the-ai-act-wont-save-us-2/

Hill, R.K. 2016. What an Algorithm Is. *Philosophy & Technology* 29: 35–59. DOI: 10.1007/s13347-014-0184–5

Kim, B. 2015. *Interactive and Interpretable Machine Learning Models for Human Machine Collaboration.* Ph.D. thesis, Massachusetts Institute of Technology.

Kripke, Saul. 1982. *Wittgenstein on Rules and Private Language.* Cambridge, MA: HUP.

Lapuschkin, S., Wäldchen, S., Binder, A., Montavon, G., Samek, W., & Müller, K. R. 2019. Unmasking Clever Hans Predictors and Assessing What Machines Really Learn. *Nature Communications* 10(1): 1096.

Lipton, Z.C. 2016. The Mythos of Model Interpretability. *arXiv preprint.* arXiv:1606.03490

Miller, T. 2019. Explanation in Artificial Intelligence: Insights from the Social Sciences. *Artificial Intelligence* 267: 1–18.

Mittelstadt, B., Russell, C., & Wachter, S. 2019. Explaining Explanations in AI. In *Proceedings of the Conference on Fairness, Accountability, and Transparency* (pp. 279–288). New York: ACM.

Nguyen, A., Yosinski, J., Clune, J. 2015. Deep Neural Networks are Easily Fooled: High Confidence Predictions for Unrecognizable Images. In *Computer Vision and Pattern Recognition* (pp. 427–436). (CVPR'15), IEEE

NJCM et al. v The Dutch State. 2020. The Hague District Court ECLI: NL: RBDHA:2020:1878 (SyRI). Online: http://deeplink.rechtspraak.nl/uitspraak?id =ECLI:NL:RBDHA:2020:1878

Páez, A. 2019. The Pragmatic Turn in Explainable Artificial Intelligence (XAI). *Minds and Machines* 29: 441–459. https://doi.org/10.1007/s11023-019-09502-w

Philipse, H. 1989. Psychologism and the Prescriptive Function of Logic. In M.A. Notturno (ed.), *Perspectives on Psychologism*. (pp. 58–74). Leiden: Brill.

Pichler, Alois. forthcoming '"Suppose You Came as an Explorer to an Unknown Country with a Language Quite Unknown to You…": From Interpreting Unknown Languages to Understanding (Other) Religion'.

Proudfoot, D. 2004. Robots and Rule-Following. In: Teuscher, C. (ed.), *Alan Turing: Life and Legacy of a Great Thinker*, pp. 359–379. Springer, Berlin, Heidelberg. https://doi.org /10.1007/978-3-662-05642-4_15

Reisman, D. et al. 2018. Algorithmic Impact Assessments: A Practical Framework for Public Agency Accountability. AI Now Institute.

Ribeiro, M. T., Singh, S., & Guestrin, C. 2016a. Model-agnostic Interpretability of Machine Learning. *arXiv preprint*. arXiv:1606.05386

Ribeiro, M.T., Singh, S., & Guestrin, C. 2016b. Why Should I Trust You?: Explaining the Predictions of Any Classifier. In *Proceedings of the 22nd ACM SIGKDD International Conference on Knowledge Discovery and Data Mining*. ACM Press, 1135–1144. https://doi .org/10.1145/2939672.2939778

Rudin, C. 2019. Stop Explaining Black Box Machine Learning Models for High Stakes Decisions and use Interpretable Models Instead. *Nature Machine intelligence* 1: 206–215.

Schulte, Joachim. 2021. Philosophische Superlative und die Maschine als Symbol. *Wittgenstein Studien* 12: 1–36.

Tamanaha, B.Z. 2004. *On the Rule of Law*. Cambridge: Cambridge University Press.

Trächtler, Jasmin. 2022. Hinges of Trust: Wittgenstein on the Other Minds Problem. In Constantine Sandis and Danièle Moyal-Sharrock (eds.), *Extending Hinge Epistemology*, 109–124. London: Anthem Press.

Turing, A.M.1950. Computing Machinery and Intelligence. *Mind* 49: 433–460.

Vilone, G. & Longo, L 2021. Notions of Explainability and Evaluation Approaches for Explainable Artificial Intelligence. *Inform Fusion* 76: 89–106.

Wang, J., Oh, J., Wang, H., & Wiens, J. 2018. Learning Credible Models. In *Proceedings of the 24th ACM SIGKDD International Conference on Knowledge Discovery & Data Mining (KDD '18). Association for Computing Machinery*, New York, NY, 2417–2426. https://doi.org/10 .1145/3219819.3220070

Wexler, R. (2017). When a Computer Program Keeps You in Jail: How Computers are Harming Criminal Justice. *New York Times* (13 June 2017). https://www.nytimes.com /2017/06/13/opinion/how-computers-are-harming-criminal-justice.html

Wittgenstein, Ludwig. OC. 1998. *On Certainty*, G.E.M. Anscombe & G.H. von Wright (eds.). Oxford: Blackwell.

Wittgenstein, Ludwig. RFM. 1998. *Remarks on the Foundation of Mathematics*, G.E.M. Anscombe, R. Rhees, & G.H. von Wright (eds.). Oxford: Blackwell.

Wittgenstein, Ludwig. RPP II. 1998. *Remarks on the Philosophy of Psychology Vol. II.*, G.H. von Wright and H. Nyman (eds.). Oxford: Blackwell.

Wittgenstein, Ludwig. Z. 1998. *Zettel*, G.E.M. Anscombe, R. Rhees, & G.H. von Wright (eds.). Oxford: Blackwell.

Wittgenstein, Ludwig. PI. 2009. *Philosophical Investigations*, P.M.S. Hacker & J. Schulte (eds.). Oxford: Blackwell.

Zeiler, M.D. & Fergus, R. 2014. Visualizing and Understanding Convolutional Networks. In *13th European conference on computer vision ECCV* (pp. 818–833). Cham: Springer.

Zerilli, J., Knott, A., Maclaurin, J., & Gavaghan, C. 2019. Transparency in Algorithmic and Human Decision-Making: Is There a Double Standard? *Philosophy & Technology* 32: 661–683. https://doi.org/10.1007/s13347-018-0330-6

NOTES ON CONTRIBUTORS

Alessandro Rossi, Assistant Professor in Philosophy, Northeastern University London, United Kingdom.

Burkhard Schafer, Professor of Computational Legal Theory, University of Edinburgh, United Kingdom.

Paula Sweeney, Senior Lecturer in Philosophy, University of Aberdeen, United Kingdom.

Alberto Rappuoli, PhD Student, University of St Andrews and University of Stirling, United Kingdom.

Mehmet Taylan Cüyaz, PhD Student, University of Rochester, USA, and Research Assistant, Middle East Technical University, Turkey.

Alice C. Helliwell, Assistant Professor in Philosophy, Northeastern University London, United Kingdom.

Richard Harper, Professor of Socio-Digital Systems, Lancaster University, United Kingdom.

Gianmarco Gori, Guest Professor and Postdoctoral Researcher at the Law, Science, Technology and Society Research Group (LSTS), Vrije Universiteit Brussel, Belgium.

Jean-Charles Pelland, Postdoctoral Fellow, University of Bergen, Norway.

Jasmin Trächtler, Assistant Professor, Technical University Dortmund, Germany.

Helene Love, Assistant Professor, Simon Fraser University, Canada.

INDEX

www.ingramcontent.com/pod-product-compliance
Ingram Content Group UK Ltd.
Pitfield, Milton Keynes, MK11 3LW, UK
UKHW011005120926
8556IPUK00027B/115

9 781839 991394